TESTIMONIALS

"Carol Henn has written a beautiful book that takes her life experiences, fictional worlds, and observations, and transports you to a place called Bethlehem in Pennsylvania. Part lush fiction, novella, and memoir, Carol weaves masterful tales in celebration of her roots, family life, and love that will delight readers everywhere."

Adriana Trigiani, New York Times best-selling author of BIG STONE GAP

"Carol Henn's Oilcloth Stories capture life in the shadow – economic, social, emotional, and cultural – of a giant steel mill. The characters are fresh and vivid. The events brim with life's lessons and meaning. The recounting is sensitive, insightful, and presented with exquisite craftsmanship."

Tim Mead, award-winning outdoor writer and photographer; author of QUETICO ADVENTURES

"Oilcloth Stories bring back the nearly forgotten world of South Bethlehem, Pennsylvania, the home of Bethlehem Steel, but they do more than that. In her uncanny recollections of a child's view of so many things – restaurants and ice cream parlors; bedrooms lit by blast furnaces; small but abundant backyard gardens; the men and women whose emotional wounds she already, preternaturally, understood as a child – Henn evokes tender stories of early and mid-20th century American life. These stories are a loving tribute to Henn's own beloved family, and to the many immigrant families who filled the neighborhoods and workplaces of Bethlehem. They are also a rare gift to us, her readers."

Joyce Hinnefeld, author of IN HOVERING FLIGHT, STRANGER HERE BELOW, and TELL ME EVERYTHING

"The little distortions that fiction writers make of their perceptions are used to bring us closer to the truths of our lives, those otherwise untellable truths of our emotional experiences. Carol Henn has used her remembered past – the experience of Middle European immigrants striving to build lives in a Pennsylvania industrial town at mid-century – to create a narrative web of characters who remind us with a visceral vividness why people came here and why they continue to come. Her prose captures a time and a feeling denied even to photos of the period."

G. Bruce Boyer, author of GARY COOPER - ENDURING STYLE

June, 2016

OILCLOTH STORIES

Carol Dean Henn

For Joyce Slavin —

With warm good wishes and with gratitude for your interest in the people and places of "Oilcloth Stories." May all of your memories be golden.

Warm regards —
Carol Henn

 **FriesenPress**

Suite 300 - 990 Fort St
Victoria, BC, Canada, V8V 3K2
www.friesenpress.com

Copyright © 2015 by Carol Dean Henn
First Edition — 2015

All rights reserved. Except for references to specific family members or actual persons, any resemblance of other characters in the book to persons living or dead is unintentional.

What A Diff'rence A Day Made (also known as **What A Difference A Day Makes**)
English Words by Stanley Adams
Music and Spanish Words by Maria Grever
Copyright © 1934 by Edward B. Marks Music Company
Copyright Renewed and Assigned to Stanley Adams Music, Inc. and Grever Music Publishing
  S.A. De C.V.
All Rights for Stanley Adams Music, Inc. Administered by The Songwriters Guild Of America
All Rights for Grever Music Publishing S.A. De C.V. in the U.S. Administered by Universal Music
  – Z Tunes LLC
All Rights for the World Excluding U.S. Administered by Edward B. Marks Music Company
International Copyright Secured   All Rights Reserved
Used by Permission
Reprinted by Permission of Hal Leonard Corporation

No part of this publication may be reproduced in any form, or by any means, electronic or mechanical, including photocopying, recording, or any information browsing, storage, or retrieval system, without permission in writing from the publisher.

ISBN
978-1-4602-4092-2 (Hardcover)
978-1-4602-4093-9 (Paperback)
978-1-4602-4094-6 (eBook)

1. Fiction, Short Stories (Single Author)

Distributed to the trade by The Ingram Book Company

TABLE OF CONTENTS

Testimonials i
Dedication xiii
Introduction xvii
Preface xxiii

Part I

Stories 1

    The Legacy 3
    The Good News 9
    At Last 13
    Lena 17
    The Violin 23
    The List 25
    The Boarder 29
    Getting Hoofty Fixed (Up) 37
    Reality 47
    Driving the Devil Away 55
    Another Lottery 61
    Losing Grandpop 77
    Theresa 83
    Ghost 87
    The Odds 91
    Go, white! 101

Intersections 115

The Steel 121

Morecz-nina 131

Treasures 137

Part II

Sweet Revenge 141

Sweet Revenge 143

Part III

South Side School Days — A Memoir 175

Central School 177

Power 179

New Worlds 183

Taking Cover 187

Mrs. DeLio 191

No Good Deed 195

"Bluck, bluck, bluck, bluck, bluck" 199

Broughal Junior High 201

The Birds and the Bees and Bellybuttons 205

Janice 209

The View from the Window 213

Afterthoughts: South Bethlehem Remembered 215

Acknowledgments 223

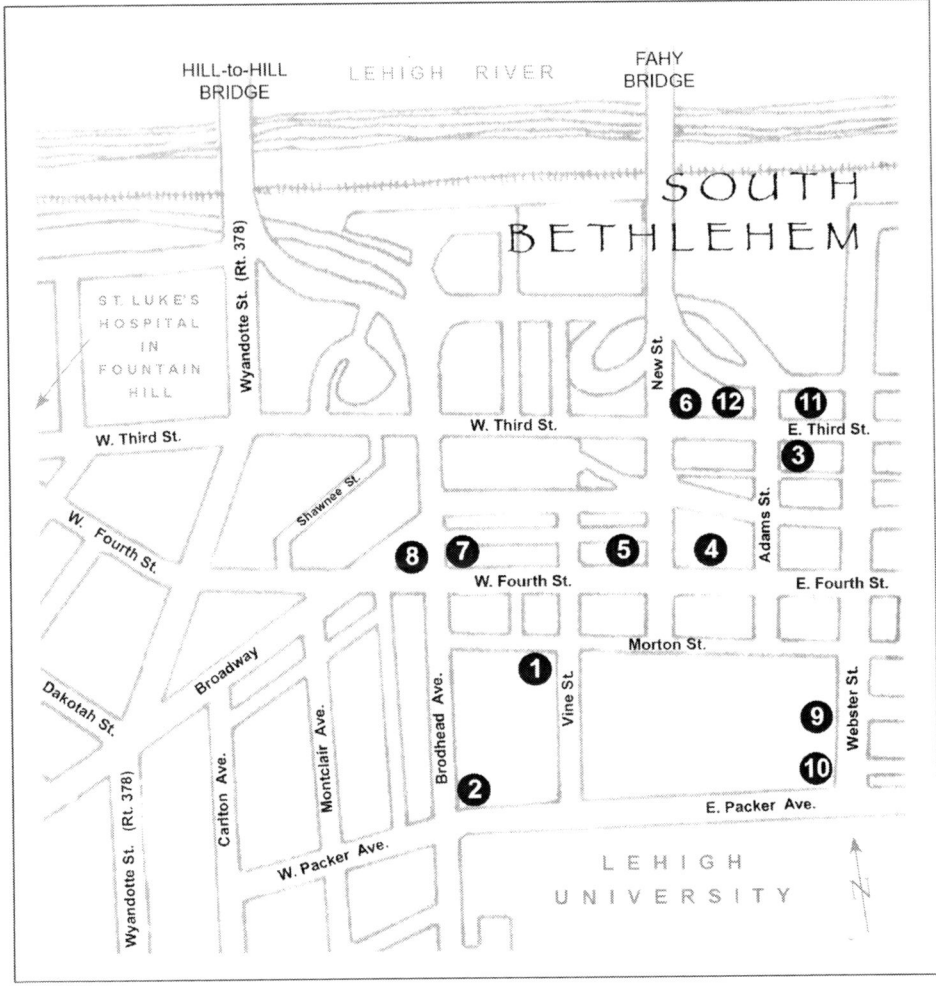

Locations west of Webster Street

1. Central School
2. Broughal Junior High School
3. Bethlehem City Market
4. Archond's Ice Cream Parlor
5. Royal Restaurant
6. Le-Roy Shop
7. South Bethlehem Post Office
8. Tally-Ho
9. Synagogue
10. First Moravian Church
11. Egan's Men's Shop
12. Josephine Harris Beauty Salon

Maps of South Bethlehem in 2014 showing some of the locations in Oilcloth Stories in the early to mid-20th century.

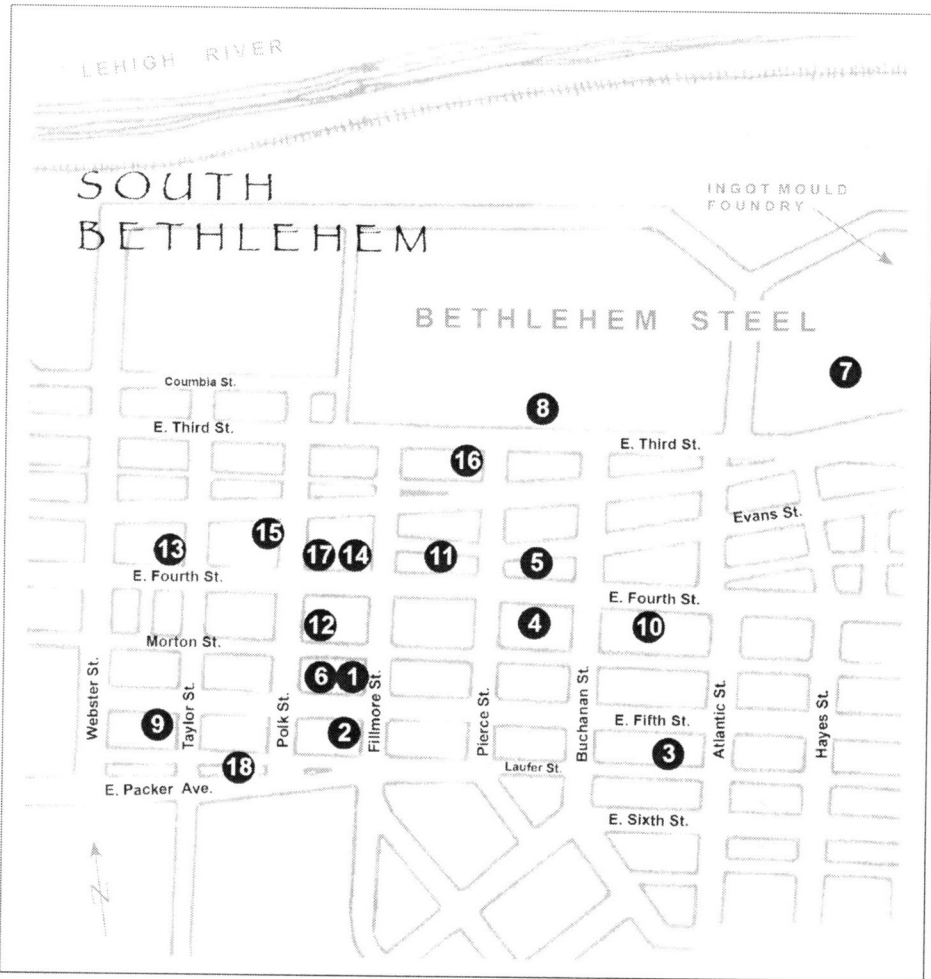

Maps by Kenneth F. Raniere

Locations east of Webster Street

1. 426 Fillmore St.
2. Theresa's Restaurant
3. 737 Laufer St.
4. Quinn School
5. St. John's W. L. Church
6. St. Joseph R.C. Church
7. No. 2 Machine Shop
8. Bethlehem Steel Main Office
9. Anna's House
10. Zavacky's Shoe Repair Shop
11. Cigar Factory
12. Lena's House
13. Holy Infancy School
14. Tammany
15. Bethlehem Bulletin Office
16. Gosztonyi's Savings & Trust
17. Zelko's
18. Windish Hall

*Their story — yours, mine —
it's what we all carry with us on this trip we take,
and we owe it to each other to respect our stories and learn from them.*
William Carlos Williams

Stories make us more alive, more human, more courageous, more loving.
Madeleine L'Engle

Joseph and Vilma Kuzma on their wedding day, April 12, 1913.

DEDICATION

He was born in 1883, in what was then the Austro-Hungarian Empire and is now Slovenia. His mother loved his father, but she was far beneath him socially. She was his mistress, not his wife, and marriage was out of the question. So was the presence of this illegitimate son in cities where his prominent father lived. Money was paid for the child to be cared for on a farm far away from Budapest and Vienna. What was actually provided for him, after his infancy, was a floor to sleep on in a drafty stable and scraps of food thrown to him when they were thrown to the barnyard animals. The animals' food was thrown into a trough; his food was thrown onto the stable floor. But work was given to him in abundance — back-breaking work from dawn until sundown, from his earliest years to his mid-teens.

Once, when the harvest was finished, he walked across the fields to the Catholic church in the distance. He stepped into the stone-arched room where a priest was teaching children from neighboring farms. "Why do you come here in rags?" the priest demanded. "This is all I have," said the child. "I want to go to school. I want to learn, like the other children." "You are not wanted here," replied the cleric. "Everyone knows who your father is. Everyone knows what your mother is. In God's eyes you are not even a person and God does not want you in his house." The child lowered his head and left the cathedral, vowing silently not to intrude upon God or his house again.

He walked away from the farm with only the clothes he wore. Needing a last name, he took it from the nearby village: Kuzma. He volunteered for service in the Austro-Hungarian army, where he became an officer. A photo from that time shows a handsome, even dashing young man — mustachioed and magnificent in his high-collared, beribboned uniform with brass buttons. When he left military service, he made his way to America, to the steel mills of Pennsylvania. Here, his hard work earned him money — money he could use to buy decent food and a clean, warm place to live. He lived among people who spoke his language, people with whom he could laugh, talk, and share a glass of slivovitz. Someone taught him to sign his name in English, with an ornate flourish, so that he could sign his paychecks. When he was in his late twenties, he met a beautiful sixteen-year-old girl with chestnut hair and ivory skin. She, too, had been sent to America to find a better life. She spoke his language and came from the same land he had come from. They married in April of 1913 and had four children, the first two of whom died in infancy.

Deprived of any trace of affection in his childhood, he loved his family deeply and devotedly. Impoverished repeatedly by the need to pay his wife's medical bills, he lived without borrowing and he died without debt. Uneducated, he knew the meaning of commitment and he embodied honor. He had a limitless capacity for joy and no room for bitterness. He respected all people but envied none. He walked with dignity and lived with integrity. True to his vow, he never intruded upon God in his Catholic house again, but he faithfully attended services in the Lutheran church. To him, work was a blessing, not a burden, and he worked in the steel mill until he died at age 71. Because he never knew his birth date, he simply celebrated St. Joseph's Day. Joseph Kuzma. My grandfather. My hero.

For my parents, Dean and Irene Henn, and my grandparents, Earl and Elizabeth Henn and Joseph and Vilma Kuzma. Especially for Grandpop. Joseph Kuzma. Still my hero.

This essay was originally published by Newsweek® in 2000, as part of Newsweek's international My Heroes series.

OILCLOTH STORIES

INTRODUCTION

I can still see their faces and hear their voices: Marika, Lena, Theresa, Mishka, and so many others. They were among the immigrants from Central and Eastern Europe who lived on the South Side of Bethlehem, Pennsylvania, during the early and mid-1900s. Their lives were a blending of the American Dream and the customs and beliefs of the 'old countries' they left behind when they came to America.

When these immigrants from Austria-Hungary, Poland, and later Yugoslavia and Czechoslovakia began to arrive in Bethlehem, in the late 1800s and early 1900s, the Bethlehem boroughs were populated with more than 21,000 residents, and the town was being transformed by industrialization. Settled in the mid-1700s by the Moravians, a Protestant denomination pre-dating Luther's Reformation and tracing its beginnings to the teachings of John Hus, Bethlehem was a cultured and sophisticated community from its earliest days. Among the prominent people who visited Bethlehem in the mid- to late 1700s were John Adams, Benjamin Franklin, George and Martha Washington, the Marquis de Lafayette, General Casimir Pulaski, and several signers of the Declaration of Independence. Music, art, architecture, and education — including education for women — flourished in early Bethlehem. Moravian College, the sixth oldest college in America, traces its history to the Moravian Seminary for Young Ladies, established in 1742 and attended by George Washington's niece, John Jay's daughter, and the daughters of many of early America's leaders and shapers. The Moravian Book Shop, on Bethlehem's Main Street, is the current setting for the oldest continuous book-selling enterprise in the United States. The Moravian Trombone Choir is the oldest continuing music organization in America. The first complete American production of Bach's *Mass in*

B Minor was performed in Bethlehem, as was the first American performance of Haydn's *Creation*.

The Lehigh River formed a natural dividing line between the Moravian community in North Bethlehem, where by 1880, commerce and retail had been flourishing for more than a century, and South Bethlehem, where the buildings and machinery — the sights, sounds, and smoke — of industrialization took hold and burgeoned. Immigrant labor was needed for the Bethlehem Iron Works, which became Bethlehem Steel Company, as well as for the railroads, the zinc industry, the textile mills, and the cigar factories that grew along the south shore of the Lehigh River. Sometimes earning no more than fifty cents a week, these immigrants often slept four to a bed, and ten to a room in South Bethlehem boarding houses.

They came from countries we now know as Hungary, Austria, the Czech Republic, Slovakia, Poland, Russia, and Slovenia, among others. In 1917, there were 64 ethnic groups in South Bethlehem. These immigrants brought strong bodies, a willingness to work long hours in hard and even brutal conditions, and a willingness to learn new work, new customs, and a new language. They also brought culinary skills and cultural traditions that are still enjoyed today. They joined the immigrants from Germany, Italy, Portugal, the British Isles, and Spain who were already in Bethlehem. In later decades, immigrants from Greece, Mexico, other Latino countries, and Asia added to the multi-cultural population of South Bethlehem.

Today, more than 270 years after its founding, Bethlehem attracts more than two million visitors annually because of its arts and history. Buildings on historic Church Street are the finest examples of colonial Germanic architecture in continuous use in the United States. America's first municipal waterworks were built in Bethlehem. The Bach Choir Festival, Musikfest, and Celtic Fest are among the many festivals and celebrations that keep Bethlehem's arts and cultural traditions alive.

What must also be kept alive are the stories of the immigrants, ordinary and extraordinary men and women who lived in South Bethlehem in the early and mid-1900s. Without them, Bethlehem Steel could never have "built America." Without them, industry in Bethlehem would have been an idea, not a reality. Without them, the economy of the city would never have thrived and prospered. These were men and women whose lives never warranted a news story, an autograph, or an award, whose names were unknown beyond their families, churches, and neighborhoods. They were men and women who lived and died in relative obscurity. But in many of their lives there were astonishing stories of triumph and pathos, devotion and brutality, tragedy and exultation. Their stories should be told, must be told.

The arc of history can be breathtaking. When my maternal grandfather, Joseph Kuzma, was born in 1883, many men who fought at the battle of Waterloo were still alive; women were alive who could recall attending George Washington's funeral. The grandchildren Joseph Kuzma doted upon, alive in the twenty-first century, use palm-sized computers that transmit data, sounds, and film images around the world in nanoseconds, and they regard as commonplace such things as MRIs, robotic surgery, and space travel. One lifetime can touch eras that are truly worlds apart. Many of the immigrants who came to America in the 1800s and 1900s touched a span of three centuries in a single lifetime. Breathtaking, indeed.

For many children of South Bethlehem's immigrants, caught in the despair and destitution of the Great Depression, attending school remained an elusive dream. The need to help support their families pulled many first-generation boys and girls from grade schools and junior high schools into factories, foundries, and whatever jobs they could find. But it was their children — the grandchildren of those turn-of-the-century immigrants — who were finally able to attend school with the hope of actually graduating. Most had realistic hopes of attending college. Many attended state universities or local schools — Moravian College, Lehigh University, Muhlenberg, Lafayette, and Cedar Crest Colleges. Some attended Harvard, Yale, and other Ivy League schools. They became teachers, engineers, nurses, pastors, managers, musicians, writers, scientists, doctors, lawyers, bankers, artists, professional athletes, and business owners. Many had distinguished careers, and some achieved national prominence. Few, if any, of the grandchildren of those early twentieth century immigrants worried about whether they would be able to find jobs or support their families. From uncertainty and poverty to security and success in two generations.

The school days of those immigrant grandchildren, from the 1940s through the 1960s, are also fading from memory. South Side School Days, Part III of this volume, is a memoir that reflects my memories of attending Central Elementary School and Broughal Junior High School in South Bethlehem. Those who attended other schools, including the many Catholic schools in the area, undoubtedly have similar memories of their school days. I recall reading books that featured Alice, Jerry, and Jip the dog ... May Days and Ice Cream Festivals ... art projects (clay ashtrays, papier mache bowls, and woven mats) that became gifts for Mom or Dad ... memorizing the "times tables" ... air-raid drills ... learning cursive writing and using no technology more complicated than a compass. We enjoyed mid-morning snacks of milk and a graham cracker, bought with a nickel "milk money." After school, there was a rush to the nearest candy store, with its overwhelming choices — Bonomo's Turkish Taffy, Necco wafers, Mary Janes, Sky Bars, Chunkies, Jujubes, Good & Plenty, and Chuckles, among others. There was also the dazzling assortment of penny candies — marshmallow ice cream cones, satellite wafers, candy cigarettes, root beer barrels, candy button strips, licorice, Nik-L-Nip wax bottles filled with colored sugar water, and scores of other treats. Most Baby Boomers still remember that unforgettable smell of a new box of crayons and the equally memorable scent of chalk being clapped from erasers. For many Baby Boomers, these earliest school days provide golden memories.

Each person, each generation, each neighborhood has its own memory lane. When we take that walk through our memories, and when we invite others to stroll along with us, we do something more than recall our past. We enable it to live again, perhaps to live forever, for generations yet to come.

This book is not intended to be a comprehensive history or overview of South Bethlehem or all of its ethnic groups. It is a collection of stories about some of the people who called South Bethlehem home. Although the stories in Part I and Part II of this book are based on actual persons, occurrences, or situations — according to my knowledge or best recollections — many of the names in these stories have been changed or fabricated, and many of the stories have been fictionalized. Some of the stories are authentic memoir, written from first-hand knowledge or involvement, and often written in the first person. Other stories, which are simply known to me, are conveyed with no first person or family references in the narrative.

Carol Dean Henn

PREFACE

*I*n the 1940s and '50s, the big kitchen at the rear of Theresa's Fillmore Street Restaurant in South Bethlehem didn't have one fancy or unnecessary thing in it. An enormous, black Garland stove spanned most of one wall, and double porcelain sinks on the adjacent wall were used to hand wash dishes incessantly, from pre-dawn until after midnight. The steam from the hot water running in those sinks created a perpetual mist in the kitchen.

In the center of the room, a large, oval wooden table, surrounded by eight unmatched wooden chairs, was the gathering place for the men who rented rooms upstairs — the immigrant boarders who worked shifts at Bethlehem Steel and who took their meals in the kitchen. Speaking Windish, Polish, Hungarian, or Slovak, they wore old sweaters, plaid flannel shirts, and steel-tipped shoes. Their hands, even after diligent washing, bore the traces of the grit and grime in which they worked. Their nails were outlined in black and their coughing filled the kitchen with the faint, unmistakable odor of the gases and fumes that they breathed into their lungs at the steel mill. Shots of liquor helped to "cut the cough," and when their meals were finished they leaned back in their chairs, lit their pipes or cigars, and talked about work, families, religion, and the old country. Women from the neighborhood sometimes sat at the table to gossip with Theresa or wait for the take-home platters she prepared for them. They, too, talked about their neighbors, families, churches, and husbands. They told each other things they would never tell anyone else. The confidentiality of the kitchen table was sacrosanct.

My parents and I lived on Fillmore Street with my maternal grandmother and grandfather. On many evenings in my childhood, after my grandfather finished his supper, he would take me with him when he walked the one-block distance to Theresa's. There, Grandpop sat at the long, polished mahogany bar at the front of the restaurant, talking with his cronies and with Theresa's husband, Steve, the amiable, white-haired bartender. After I'd finish my foam-topped glass of birch beer at the bar, I would climb down from the barstool and make my way to the kitchen. Theresa always allowed me to open the doors of the big refrigerator and take out a paper cup of ice cream from the freezer. I sat at the crowded kitchen table, eating my ice cream with the flat wooden spoon that came with the paper cup, and I listened as the men and women talked and told their tales.

The table was covered with patterned oilcloth, ripped in spots and missing pieces here and there. Above the table, a frayed electrical cord hung down, holding the dome of an ivory glass light shade with one light bulb in it, creating a muted yellow glow that hovered over and enfolded those gathered at the table. I listened to the conversations at that table, understanding what was said in Windish and broken English. Much of what was said concerned the ordinary business of life. But often enough, the conversations revealed vignettes from the human drama — passion, courage, hatred, revenge, obsession, love, and loss. I've never forgotten those stories, or the many other stories that unfolded as part of life in South Bethlehem. I always knew that the stories had to be told. There is only one way to think of them and to present them: as Oilcloth Stories. It is easy to go back to the steel town that was Bethlehem, to blue-collar, immigrant-graced South Bethlehem … to the table in Theresa's kitchen, under the yellow glow of the light bulb.

Part I
Stories

THE LEGACY

"How much money you got now, Mishka?" The skinny man with his deeply lined face and grizzled salt-and-pepper beard asked the question with more than a hint of a smile. The men around Theresa's kitchen table had finished their suppers and were ready for relaxation and conversation. It was pay week and Theresa had given them steaming chicken noodle soup, roast beef with brown gravy, potatoes fried with onions, green beans, creamed cucumber salad, and the unexpected treat of warm marrow spread on thick slices of fresh-baked rye bread. They salted the marrow liberally and finished it quickly, using the remaining rye bread to sop up the rich beef gravy on their dishes. The marrow sufficed for dessert. In fact, it was better than dessert.

Mishka had come to the kitchen to join the men, as he usually did a few times each week, when supper was over and it was time for cigars and slivovitz. Mishka's starched white shirt was a sharp contrast to the flannel shirts and threadbare vests that the other men wore. He looked as if he had just come from a good bath. His wavy hair was combed back and slicked with hair cream. Mishka was also a single man and a boarder, but he rented a room in a house a few blocks away. He ate his meals with the family at the house, and the matriarch did his laundry and cleaned his well-furnished room. He felt a kind of superiority over the men who lived here, above the restaurant, with less privacy, less comfort, and less privilege.

Mishka heard the question but waited a long moment to respond. Finally, he said, "More money than I had last week and more than you'll ever have." The men laughed at the familiar question and even more familiar response. If they envied Mishka, they didn't show it. Like them, he worked at Bethlehem Steel but he didn't do skilled or hard physical labor. He had an office job inside the plant and his hands never looked grimy.

Mishka lived frugally despite the splurge of renting a room in a private home. He would have one glass of beer — no more — in Theresa's kitchen, with these men, and then he'd walk home. There, he would sit with the family in the living room to listen to the radio — and in later years, watch television — until it was time to go to bed. In that way, he knew he wasn't wasting their electricity. He saved his money. He told his landlady that he had family in the old country, and he would send them money occasionally. But he was really saving most of it to move back to his home country after he retired. He wanted to return as a rich man, a man who could take care of his sisters and their children, a man who would be respected and loved by them, taken care of in his old age, and remembered in his village as a good and great man.

Rumors about Mishka's wealth surfaced from time to time, with some people guessing that he had nothing at all and was merely pretending, while others ranked him somewhere just south of the Rockefellers. When he walked down our street, he would always nod or wave, stopping occasionally to talk with my parents and grandparents. Soft-spoken and shy, he kept his business to himself. Once, as he walked down our street at night, he saw what appeared to be lights moving around inside our house. He knew that no one was at home, that we had gone to St. Luke's Hospital to see my grandmother. Fighting his natural inclination to not get involved, Mishka went home and phoned the police, hesitating at first to give them his name. The police arrived at our home a few minutes later and caught the burglar in the midst of his attempted robbery. My parents thanked Mishka profusely and bought him several shirts and sweaters at Egan's Men's Shop. He was speechless. He said that he had never received such gifts and seemed genuinely embarrassed. But the episode created a kind of bond between Mishka and my parents, and he stopped at our house to talk more often after that.

One day, Mishka's landlady, Mrs. Kutos, came to see my grandmother. She said that she was worried about the money Mishka kept in his room. "You mean he really has a lot of money?" my grandmother asked. "Come with me," said her friend.

When they got to Mrs. Kutos's home, she led my grandmother upstairs to Mishka's room. It was the middle of the day and he was at work. There was no chance that they would be interrupted. The room was immaculate, with a double cherry wood bed and matching dresser, a cherry bureau, two small bedside tables with matching, blue-shaded hobnail lamps, and a rocking chair with tufted blue cushions. White curtains with hand-crocheted trim bordered the windows and matched the white daisies in the pale blue wallpaper of the room. Some framed photographs, a milk-glass vase of flowers from the garden, and two framed samplers on the walls completed the room's coziness. Mrs. Kutos walked over to the perfectly dressed bed and lifted the embroidered bedspread. "Look here," she said as she lifted the edge of the mattress. My grandmother gasped. Underneath the mattress, on top of the box spring, were stacks of neatly bundled currency — scores, maybe hundreds of bundles.

"It must be a fortune!" my grandmother exclaimed. "So it's all true — he is rich! Very rich! How much money is there? Do you know?"

"Yes," Mrs. Kutos said, "I know. He showed me the money many years ago when he started putting it here. He wanted me to know where it was in case anything happened to him. I begged him to put it in the bank, but he said he doesn't trust the banks. I don't want to be responsible for this much money. What if there was a fire? What if someone found out and stole it? Someone could come here and kill us all for this kind of money. The last time he counted it, it was $75,000. My God, you can buy a big, new house for $10,000."

"Who else knows about this?" my grandmother asked.

"Just the family — my son and daughter-in-law," replied Mrs. Kutos. "And I told the minister and now I'm telling you, in case anything happens to me or to any of us."

"You have to make him move it," my grandmother urged. "It is too dangerous to have this much money around."

Mrs. Kutos worried about the money and tried to talk to Mishka about it repeatedly for the next four years, to no avail. He insisted that he wanted the money to be kept safe, because he wanted to take it home with him to Hungary when he retired. He needed it for his life there and for his sisters. As time passed, Mrs. Kutos pushed her worries about the money to the back of her mind. She knew she would never convince Mishka to take his money to the bank.

Mishka's cough started insignificantly enough. He wasn't worried because he was only in his fifties. He was still a decade away from retirement. He still thought of himself as a young man. He simply smoked fewer cigars and believed that would stop his coughing. It didn't. His cancer came with lightning speed and took him quickly. He died before he could even contemplate the possibility of dying. By then, there was more than $88,000 under the mattress.

It never occurred to Mrs. Kutos or her family to keep the money. They knew Mishka would want it to be given to his sisters. They also knew that he always assumed he would take it with him when he returned to Hungary. Sending money, sending anything, to Communist countries was a risky proposition. Many immigrants in South Bethlehem sent clothes and shoes back to their families in Europe, but they could never be sure that the packages would arrive. Usually, they would write to their relatives telling them exactly what to expect. Sometimes, the families in Europe could pressure the authorities for delivery of their parcels.

The families in America would pack the clothing carefully in a large cardboard carton and take it to Mrs. Kardos for wrapping. She would wrap the carton in layers of white muslin and carefully sew all the edges closed, by hand, in small, uniform, looping stitches. It might take a day to wrap one package. Then she would neatly print the address on the package with a purple indelible pencil, in English and in Windish or Hungarian as well. The families would pay her for her services and then take the large white cartons to the post office for mailing. Most packages got through; some didn't. Some found their way into the hands of unscrupulous officials on the other side. Sending money was a virtual impossibility. Money was sure to be pocketed before it could ever get to the families that needed it. All of this was on Mrs. Kutos's mind as she left the hospital on the day Mishka died.

The undertaker was surprised by her question. He had never been asked to ship a body to Europe. Mrs. Kutos explained that Mishka's only wish was to be buried in his native village. It was close enough to the truth, she thought, and the undertaker didn't need to know any more.

"It will take a lot of paperwork," he said, "and it will be very expensive. We can store the body here until we have all of the approvals, but that will add to the cost as well. And don't forget, the body will not be reliably refrigerated during its shipment. We will have to mark the coffin so that the family knows the body can't be viewed."

"No matter," said Mrs. Kutos, seeing the solution to her dilemma more and more clearly.

While the paperwork and approvals were in process, aided by local political officials who wanted to keep the good will of the immigrant voters, Mrs. Kutos and Mrs. Kardos began their handiwork. The many twenty- and hundred-dollar bills under the mattress were taken to the bank and exchanged for five-hundred-dollar and thousand-dollar bills. The women carefully folded some of the bills and sewed them into the puckered waistband of a pair of Mishka's blue plaid undershorts. Other bills were tightly pressed into the seams of the cuffs of his trousers and many were sewed flat into the lining of his best sport coat.

When Mrs. Kutos asked the undertaker if she could dress Mishka's body for his final trip, the undertaker didn't question her. With the undertaker's help the job went quickly, and she knew that no one had seen — no one had suspected — that Mishka's clothes were anything other than the last outfit he would wear. When she left the lower level of the funeral home with the undertaker, Mrs. Kutos knew that her secret was safe and her plan would work. Next, she wrote carefully worded letters to each of Mishka's sisters in Hungary, letting them know that in each of their letters there was part of a message that they needed to have.

Approvals and paperwork completed, Mishka was sent on the trip he always hoped he would make: the trip home. He took with him the money he had so carefully saved, for the sisters and family he loved. There was little chance that officials in Hungary would touch or tamper with a body that was labeled as having been in transit for many days. Nevertheless, Mrs. Kutos breathed a sigh of relief when she received a letter from Mishka's oldest sister, telling her that Mishka had, indeed, arrived home, and that he had been placed to rest in the soil of his native village. Before they buried him, his sisters changed his clothing. They found what they were told to look for, and with the help of a well-educated and well-connected relative, they exchanged the American money for Hungarian forints at a bank in Budapest. They promised Mrs. Kutos that they would honor and remember their brother always, and would treat his generous legacy with respect. It had never occurred to Mrs. Kutos to keep the money. That is *her* legacy.

THE GOOD NEWS

The fifth floor solarium at St. Luke's Hospital was empty and quiet. July's heat had made the air as heavy inside as it was outside, and the solarium had that hospital smell, which was a mix of flowers, disinfectant, and medicines. The solarium's old wicker furniture, with its 1940s overstuffed, flowered cushions, waited like an old dowager who had received too many guests but was still trying to keep up appearances.

I entered the solarium and settled down at a puzzle I'd worked on several times that week. Daily visits to see my grandmother, hours at a time, day after day, had given this place a familiarity with which I had made my peace. And a puzzle was always a welcome diversion.

In the midst of my search for another sky-blue puzzle piece, the solarium doors yawned open. In they came — a half-dozen members of a family, with tight faces and holding twisted handkerchiefs in twisted hands. They carried tension with them like a tent ... like a cloak that enshrouded them. Oblivious to me, their words came softly.

"She had a long life, a good life."

"She always tried to do the best for everyone."

"She's at peace. It's better this way."

I curled even more intently into my chair, wanting to become invisible. Leaving the room would have been awkward, disturbing, and I knew their grief was too fragile to be interrupted by a stranger.

"What a good mother she was!"

"Yes, a good Slovak mother from the old country."

They moved around the far end of the solarium, finding their places, as if some protocol within the family group had preordained their positions. Soon, the level and tone of their voices changed.

"I suppose you'll get the house."

"I should. I stayed with her."

"You could. We couldn't. It was no more than we would have done if we didn't have our own families to think of."

"Well, I know what insurances Pop left her so I won't be fooled on that score."

"Who'd try to fool you? You think you're the only one who's entitled to something?"

"What about the land on Spring Street that she and Pop never built on?"

"We'll sell it and split the money. It's only fair."

"Again, you're making the decisions? Or do you know something we don't?"

"Well, Mom always wanted me to have her diamond ring, and there are other things I know she'd want me to have. Things I want. Things we talked about."

"Things you talked about? When? On your twice-a-year visits? When you managed to make the whole two-mile trip from your house to hers? During your ten-minute stops on Mother's Day to hand her a goddamn geranium? Is that when you talked?"

"You'll probably get the house. Do you have to begrudge your sister a few things?"

"Yes, I do. Because fifty lousy rings wouldn't make up for running Mom to the doctor every week, washing her soiled bedding every day, giving her those insulin injections, feeding her, putting up with her moaning and groaning. You never had any of that. I did. I had it all."

"And we had our own families, our own work, and our own troubles. Mom was only a burden to you in the last couple of years. Before that you had more freedom than any of us. She did everything at home while you went to work and ran around at night."

"Ran around? I only went out for coffee or to the movies or to the Legion a couple of times a week. Ran around? I'm hearing this from you? Just how many Lehigh fraternity parties did you go to when you were single? Or maybe Harry doesn't know that you were 'queen of the hill.'"

"Shut up, you bitch. You were always jealous of me. Jealous because I got Harry. Jealous because I got married and you never did. Jealous. Even jealous about Mom's ring."

"Did she ever say who'd be executor? We ought to know that. We can't guess at what's in the will. I assume she had a will."

"We'll know soon enough."

"I still think we should sell the house and the land and split it. It's the only thing to do."

"She better have a will and it better be fair. I don't want to work for the rest of my life. I want to retire. I want to move to Florida and we need money to do that."

"I need a new car and I need it now. I haven't had a decent raise in five years. You're damn right she better have a will and it better be written the right way."

I hadn't planned to hear any of it, but I did. Then, as if they had been meticulously choreographed, each person in the family turned toward the solarium door and the hallway that stretched beyond it. In another second, the footsteps in the hallway were audible … footsteps that grew louder and more authoritative with each step. In the solarium, movement and sound ceased. The door flew open and the green-garbed surgeon interrupted the moment shamelessly with his loud voice.

"I knew you would want to know right away — it went splendidly. No problems. I knew you'd be glad to hear it. She's going to be just fine!"

AT LAST

I first saw Anna in 1957, when she was well into her thirties. I was ten years old and had been sent by my grandmother to take some apple strudel to Anna's mother. My grandmother had told me to pay no attention to Anna, simply saying that she was "funny in the head." Anna's dark eyes stared at me. Her pixie-ish, brunette hair suggested that in her younger years she must have been pretty. Her clothes were dated, however, and made her look as if she had been caught in a time warp. That dated look and her empty stare were the first clues that something was wrong with her.

Anna's mother was a shy, soft-spoken woman with neatly waved gray hair. She smiled and thanked me for the strudel, and gave me some pink roses from her garden to take home for my grandmother. But I couldn't get Anna or her stare out of my mind. When I got home, I asked my mother what was wrong with Anna. I asked if she was mentally ill.

"No," said Mom, "she isn't mentally ill. Not really. That's not the problem. It is a much more complicated situation. We know what happened because Mrs. Novak, Anna's neighbor, was there and she told us what happened."

Mom explained that Anna had finished tenth grade, but like so many Depression-era children, she had to quit school to go to work, to help with family expenses. An only child, she had no brothers or sisters to share that financial burden. Anna worked in a textile mill, spreading cloth for the pattern cutters. She dutifully brought her pay home to her parents every week. They gave her a small allowance and she was content. Cute and vivacious, she was a member of the church choir and used her allowance to go to the movies and to Archond's Ice Cream Parlor on Fourth Street. Mom remembered that Anna's favorite song was

"At Last" from the film *Orchestra Wives*. She said that Anna had gone to the movies to see that film at least a half-dozen times just to hear that song.

Anna's Hungarian father was a hard, fearsome man. Muscular and quick-tempered, he expected absolute obedience from his wife and daughter. His black hair, heavy eyebrows, and thick mustache gave him a perpetually menacing look. He didn't allow Anna to invite friends to their home. Dating was absolutely forbidden. Had her father's attitude been different, Anna might well have met a young man and been married. But then she would not be bringing her weekly paycheck home.

The years passed, and the 1930s turned into the 1940s. Anna continued to work at the factory and bring her paycheck home. In the late 1940s, she asked her parents if she could buy a television set. She'd pay for it, she promised, out of her allowance. Her father said that he wanted no such devil's contraption in the house. "But it's her money," the mother had said, interceding for Anna. "She should be able to buy something from her own money." The father said no more. And so, Anna began to save quarters, dimes, and dollar bills. She didn't go to the movies as often and she stopped going to Archond's after choir practice. It took five years, but Anna finally filled two cigar boxes with enough dollar bills to afford a black and white television set. She asked her father to help her choose one, but he refused, saying again that he wanted no tool of the devil in his house.

Anna's mother went with her to an appliance store on Third Street to pick out a television. They chose a GE console model costing $320. Never had Anna been happier. She could imagine herself coming home from work and watching *The Jack Benny Show, Arthur Godfrey*, and all the programs her co-workers at the factory talked about. She told herself that she would watch *I Love Lucy, Burns and Allen,* and *Texaco Star Theatre*. She had the exotic sounding names memorized.

On the day the television was delivered, Anna brought her cigar-box savings down to the living room. Before she could pay the deliverymen, her father brusquely took the cigar boxes from her hands and went into the kitchen. He ordered Anna to sit down at the kitchen table.

"You think you will defy me?" he growled. "You think you will bring the devil in here?"

While the deliverymen looked on quizzically, Anna's father opened the circular iron top of the coal stove, took a dollar bill from one of the cigar boxes and dropped it into the searing flames. Anna shrieked and ran toward the stove but her father shoved her back onto the kitchen chair. Her mother tried to stop him, but he slapped her hard across the face and she flew backward, slamming into the kitchen wall.

Hearing Anna's screams, Mrs. Novak rushed over from her house next door. When she saw the scene in the kitchen she instantly understood what was happening.

"Louie!" she demanded. "Are you crazy? What are you doing? You can't take that money from her!" But Anna's father paid no attention. He seemed to not even hear her. His hands moved slowly, mechanically, from the cigar box to the scorching, glowing opening of the stove. He stared fixedly at the flames, watching as each dollar bill burned. Anna sobbed and wailed as she watched the paper bills curl into gray cinders. Her father moved as if he was in a trance, oblivious to his neighbor's pleas, his wife's tears, and his daughter's shrieking. One by one, dollar bill by dollar bill, with excruciating slowness, Anna's father dropped her five years of savings into the licking red flames, making something of a ceremony out of this torture.

The deliverymen left soon after the burning began, taking the television with them. Anna never saw them leave.

Soon, Anna's sobbing ceased and a terrible stillness came over her. Mrs. Novak, who watched this drama unfold, told my mother that, "it was as if her soul drained out of her."

After an hour or so, the cigar boxes were empty. Satisfied, Anna's father left the kitchen, throwing the empty boxes to the floor. Her mother tried to talk to Anna, to console her, but Anna was past being consoled, past hearing, past being reached.

Mrs. Novak said that Anna sat on that kitchen chair, silent and motionless, for three days and three nights. Her mother eventually picked her up and carried her to her bed. The doctor said that he could do nothing — said he had never seen anything like it. Anna never went back to the factory and she never spoke again.

Anna's mother bathed and dressed her. She helped her to eat until that function returned. When the weather was pleasant, Anna's mother led her outside to sit in the sun, on the green wooden bench at the back of the house. She spoke to Anna as if her daughter heard and understood, and she made sure that the radio in the living room was played all day for Anna.

When her father died three years later, in 1955, Anna showed no emotion, no recognition of the fact that he was gone. She wasn't taken to the viewing or the funeral. Mrs. Novak stayed with Anna while her mother attended the services.

In 1959, two years after I first saw Anna, her mother died. There was neighborhood chatter about what would become of Anna and who would take care of her. A few weeks after the mother's funeral, my grandmother asked me to take some pastries to Anna. "She must be eating," my grandmother reasoned, "and it will be good for her to see someone."

I cautiously knocked on the wooden screen door at the back of Anna's house, half afraid of what I would find. The screen door was unlatched, so I opened the door and stepped into the kitchen. I called Anna's name and announced that I had come with turnovers and poppy-seed rolls from my grandmother. I saw a bright light glowing in the living room. There sat Anna, in front of a large, console color television set. I placed the pastries on a table nearby and gestured that they were for her. She gave me a wide smile and turned right back to the television. I sat with Anna for a while and was pleased that she laughed and smiled at the shows on the screen. I brought her a glass of cold milk from the kitchen and gave her one of the cherry turnovers I'd brought. Again, she gave me a warm smile. Again, her attention turned back to the TV immediately.

Anna lived for another twenty years after that visit, attending to her basic needs herself, with some help from Mrs. Novak. She spent most of every day and evening in front of her beloved television, its sights and sounds and stories filling the space where her mind used to be.

LENA

Lena had the gift of second sight, or so they said. Quiet and reclusive, Lena had her hands full with one child who was crippled from birth and another who was mentally ill.

Born in 1896, in that part of Austria-Hungary that would remain Hungary, she had emigrated to America in 1914. She met and married a man from Bratislava who, after siring her two seriously disabled children, committed suicide because he could not face the burden of caring for them. The irony was not lost on Lena.

She worked as she could, doing housekeeping for some families, sewing and cooking for others, always looking for work that would allow her time to care for her children. Friends and neighbors looked after the children if Lena couldn't do so. Her house, in an alley near Polk Street, looked like a miniature house. It was what she could afford.

Lena was not unfriendly. She was simply too busy and too burdened to have time for visiting or talking over the fence on wash day. She knew my grandparents and exchanged greetings with them as she hurried to her house or to work.

One day, in the spring of 1946, Lena knocked on the side door of my grandparents' home. She was invited to come in and have something to eat. Surprisingly, she made time to do both. As my grandmother gave her a cup of fresh coffee and slices of nut roll, Lena placed a small item on the kitchen table, an item wrapped in soft, white paper.

"I'm bringing a gift," she said, "and I must explain the gift. This is for the child your daughter will bear. It will be a girl and she will be born next January. She will be a special child, but I don't know why or how. I only know that I must give her her first gift and it must be this gift, something I brought from the old country ... something that was given to me."

Lena carefully unwrapped the paper to reveal a hand-painted, embossed metal cup, showing some flowers and a child with a red cap, with a metal handle trimmed in red. My grandparents admired the cup and thanked Lena for her gift.

"But I don't think Mary is pregnant," said my grandmother. "And if she is, she doesn't know it yet. But after having two boys she'll be so happy to have a girl."

"Mary isn't the one who will have the baby," replied Lena. "Irene will."

My grandparents exchanged knowing glances, not certain how much to tell Lena. Finally, my grandmother said, "That can't be. Two doctors have told Irene that she can never have children. Her uterus is not shaped to make that possible. They have told her she can never have children."

Lena smiled gently, knowingly. "January," she said. "A girl. And this is the child's first gift." She rose from the table, said her good-byes, and left the house.

My grandmother quickly picked up the cup and reached for her coat. "Where are you going?" my grandfather asked.

"To Mary's, of course. I have to tell her the good news."

That evening, when my parents came home from work, Lena's visit was the main topic of conversation around the dinner table. Everyone was pleased with the idea that Mary would have a daughter, but there was also the recognition that Lena's second sight was flawed. She might have seen a little girl in the family's future, but she saw her with the wrong mother.

Two months later, Dr. Frederick Pearson told my mother that, against all odds, she was pregnant. The baby would be born around Christmas. The metal cup was brought back from my Aunt Mary's house and placed on the kitchen shelf in the home where my parents and grandparents lived.

As the months went by, Dr. Pearson continued to talk about a late December delivery. My mother kept Lena's comments about January to herself. A medical doctor is not someone to whom one speaks about an old woman's predictions. Christmas came and went. The New Year came and went. I was born on January 30, 1947.

I was told the story of Lena's prediction sometime in my childhood, and I liked to look at 'my' cup, placed on a high shelf in the kitchen cupboards. Occasionally I would see Lena's crippled son making his way around the neighborhood on a small cart, running errands for Lena or for someone who would pay him a few cents. Lena still struggled to support herself and her children, and we seldom saw her. Her prediction of my birth gave considerable credence to the idea that she had the gift of second sight, but no one dared to ask Lena what was in their futures. She had a gift, and if she believed she had to tell someone something she did so. But she never responded to questions about the future and never took money for her visions.

During the summer after my graduation from college, Lena again knocked on the side door of our house. My grandmother welcomed her in and Lena asked to see me. She had official-looking papers with her, papers she didn't understand.

"I know Carol will know what these are," she said, "and what I should do."

I sat with her at the kitchen table and looked over the papers. They were simple enough policies and instructions relating to Social Security and disability benefits for her son, but they were complex for an elderly woman who could barely read English.

I explained all of the questions, and I filled in the forms as Lena wished. She signed where I told her to sign, and I told her I would mail the forms for her. She thanked me heartily and reached for my hand. She said that she would "look ahead" for me as her thanks for my help.

"No, thank you," I replied quickly, my thoughts swirling. "I'm happy to help you anytime. You don't have to do anything for me."

"But I must," she said. "You don't understand. There must be a gift in return, and this is what I can give."

Stalling for time and knowing that I was very uncomfortable with the idea of anyone looking into my future, I asked Lena when she first knew she had "the gift."

Lena leaned back in the kitchen chair and was silent for a moment. Her thoughts traveled back in time and then she began her story.

She told us that her parents had a small farm. They raised enough food to feed the family, with a little left over to sell. Lena's mother was a strong woman, physically and spiritually, with great wisdom and common sense. She was respected by the villagers and her counsel was frequently sought.

At the outskirts of the village, groups of gypsies often camped. There was an abiding hostility between the villagers and the gypsies, with each group careful to stay clear of the other.

On one summer day, a woman from the gypsy camp did the unthinkable: she came into the village and approached the women she encountered. She told them that she had just given birth and needed to have someone serve as godmother to her newborn child. "Why doesn't someone from your tribe do this?" they asked her. She explained that this was her thirteenth child and it was a man-child. For these gypsies, the number thirteen was almost a curse, and no one from the tribe would "stand up" for her baby.

Word of the gypsy woman's request flew around the village. Soon, Lena's mother heard of it. She walked into the village and asked if anyone had gone to the gypsy camp to do as the gypsy had asked. The village women were astonished and said that they would never do such a thing. "Are you mad?" Lena's mother exclaimed. "This is a baby. A baby to be placed in God's hands and God's care. God does not count numbers as humans do and he does not have prejudice as humans do." She strode off angrily toward the edge of the village.

As Lena's mother approached the gypsy camp, all activity there stopped. They stared at her as suspiciously as the villagers had stared at the gypsy woman who intruded into their territory.

"Who is it that has the child?" Lena's mother asked.

A woman appeared holding an infant in her arms.

"You would do this for me?" the woman asked incredulously.

"Of course," said Lena's mother. "This baby is God's own creation and he belongs to God more than to you or to the tribe."

The two women embraced — the gypsy men dared not interfere — and a small ceremony was conducted by which the baby was consecrated to God and given his name.

The gypsy woman turned to Lena's mother and said, "I know you will not take coins or ornaments for this honor that you have paid me, but I must give you a gift, and I know what it must be. I cannot give you the gift of second sight. That must be done before a child is born. But you will bear a girl-child and she will have the gift." The gypsy paused as if looking through the mists of years to come. "But I know already that it will bring her little solace in this life. Her life will be hard. She will live far from here and she will work hard all her life. Her children will be broken. I do not know how, but I can see that they will be broken. Your daughter will have much sorrow in this life and much peace and joy in the next life."

When the gypsy woman concluded her reverie, they embraced again and Lena's mother walked back toward her home, half believing and half denying what she had just been told. Less than a year later, Lena was born.

Her mother told Lena about the gypsy's words many times. She taught Lena to value and use her gift wisely, and never to use it in exchange for money. She never told her about the broken children. She hoped that part of the gypsy woman's prediction would never come true. Many years later, when Lena wrote to her mother from America and told her about the birth of each child, her mother finally told her what the gypsy had seen foreshadowed for her.

"And so," Lena said to us, "I was born as the gypsy said I would be, with the gift of sometimes knowing what will come. I must use this gift to thank you now."

I explained that I did not want to look ahead, did not want to know what was to come. I wanted life to reveal itself to me without my looking for predicted outcomes. Lena understood.

"Then I will tell you about someone close to you. Perhaps a good friend?"

I immediately thought of my college classmate, Patricia, then doing graduate study in Denmark. We were good friends and exchanged letters regularly. I knew that Pat was deeply involved in her research, and I wondered if Lena could imagine Pat's life of study and reading. Lena asked to see a picture of my friend. I brought her Pat's graduation photo. She stared at the picture for a long while. Finally, she spoke.

"Your friend is far away now, but she is distressed. She has work to do, much reading to do, but she can think of nothing except a young man she has met. He is tall and handsome, with blond hair. She is completely entranced by him and can think of nothing else. It will come to nothing, and that will be a good thing. But for now, she is … as we say, 'sick with love.'"

Having given me this obligatory gift, Lena left our house.

"Well," I said to my parents, "we can finally know that Lena's gifts are flawed at best. Pat hasn't had a crush on anyone in her life, except for the actor Peter O'Toole, and she's too busy to start now. She always thought that my infatuations and romances were a waste of time. This time, Lena is way off base."

Pat's weekly letter arrived a few days later. I sat outside in the sunshine as I opened the familiar, blue air-mail envelope.

"Dear Pal — I haven't been able to concentrate on my work for several weeks now. I know this will sound crazy, won't sound like me at all, but I've met this student from Norway. His name is Haakon and he is handsome and blond and …."

THE VIOLIN

On Bethlehem's South Side, the shoemakers' shops have always been more than places of business. The old, retired men gather there, in shops in their own neighborhoods, and they talk in Windish or Hungarian or Slovak. They wear felt hats and flannel shirts, and they sometimes just sit, in silence and ceremony, on wooden chairs that have been there since the days of cigar factories and silk mills along Fourth Street.

I expected to see the venerable gathering one summer day when I pulled open the screen door of one of the neighborhood's cobbler shops. Surprisingly, no one was there, and in chatting with the shoemaker — an old family friend — about the absent, elderly men, a long and varied conversation began. I learned that our shoemaker had once intended to study music in Vienna. As a child, some sixty years before, he had played a family violin well enough for his parents to admit that he deserved special training. But as with so many wrenchingly poor families in Hungary, Yugoslavia, Austria, Poland, and Czechoslovakia, the thought of advanced education was out of the question. So he learned a trade and came to America and opened his shop here. In Bethlehem, at least, he found people who could appreciate music as he did.

Did he still play at all, I asked. His face beamed like Christmas morning. Would I like to hear? Of course I would, I told him, and settled back on a particularly ancient chair while he reached under a cluttered, wooden counter piled high with shoes and bits of leather. He emerged with a black leather case, pieces of which had flaked off at the sides and near the handle. He opened it carefully and took the violin out.

I have no idea how long he played. I only know that I was eight years old again, sitting in our backyard on a quiet Sunday night filled with fireflies, listening to our down-the-street neighbor, an old Hungarian, as he played "When a Gypsy Makes His Violin Cry." I looked at the shoemaker. His eyes were closed and I knew that he was twenty-five again and in Vienna and the Emperor was in the audience. I closed my eyes and went there too, as waterfalls and carriage rides and moonlight poured from that violin. When he stopped, there was a brief second of transcendent quiet, and then the moment was punctured by applause.

We looked toward the screen door to see that a small crowd had gathered — a few bearded and blue-jeaned Lehigh students, some Puerto Rican children, a policeman, the grocer from across the street, and a half-shaved man from the barber-shop next door. One lady in a flowered dress put her bag of groceries down on the sidewalk, wiped at her eyes with a chubby fist, and then joined the others as they smiled and clapped, and for one moment, made the world so tender that its promise could break your heart.

In a few seconds they were gone and traffic noises came to the screen door once more. I was silent. What do you say when you've just been in a scene on Hallmark Hall of Fame? I mumbled something about the violin being so handy, there under the counter. "It's always with me," the shoemaker said, as he cradled it. "It's the most precious thing I own." He held it toward me and tilted it so that the afternoon sunlight streaming through the shop window made the wood glow. There, visible in the deep, warm interior of the violin, was the testimony: Ant. Stradivarius Cremonen.

This article was first published in the Moravian College Magazine, November, 1973

THE LIST

*I*f the old woman who had come to visit my grandmother had spoken in normal tones, I wouldn't have paid any attention to their conversation. But from the moment she came through the side door and into our kitchen, her excitement was undisguised.

"I have something amazing to tell you," she said breathlessly to my grandmother in Windish. "You'll never believe it!"

As soon as I heard those words, my child's curiosity was aroused. I was sitting in the kitchen and couldn't help overhearing their conversation. My grandmother poured a glass of red wine for her visitor and encouraged her to tell her story.

I understood Windish very well, and I wanted to know what this woman's amazing news was. I could understand all of the words she spoke, but I couldn't connect them for meaning. The woman talked about a group and a list and the priest. The woman was Catholic, and it wasn't unusual for Protestants and Catholics of the same ethnic background to be friends, as my grandmother and this woman were friends. There was the fundamental understanding that you would never marry outside your religion, but for business, neighborhood matters, or simple friendship, the Protestant/Catholic line could be crossed.

"She told them that if they didn't take her in she would show the priest her list," Gram's visitor said dramatically, leaning forward and pulling her white shawl more closely around her shoulders.

"No!" exclaimed my grandmother, shocked. "But she would never do that. She would never point the finger at herself."

"Yes, she would," Gram's friend said authoritatively. "After all these years, and all that snubbing, she would do it. I believe that and they must have believed it, too."

The two women talked excitedly for a while longer, and then Gram's friend left, obviously on a mission to carry her news to other women in the neighborhood. I turned their words over and over in my mind but I still could make no sense of what I'd heard.

When my mother came into the kitchen, I asked her what the women had been talking about. She had heard their conversation from the dining room where she had been putting dishes into the china cabinet. She then realized that I had also heard their conversation. I told her that I knew it was something about a group and a list and telling the priest something, but I couldn't understand how all of this fit together. My mother and grandmother exchanged long looks and my mother was silent for a moment, obviously assessing what she should tell me and how. It was the first time she had hesitated in answering one of my questions. Finally, she sat down at the kitchen table and spoke.

"There is a group in the Catholic church that some of the ladies of the church belong to," she said. "It is called the Sodality and it is an important organization to the ladies who belong to it."

In my child's mind, I thought that anything that had 'soda' in its name sounded like fun, but I said nothing and waited for Mom to continue. She sighed, hesitated again, and then seemed to speak especially slowly and carefully.

"You know that when a man and a woman are married, they often have babies. Well, sometimes women find out that they are going to have a baby even though they're not married. And sometimes," Mom went on, "they don't want to have the baby."

"But why wouldn't they want to have a baby?" I asked, picturing cute little bundles in blankets and wishing I had a little brother or sister.

"Almost always," Mom said, choosing her words carefully, "it's because they are afraid. Afraid of what people will say, afraid of bringing shame on their families, perhaps afraid of the baby's father. And because they are so afraid, they think that not having the baby is the only solution."

"Sometimes," she continued, "they have an operation that makes the baby go away. But that operation is against the law. It isn't legal. And if the person doing the operation is caught, they could go to jail."

"But why would they do something that could get them into that kind of trouble?" I asked.

"Because they are more afraid of what will happen to them if they have the baby than they are afraid of doing something illegal. One fear is greater than the other."

"How does this operation fit in with what the lady was saying to Grammy?"

"Well, there is a woman who has wanted to be a member of the Sodality for many years. But the ladies who belong to the group wouldn't allow her to join. She asked and tried many times but they wouldn't let her join."

"Why?" I asked.

"Perhaps they thought she was beneath them ... thought she wasn't as important as they are. Perhaps they don't like her or never had the chance to get to know her."

"But she got into the group now?" I asked, still trying to connect the dots of the women's conversation.

"Yes. You see," said Mom, almost painfully, "the lady who wanted to get into the group does the operations I just told you about. And she has done those operations for some of the families, some of the women, in her church. She was tired of being kept out of the group and she finally told them that, if they didn't let her join, she would show the priest the list of the families for whom she has done this operation."

I understood. I was only nine or ten years old, but I understood.

The next Sunday afternoon, the lady who had the list, the lady who had done the operations, walked past our house while my grandmother was outside gardening. They exchanged greetings and Gram asked if she wanted to come in and have something to eat.

"I can't," said the dressed-up woman, smiling widely under her obviously new hat. "I have to go to a meeting of the Sodality," she said proudly.

I wondered if she was using the same route for her announcements that my grandmother's friend had used the week before.

THE BOARDER

When the twentieth century hit its mid-point, in 1950, Rudy Czsazar was 62 years old and had lived with the Horvath family for thirty years. He was a boarder, renting a room on the second floor of the Horvaths' large and immaculate home on Packer Avenue. He ate with the family and sometimes sat with them in the living room in the evening. Mr. and Mrs. Horvath were approximately Rudy's age — in their mid-sixties — and like Rudy, had emigrated to America from Hungary in 1917. Also living in the house were the Horvaths' son, John, his wife, Flora, and their daughter, Terry.

The son, John, was short and slight in stature, with a nervous laugh, a hawk-beaked nose, and slicked-back dark hair. Taller and heavier than her husband, Flora had sleepy, languid eyes. Her lips were always colored bright red, and her shoulder-length brunette hair was a mass of permed curls. Their daughter, Terry, had short, dark hair and she had her grandmother's beautiful complexion and warm smile.

Rudy and Mr. Horvath worked at Bethlehem Steel, but John worked in a shoe store on Third Street in South Bethlehem. John had worked at the Steel for a few months after he graduated from high school, but he didn't have the physical strength for the labor of the foundries and he didn't have the skills for office work within the plant. Although it was never acknowledged, he also didn't have the temperament for the natural camaraderie and teamwork of a steel mill. John could be pleasant to customers at the shoe store and friendly enough to his two co-workers, but that was the extent to which he could be outgoing. Even his marriage to Flora happened because she told him, initially, that they would date, and later told him that they would be married. John never could have navigated that journey on his own initiative. John prided himself on having a white-collar job and wearing a suit and tie to work. He didn't allow himself to think about the fact that his miniscule earnings required him and his wife and daughter to live with his parents. He thought of himself as a professional and that was success enough for him. It even allowed him a modicum of conceit.

Mr. Horvath had suffered from crippling arthritis for years, and accommodations had been made for him at the plant to ease his strain. By the time he came home each day, in late afternoon, he simply wanted to have his supper and take enough aspirin to blunt the pain until bedtime. Mrs. Horvath — chubby, energetic, and good-natured — was the center of gravity for the family, and she tended to everything from cooking to bill paying. Flora had no inclination to compete for the title of woman of the house, and she occupied herself with reading magazines, polishing her nails, and having card games with her friends several times a week. If John could fancy himself a professional, Flora had no intention of spoiling the image by being a working woman.

It was, perhaps, inevitable that Rudy Czsazar would be drawn into this vacuum of family leadership despite his protests that "I am only a boarder." When the family listened to the radio or watched television, Rudy made no requests or suggestions regarding the shows selected. When visitors came to the house, he stayed in his room and did not interrupt the social interactions of the family. But when Mr. Horvath had to seriously consider retirement because of his arthritis, it was Rudy, not John, who was consulted about the decision. When the increasingly frail Mr. Horvath had to be helped with his bathroom needs and getting dressed, it was Rudy who assisted him, not John. (John informed his parents that he was too sensitive to help with such personal needs and that it upset him to see his father's frailty.) When there were major repairs to be done to the house, it was Rudy who was asked about the feasibility of the project, the amount to be spent, and the workmen to be hired. With each inquiry, he repeated his disclaimer of being "only a boarder" before offering his opinion or his assistance.

When Mr. Horvath died, it was Rudy who assisted Mrs. Horvath in choosing a cemetery plot and making arrangements for the funeral. John was burdened enough by having to choose a suit to wear to the funeral and worrying about what he would say to those attending the viewing.

As years passed, more and more decisions were brought to Rudy for resolution. Even Terry asked his opinion about her job choices after graduation from high school. "I am only a boarder," Rudy said for the millionth time, "but I think you should continue your schooling. I have some money saved, and it would please me to pay toward college for you." He gave Terry more than half of the amount she needed for tuition each year, and with school loans and a part-time job, Terry was able to get a degree in education and begin work as a second-grade teacher at Donegan School. Rudy reluctantly accepted her invitation to attend her college graduation, but he sat at the rear of the auditorium because he was not a family member, but "only a boarder."

As Mrs. Horvath entered her mid-seventies, she began to slow down, and for the first time, show signs of age and infirmity. Flora declared that she had no talent for cooking and would be just as happy with canned soup or take-out. It was Rudy who kept Mrs. Horvath company in the kitchen and followed her instructions for preparing meals, enabling the whole family to continue to enjoy the home cooking that had nourished them for decades. Rudy also took over the garden, and while Mrs. Horvath sat outside and enjoyed the sun's warmth, he planted the spring pansies and pinched back the mums by the 4th of July, as she directed. Inside the house, Rudy dusted and ran the vacuum, occasionally disturbing Flora's naps or magazine reading, for which he dutifully apologized.

When Mrs. Horvath was diagnosed with diabetes, it was Rudy who learned how to give her daily insulin injections. Both Flora and John said that they were terrified of needles. John also said that the store had begun to take credit card payments and he was under great stress to learn this new system. He did not want to try to learn anything more right now. Rudy read the menu guides and food labels for Mrs. Horvath and organized her weekly pill container. "What would I do without you?" she frequently asked him. "You would be fine," Rudy answered, knowing better. Then the inevitable: "I am, after all, only a boarder."

One evening when John and Flora had gone to the movies, Mrs. Horvath patted the sofa cushion next to hers and said, "Rudy, please, you come sit here with me." Rudy rose from his chair and joined her on the sofa.

"I am not stupid," she began. "Like you and my dear, dead Janos, I have no schooling. But I am not stupid. I see how things are, how they have always been. You see these things, too, I know. I want to make things right. I want to do for you some of what you have done for me, for Janos, for Terry, for all of us. I want you to marry me. We can go to the priest and he will take care of things."

After his initial shock, Rudy smiled and said, "I hope you aren't counting on having children, Mrs. Horvath." After they enjoyed a hearty laugh at his joke, she said, "Perhaps you should start calling me Helen."

"But what will your son say?" Rudy asked. "What will he and Flora think of this?"

"It is none of their business," Mrs. Horvath said firmly. "This is my house. The money I have is my money. They have contributed nothing toward it, nothing toward the house. You have given me rent money for more than forty years, so part of my money is already your money. And if it pleases me to have companionship in these last years of my life, to have someone to sit with me on this sofa, someone to hold me as I sleep, that, too, is none of their business."

"Are you sure about this, Mrs. ... Helen?" Rudy asked. "It seems to be a very big decision."

"It has been a long time coming," she replied earnestly, "and, yes, I am sure about it. But you have not given me your answer to my question."

Rudy paused for a long moment. "I think you are a fine woman," he said gently. "I have always admired your love for your husband and your good care of your family and me. In these last years, I have felt affection as well as respect for you. It would be an honor to be your husband. And I will honor and care for you for as long as I live."

"Then that settles it," said Mrs. Horvath, smiling. "We will go to the priest tomorrow and he will tell us what we have to do. I am happy, Rudy. I am truly happy that you have agreed to this."

When Mrs. Horvath told John and Flora about her plans, they were stunned. While John had no ability to see three steps ahead, Flora seemed to wake from her quarter-century lethargy to ask, "What will this mean for us?"

"You may continue to live here if you wish," replied Mrs. Horvath. "More I cannot say and more I will not promise." Flora began to worry for the first time in her life. She felt a tightening at her throat and could only think of John's small salary.

After their visit with the priest, Helen told Rudy that they had another stop to make. They walked five blocks farther and entered the offices of Neil Stangl, Attorney at Law. Stangl greeted Helen cordially, obviously having met her before, and Helen introduced Rudy to the attorney. She then asked Stangl what happens with home and property ownership when there is a marriage. Before he could reply, Helen said, "What I want is for Rudy to have co-ownership of everything I have while we are both alive and I want him to get everything if I die. The money, jewelry, and other items that I have given to Terry in my will should remain that way. But everything else must go to Rudy."

Stangl explained that, with such clear directions, in addition to the community property rights attendant to marriage, Rudy would have the security of a newly drafted will, which he would prepare. When Stangl asked Helen about her preferences if Rudy predeceased her, she refused to discuss the matter. "That can wait for another day," she said.

Whether she had an actual feeling about her mortality or was just making a good guess, Helen was right to say that alternate provisions in her will could wait for another day. Helen and Rudy had seven years of peaceful and joyful marriage. Laughter sprinkled itself through their days, and they enjoyed church trips, a cruise to Bermuda for seniors, and the simple pleasures of sitting on the porch or on the sofa holding hands. Helen died quietly in her sleep a few days after their seventh anniversary. She was 84 years old.

Absorbed with his grief and loss, Rudy didn't notice John's and Flora's nervousness in the days following Helen's death. It was Flora who was bold enough to finally ask the question. "Will you be staying here, Rudy, now that Helen is gone? Perhaps you'd prefer to rent a room somewhere else, somewhere where there aren't so many memories."

"Why would I wish to leave such wonderful memories?" he countered. "Why would I leave the place where I have known such peace and happiness? Why would I leave my own home?"

That last statement hung in the air like a sword suspended above John's and Flora's lives. Not wishing to tease or torment them, Rudy told them what Helen had done when they visited the lawyer. He retrieved a copy of Helen's will from their bedroom and showed it to them. The meaning of it eluded John for a long while, but Flora understood instantly.

"This is outrageous! You are nothing but a thief!" she shouted, her red mouth twisted into an accusing sneer. "This is our house. It should be our house. John is their son. We always planned that, when they were both dead, we would sell the house and move somewhere else."

"You are free to move now," said Rudy, calmly. "Or you may stay if you wish. But this is not your house. Helen did not want you to have it. That was her choice. She saw ... she knew ... that you did not value this house; you did nothing to help maintain it; you contributed no money toward it or toward its expenses. Perhaps she also guessed that you would do as you have said: you would move as soon as you could. You did not love or appreciate this home as she and Janos did. What I saw," Rudy continued, his face reddening and his voice growing thick, "is that you did not love or appreciate them. You had no time for them, and no desire to help them in their times of need. If Helen was pained by your lack of appreciation for this home, I have been pained by your lack of love for her and for Janos."

"What will we do?" asked John, stirring from his silence and falling back instinctively on the habit of asking for Rudy's advice.

"Whatever will make you happy," responded Rudy. "But know this — if you stay, you will pay something toward the expenses of the house and you will do some of the work needed for cooking, cleaning, and maintaining it. You will not insult Helen and Janos in their deaths by continuing your lazy and uncaring ways. If that is too much for you, then perhaps you should leave."

"Pay? Pay??" shrieked Flora. "Never! Why, that would make us ... make us ... mere ...."

"Boarders?" suggested Rudy. "No, you will never be thought of as boarders. You will always be family. You will always have a place here if you wish. It is simply that I am no longer just a boarder. After fifty years ... I am no longer 'only a boarder.'"

GETTING HOOFTY FIXED (UP)

He was a fixture in South Bethlehem. Known to almost everyone by his nickname, Hoofty, he was a middle-aged man who was slow and simple. Like a half-dozen other off-center characters, he was part of the landscape and the flavor of the South Side.

Hoofty and the others — Whizzer, Lehigh Leon, Gabor, and Claudie — lived with their families. At night, they made their way home to their suppers and to a safe, warm, comfortable place to sleep and be cared for. During the day and into the evening, they had their routines, their pals, and their resting places. They could go anywhere. People knew they weren't quite right to one extent or another, and allowances were made for any confusion they might have or create.

When they could, they ran errands for residents and shopkeepers and earned a few cents, sometimes a few dollars, for their efforts. Most of the time, they were happy to simply be part of a group, accepted as one of the guys by people who, they knew instinctively, were somehow smarter and more normal than they were.

Hoofty was quiet and shy, and he looked, more than anything, like the cartoon character Sad Sack. His ears stuck out more than they should, and his eyes drooped down at the outer corners. Friendly to those he knew, he would avert his gaze if he saw someone unfamiliar walking by. He knew that he was different and he didn't need a stranger's stare to remind him of that reality. Hoofty's clothing gave him a comforting predictability. In fall and winter, he wore corduroy slacks paired with a plaid flannel shirt and a sweater or jacket. In spring and summer, he wore khakis and a cotton T-shirt in subdued colors. Hoofty's clothes were always immaculate and neatly pressed — a point of pride for his Windish mother, with whom he lived. When he was amused, Hoofty erupted into a hearty, guffawing laugh that made everyone in hearing distance laugh too.

Hoofty's daily routine involved checking in at the South Bethlehem post office at Fourth and Brodhead to see if there were any errands he could run. There never were. Then he stopped in at the Tally Ho tavern to ask if there was any work he could do. Sometimes there were cartons to be unloaded or trash barrels to be taken out back. Helping with such work made Hoofty feel useful. Next, he would check in at the newsstand to listen to the guys talk about sports and to have a donut, always a crème-filled donut. Sometimes, a voice from the back of the newsstand, from the big room behind the striped curtain, would call to him. It was in that backroom that the daily numbers play was tracked, along with the money that was bet on the numbers. Hoofty might be told to go to the bank and get change, or less frequently, be asked to go next door, down to the basement of the apartment building where one of the established poker games would be in progress. Gambling flourished in Bethlehem long before it became legal and before it became a marketing extravaganza. If you knew where to go, you could bet on the three-digit daily number. If you didn't know where to go, you could just ask someone. Anyone in South Bethlehem could tell you who the numbers runners were and where you could find them. Getting into the poker games was trickier. One of those games, played weekly on a Wednesday afternoon in the backroom of a downtown store, was reserved for businessmen and men from City Hall. The other, in the basement of the apartment building, was reserved for big-time betters who could put $100 on the table for a hand. You had to be invited to join either of those games.

When Hoofty's rounds were done, he would make his way to the firehouse. There, he would sit with the firemen and listen to their stories and laugh at their jokes. Hoofty was never the butt of a joke, at the firehouse or anywhere else. No one ever treated him or any of the other South Side eccentrics unkindly or disrespectfully. If someone had tried, a fireman, policeman, or shopkeeper would quickly have straightened out the miscreant.

From the firehouse, by mid-afternoon, Hoofty walked to the office of the *Bethlehem Bulletin*. A small, neighborhood-based newspaper, the

Bulletin didn't try to compete with the *Bethlehem Globe-Times* or the Allentown newspapers. The *Bulletin* covered South Side events: church dinners and celebrations, and local political news. It had a niche and filled it effectively. Hoofty had his own chair at the *Bulletin* office, along with the other regulars who sat there to pass the time and talk about local happenings.

Hoofty's last stop was usually at Tammany, a bar at the corner of Fourth and Fillmore Streets. There, someone would invariably buy him a beer, and he enjoyed the talk and laughter of the men at the bar. On warm summer nights, if some of the men decided to stand outside, Hoofty took his place beside them, bending his knee to prop himself against the brick wall, just like the other guys.

One evening, as the regulars left the *Bulletin* office, one of them, Billy, for no particular reason, asked, "Hey, Hoofty, you ever been with a woman?" Hoofty looked confused and didn't answer. The chuckles of the other guys prompted Hoofty to smile, too, although he wasn't sure why. The question hung in the air as the little group paused on Polk Street, on its way to Tammany.

"You know what I mean by 'being with a woman?' " Billy continued, asking the question slowly.

Hoofty certainly knew that he was with his mother and his sister when he was at home, and he knew that he was with women in the shops when they asked him to run errands. But he sensed that Billy and the others meant something else. "I don't know," he said softly, staring down at his feet and shuffling self-consciously.

Suddenly the question and the possibilities seemed to take on a new level of importance for the men. They paused in their questioning and walked silently up the Polk Street hill. When they got to Tammany, they sat quietly at a table, an unspoken agreement hovering around them. After their beers arrived, they thought about how to ask Hoofty the question again and how to explain to him what they meant.

"Hoofty," said Mike, an older guy, gently, "when you see a woman, a really nice-looking woman, do you ever get, you know, feelings? Urges? Do you want to kiss her or touch her?"

Hoofty's face flamed crimson, matching the bright red in his plaid shirt. He continued to look down and he started to stammer. He seemed to understand now what they meant, but he didn't know how to answer. His mother told him long ago that those feelings were wrong, that such feelings were only for married people and he would never be married.

"Did you ever kiss a girl?" Mike persisted. "Did a girl ever try to kiss you?"

Hoofty shook his head and continued to stare down at the table.

"How old are you, Hoofty?" asked Harry.

"Forty-four," mumbled Hoofty, in a barely audible voice.

So that they could talk among themselves, the men sent Hoofty to the bar to get pretzels. As soon as Hoofty left the table, they leaned forward to discuss the situation. "Jeez," moaned Mike. "Forty-four and never been laid. It's almost a crime. It's what they call a tragedy."

The others nodded in solemn agreement and they began to think of how they could solve Hoofty's problem. They looked around the bar and saw some familiar female faces but none that qualified for the project that had now taken on a life of its own.

"We gotta do this right for him," declared Frankie. "This has to be like a gift for him. A gift he'll never forget."

"We'll have to pay someone," said Harry, introducing the financial theme. "And if we're paying, we get to pick someone nice for Hoofty."

"We could go down to the Gable House," suggested Mike. "You know those girls have been around the block. They know how to handle any situation in the bedroom. And some of them are really good looking."

"Yeah," agreed Harry. "Those girls have been getting guys to leave their paychecks at the Gable House for years. Old Grace wouldn't have them there if they weren't good looking and 'good.'"

By the time Hoofty came back to the table with the basket of pretzels the basic plan was in place. The next day, Billy, Mike, Harry, and Frankie went to the Gable House after they finished their day shift jobs at Bethlehem Steel. They explained their need to Grace. They would pay — more than usual if they had to — to be sure that Hoofty had an experience they believed was long overdue. Grace understood instantly what they had in mind and smiled at their awkwardness in asking for the service.

Grace, who had come to Bethlehem from Budapest, had owned the Gable House for many years, taking over its management after her husband died in the early 1930s. For decades it had been a popular restaurant and bar, and also a place where some of the girls who provided company at the bar could provide a more intimate kind of companionship in their rooms upstairs. Under Grace's guidance, all of this was done quietly, discreetly, and even elegantly. Few, if any, of the individuals and families in the dining rooms ever knew about the other services available at Gable House. Grace herself was the image of propriety, refinement, and quiet good taste. A tall, statuesque woman with a porcelain complexion and dark blue eyes, Grace always dressed stylishly in expensive clothing bought in New York or Philadelphia. She invariably wore her signature pearl necklace from Tiffany's as well as diamond earrings and rings. Her blue-gray hair was beautifully styled at all times, with never a hair out of place, courtesy of three visits per week to the hairdresser. Grace was a shrewd and successful business woman, but she also had a sense of humor and an innate thoughtfulness. "I think it is nice of you to do this for him," she said to the men. "And I will ask the girls if one of them might want to do this, you know, as a kindness. You will pay, of course, but the kindness should be part of it anyway."

After a brief visit to the second floor of Gable House, Grace came down to tell the men that Margie — dark-haired, bright-eyed, and petite Margie — would accommodate their needs. There would be no extra charge.

When Hoofty came to Tammany that night, the guys told him that they would have a special surprise for him the next day. They told him to shave before he came into town, to "wash real good," wash his hair, and wear something nice for his surprise. Hoofty had no idea what they had in mind but he was happy and excited. He couldn't remember ever getting a surprise before. They also told him to come to the *Bulletin* office early — by four o'clock at the latest. They wanted to allow enough time for Hoofty to get his surprise and still be home by ten.

The next day, when Hoofty arrived at the *Bulletin* office, the guys were amazed at how good he looked. He was shaved, he had gotten a haircut, and his hair was neatly combed and slicked down. He was wearing his best navy blue trousers, a neatly pressed light blue shirt, and his red tie with the navy blue stripes. His good shoes were polished to a bright shine. Even his socks were new — the dark blue socks from the back of his dresser drawer. When Hoofty asked for his best clothes, telling his mother that the guys had a surprise for him, she assumed they would be taking him to a nicer place for dinner, maybe to the Royal Restaurant. As she laid out his clothes for him, the idea of her son ever being inside Gable House never occurred to his mother. After surveying Hoofty's transformation and acknowledging his improved look, the men escorted him from the *Bulletin* office to the Gable House. As they walked west on Third Street, they were all smiles, Hoofty included, and the guys repeatedly patted him on the back, telling him it would be a special night. It looked and felt like an old-world wedding procession, lacking only a bride.

When the little group arrived at the Gable House, Grace gave them some dinner and said that drinks were on the house. They decided to limit Hoofty to one beer. They didn't want him to pass out in the middle of his surprise.

Around six o'clock, Margie came downstairs to meet Hoofty. She looked as fresh and pretty as a flower. She wore a pale yellow cotton dress with a white scalloped collar and a pearl necklace. Her black patent high heels gave her a little more height and matched the patent belt at her slim waist. Her lips were the color of maraschino cherries. She smiled warmly at Hoofty and gave no indication that there was anything different about him. She gazed at him as if he was Clark Gable. She took his hand and tenderly asked him if he wanted to go upstairs. Hoofty was mute with instant infatuation and followed her meekly up the stairs. Hoofty's pals and the other men at the bar stood and raised their glasses in tribute to a Great Moment.

Once upstairs, Hoofty forgot to be nervous. He was too entranced with Margie to think of anything else. He had never seen anyone so pretty. She told him to sit down on the sofa and relax. With great gentleness, she took his hand and stroked it, telling him again not to be nervous. Hoofty thought she was the nicest new friend he had ever met. Then she leaned over and gently kissed his ear lobe. All thoughts of friendship flew from Hoofty's thoughts and he yelped with shock and with new, unexpected pleasure.

Moving slowly enough to not scare him, Margie ran her polished red nail down his cheek and under his chin. Hoofty trembled. He was afraid he was going to pee. She touched her fingertip to her lips and then placed it on Hoofty's lips. Her smile told him that this was permissible.

She stroked his other cheek and ran her practiced finger around his lips. He closed his eyes and gurgled, feeling as if he was drowning in sensations he had never felt before.

"Would you like to come to the bed?" Margie asked. He nodded 'yes' and reclined on the bed, fully clothed, curling the pillow under his head and pulling the blanket over his completely happy body, eyes closed, ready for sleep.

"No," Margie murmured. "Not to sleep ... to *enjoy*. Would you like to take your clothes off?"

"No," replied Hoofty, "I'd be cold. And these are my best clothes."

"Would you like to take my clothes off?" she asked.

Hoofty laughed. "They wouldn't fit me!" he said, sensibly. "They're for a girl!"

"Maybe I should take my clothes off," Margie suggested.

"But then you'll be cold. And you're too nice to be cold. If you take your clothes off, you can have the covers," Hoofty offered.

Sensing that this might be slightly more complicated than most of her other assignments, Margie decided to be more direct. She grabbed Hoofty's face, kissed him smack on the mouth and plastered his head against the pillow. When she raised her head from his face, he looked like a flattened cartoon figure, his hair splayed out on the pillow on either side of his ears. She then removed his tie and began to unbutton his shirt, smiling all the while and reassuring him that everything was all right.

Margie scattered kisses across Hoofty's chest and he gurgled again, making a sound like a sigh crossed with a giggle. "Again," he requested and she complied. More gurgling.

Margie decided not to proceed below the belt until she had some idea of whether Hoofty was actually interested in his surprise. She unbuttoned her dress and slipped it off, watching his eyes grow wider. She snuggled up to him and told him to hold her. He reached under her and lifted her from the bed. "Not like that," she said, stunned, "just hold me close to you while we're in the bed."

Several minutes of snuggling seemed to restore the mood. When Margie slipped out of her brassiere, Hoofty turned away. She turned his head toward her and again said that it was all right. She asked him if he wanted to take anything off. He nodded in the affirmative. "What do you want to take off?" she whispered. "My socks," said Hoofty. "They're making my feet real hot."

Suppressing a laugh, Margie encouraged him to remove the offending socks. "Why don't you take your pants off, too?" she suggested.

"Because I'll need them to go home," Hoofty replied wisely.

"You can have them to go home," Margie assured him. "But for now we can put them on the sofa so they won't get wrinkled." That made sense to Hoofty, and he left the bed to carefully fold his pants across the cushions of the sofa. When he turned back toward the bed, he saw that Margie had taken her pants off too.

She smiled at him and crooked her finger, gesturing that he should join her in the bed. This customer might not be the easiest one she ever entertained but she was determined to do her job.

Hoofty moved mechanically toward the bed and stretched out beside her. Margie now took command of the situation and initiated a self-guided tour of Hoofty's body. Suddenly, all the lights in Hoofty's life and body and being went on in a blaze of insight and glory. He knew instinctively how the marvelous pieces of their human bodies fit together and he proceeded to complete the puzzle. Hoofty's newly discovered skills propelled him to heights he didn't know existed. Margie had never ascended to such heights either. Their climbing and soaring seemed to go on forever. Margie was, for the first time in her professional life, speechless and very much the passenger rather than the pilot on this wild ride.

"What d'ya think is going on up there?" asked Frankie, after an hour had passed.

"Probably taking her a long time to calm him down or show him what to do," guessed Mike. "I kinda feel sorry for her."

They saw Grace glance up the stairs a few times, probably asking herself the same questions that perplexed them.

After two hours had passed, Grace tip-toed up the stairs and listened outside Margie's room. When she came down, the guys looked at her questioningly. "Well," she said, "it's certainly noisy enough in there. Haven't heard anything like it since my own wedding night with Julius; God rest his soul."

By nine o'clock, Harry was beginning to worry about getting Hoofty home before his mother would worry and start looking for him. Mike was elected to climb the stairs and knock on the door. When he was half-way up the stairs, the door to Margie's room opened. Hoofty stood there in his perfectly pressed pants and new shirt, sockless, with his hair still sticking out at right angles to his head, and with a beatific look on his face. He had been to Heaven and he knew it. Margie lurched out behind him in a half-closed robe, her lipstick long gone and her hair completely disheveled, wearing the same satiated look. Seeing Mike she exclaimed, "What a surprise!"

The guys decided to walk Hoofty home just to be safe. When they were almost at his house, they finally asked him if he had liked his gift. Hoofty smiled shyly, stared down at his feet, and asked if he could have the same surprise for Christmas.

REALITY

When he left, it was not real. It simply could not have happened, Kathryn told herself, not like this. And because it could not have happened ... it was not so. It was not real. Although she settled the matter with herself in this way — by deciding 'it was not so' — somewhere in the center part of herself Kathryn was numb. Numb in the way, she supposed, an amputee was numb when the surgeon cut or the grenade exploded or the shark bit. Numb. Yes, if this had really happened, if her husband had really left her, that sense of numbness would describe it well.

But it was not so. It could not be. Just a month ago, Kathryn and Clark had talked about their Christmas gifts to each other, and Christmas was still four months away. They had talked about her traditional birthday dinner, and her birthday was six months away. She remembered clearly how that tradition began. Experimenting one evening with a new recipe — gourmet cooking was an interest that Kathryn and Clark shared — they had been especially pleased with a veal and mushroom dish, and she had asked him to prepare it for her birthday dinner. That was eight years ago, and it had become a birthday tradition for him to prepare 'veau a champignon a -`la Clark' each year for her. He promised he would do so again next year. How could he do that if he was gone?

It was something of a bother, in the days after they last talked ... after he said something about leaving ... for Kathryn to decide what to wear in the morning. She was not accustomed to being indecisive, not accustomed to being bothered. Still, she looked poised and elegant each day when she went to her office. Silk shirts and stylish suits, paired with gold chains and diamond stud earrings, gave her an impeccable look, with no indication of the derailment that had occurred within her. Nor did she think there should be any such sign. After all, the matter would be explainable sometime. Why permit signals of change to surface? Why invite questions that could not be answered?

His absence buzzed in the background of all that she did, distracting her, confusing her, but she couldn't fine-tune the sound, couldn't quite remember what he had said. That, too, was bothersome, but she could do nothing about it now.

At her office, the details of projects that used to be stimulating now had an irritating effect. The mindless office chatter that she hadn't noticed before now struck her as particularly unnecessary. The meetings with their agendas were so blatantly pretentious that she wondered why she hadn't noticed their uselessness before. She was tempted to remind her colleagues that there was work to be done and they had better get on with it. But such a reaction wasn't really like her and she did not want to arouse undue curiosity. Even her concern about arousing curiosity was foreign, was unreal to her, as unreal as her last hours with Clark. Coming home from the office no longer cleansed the day of its debris. Somehow, coming home only reminded her of his absence and the fact that she could neither confront nor comprehend the reasons for that absence.

Such thoughts started Kathryn musing about reality — levels of reality ... that which we do or do not allow to be real for us. Like Jerry Lewis's Telethon kids in their wheelchairs, she thought; remembering those traditional Labor Day telecasts. Apart from that annual TV show and the action of sending a check, how real were those children? How real had they ever been, could they be, to her? If she had really thought about their pain or their prospects, her courteous sympathy would have been moved to a different level of reality, one that would be unbearable when multiplied by all of the wheelchairs, all of the homelessness statistics, all the pictures of caged puppies, and all of the children's faces appearing above empty bowls on all of the appeals that arrived almost daily in the mail.

No one could respond to all of that pain ... all of that need. Kathryn knew, instinctively, that one selects what will be real. It was a matter of defending one's sanity against all of the wheelchairs in the world. For a fleeting moment, she wondered why there had never been a poster child

... poster lady? ... for all of the abandoned women in the world, but she dismissed the thought before its irony could leaven her mood.

At one point, in the second week after he'd left, Kathryn wondered if she should have her hair cut. But that idea brought the instantaneous question of whether Clark would have preferred her to wear it shorter all along. And that was too foolish a thought to warrant her attention. She pulled back her pale blonde hair into a small ponytail at the nape of her neck and secured it with a navy grosgrain ribbon. "Classic," she allowed herself, and winked at her image in the mirror. A navy Chanel suit, white silk blouse, and large, blue Tahitian pearl earrings — the ones he bought her at the Halekulani — completed the look. Classic.

"How's Clark?" her sister Margaret asked when she phoned.

"Oh, fine. Still putting on weight and still complaining about it, but fine," Kathryn answered.

"Are you two going to the Chamber Orchestra concert next week?"

"I'm not sure. We haven't talked about it, and we'll have to spend most of Saturday with the gardener to discuss the shrubs and spring bulbs we'll want him to plant."

"Let me know if you decide to go," said Margaret. "You can join us for a late supper after the concert. I want you to see Brooke's room now that the murals have been finished."

"Sounds fine. I'll let you know."

Kathryn wondered when she would know. When? When would she know more than she did now? When would reality begin to shape itself for her ... quite apart from any shaping or forming that might be required of her? A phone call would do it. An accident. Cold, informative, impersonal words from a hospital representative would easily delineate reality for her, would define his absence and the reason for it. "I'm sorry to tell you, but there has been an automobile accident." That would do it. There was nothing strange, in Kathryn's mind, about the thought that even an accident would be preferable to this bothersome not knowing. How often, in that third week after he had left, had she actually pictured an accident ... pictured him dead. Or lost. Perhaps wandering around or hiding somewhere. Self-exiled, temporarily, by some professional failure or anxiety, some male ego problem that could be explained in terms of promotional plateaus or declining libido. Occasionally, when she permitted herself the whimsy of it, she pictured him choosing an unaffordable mink or sable to accompany his penitent return. She preferred the sable.

His last lavish gift to her, the three-carat diamond stud earrings from Cartier, never left her now. She savored them as she looked in the mirror. Her finely boned face and porcelain beauty carried the earrings well. They suited the new touches she was allowing herself in her appearance: upturned collars, silk scarves tied at her slim waist, hand-woven tunics resurrected from the back of the closet and worn now over favorite cashmeres — things she had worn in the years when they first met and dated. She looked very good and felt very good.

Kathryn had a disconcerting impulse to write some poetry or to begin a journal, but she knew that this wasn't the time for real writing, for the polished kind of prose or poetry to which she would want to attach her name. Ventilation. That's what any writing produced in these days would be. Just ventilation. And she could still hear the disdainful voice of her college English professor, as he waved a sheet of paper with a poem written by one of her classmates, saying, "Ventilation is not art."

Occasionally, a phrase or sentence would slip forward, without warning, to the front of her mind. A sentence spoken in Clark's voice. Unbidden, coming when she had just been deciding if there was too much white space in a layout, coming when she least expected it.

"I can't give you what you want, what you need. And I need more than you can give."

There. Like that. Like a razor-sharp slice of memory suddenly thrusting itself through Kathryn's brain like a dagger, slashing and paralyzing her with its cutting authenticity. When that happened, she couldn't breathe. She had once broken a rib, and anything more than the shallowest of breaths had caused great pain, so Kathryn had learned not to take deep breaths. She took no deep breaths now. No deep thoughts. Nothing that would bring the pain back.

"Are you sure everything's all right?" Margaret asked, concerned, over a shrimp cocktail and mimosa at lunch. It was the sisters' custom to have lunch together on the first Saturday of every month.

Margaret had a way of knowing. Ever since their childhood, in a modest neighborhood in South Bethlehem, Margaret had a way of knowing, of being able to guess at the unspoken. She did so now.

"Is everything all right with you and Clark?"

"Not really 'all right,'" Kathryn responded, "but it will be. You know, everyone has these episodes."

"What kind of episode? What happened?"

"I don't know, really. He said some strange things. I can't really remember. Maybe it's a phase men go through, or couples go through. I don't know, really."

"Well, you look all right. Whatever happened, you seem to be handling it well."

"Of course," replied Kathryn, smoothly. "Don't I always handle things well? I am never thrown off course. Look where I — where we — came from ... from the South Side. Do you remember those small row houses we passed on our way to Holy Infancy? Old homes filled with kids and with the laundry hanging on clotheslines out back? Look at where we are now: Hillsborough, California, having lunch at our country club. That kind of attainment comes from discipline, from focus, from self-control, from *not* being thrown off course. It will all work out, really."

The days slipped into a comfortable sequence. Nothing at Kathryn's office called undue attention to her, nothing disturbed her, nothing caused her to breathe deeply or to feel pain. She renewed their subscription to *Paris Cuisine*, annoyed momentarily, because Clark had talked about dropping that subscription and now she didn't know what he wanted to do.

Kathryn's newly free hours were beginning to feel good, almost luxurious. Self-indulgent, restful hours. Hours and days that would have been good for thinking, but all of her thoughts seemed to circle back to that central and un-thinkable consideration that involved him. And how can one think rationally about an absurdity? About something that isn't real? There had to be a basic level of common sense or reason or motive to build a thought structure that would lead somewhere. Kathryn wasn't afraid to think. She thought of herself as an intellectual, prided herself on her intelligence. But now she had nowhere to begin and nowhere to go with her thoughts. There are some things, she knew, that only time could make sense of. She knew what she could do and what she could not do ... and she could do nothing with this. It was not real.

Unclaimed evening hours offered themselves to her for long-neglected needs, such as re-arranging the bookshelves and sorting through boxes in the attic. Kathryn decided to intersperse some family memorabilia with the modern art and minimalist pieces around which she and Clark had developed their décor. She retrieved some of these family pieces from the attic now — her grandparents' sepia-toned wedding portrait, the family Bible in Polish, the old coffee grinder from her grandmother's kitchen, the antique pistols and folding rulers that had been her grandfather's. She touched these respectfully, almost acknowledging the comfort they represented, the sense of continuity, strength, and survival in the midst of change. She realized then that she hadn't thought about her grandparents for many years.

Kathryn's grandparents had certainly seen much change. Sent from Poland to America as teenagers, they somehow made their way in their new country. Her grandfather worked in the Number Two Machine Shop at Bethlehem Steel, and her grandmother worked long hours in the Bondy and Lederer cigar factory on Evans Street, pressing and rolling the tobacco leaves into cigar shapes and then licking the seams shut until her senses reeled and her stomach heaved from the potent taste and smell of the tobacco. Kathryn's grandmother had told her that when she was too sick to continue licking the cigars, she would take a small cup — one that she had brought from home — from her apron pocket and hurry down the backstairs to the rain barrel outside the factory to get water for the cup. Then she could moisten her fingers and apply the water to seal the cigars. The foreman didn't like it when the women did this. It wasted too much time. But her grandmother was always clever in waiting until the foreman was distracted, and she moved swiftly enough (despite her tight, buttoned shoes and long dress) to be back at her place before he saw that she was gone. For some reason, these memories came back to Kathryn now. She thought of how her grandparents had to learn a new language, new customs, and find their way around an unfamiliar city with signs in a language they didn't know. They had to work two or three jobs just to earn a modest living. But they had made a life for themselves, a life strong enough to love and nurture children and grandchildren, resilient enough to sustain them through times of poverty, illness, and the grief of losing infant children ... to uphold them through more than 70 years of marriage and into old age.

Kathryn proudly hung her grandparents' wedding portrait near the window, above the rosewood demi-lune table on which her own glass-enclosed wedding bouquet had been placed. She stepped back to evaluate the effect. She was pleased with it. Her grandmother's old oak coffee grinder looked appropriate on the center bookshelf, near the books about antiques, and she artfully arranged her grandfather's wood and brass folding rulers on the shelf below. The old Montenegro revolver was heavier than she thought it would be. Her grandfather had told her of its use in the old days, in the old country. Tall tales, to be sure — not real — but the stories had amused her as a child.

Kathryn studied the intricate detail on the silver-toned revolver — deeply etched vines, leaves, and tendrils curled into all of the metallic spaces near the ivory handle. She lifted the weight of the weapon in both hands. She aimed it at the ebony-edged mirror, recalling instinctively, as she always did with all of their possessions, where she and Clark had bought that mirror: at the Design Center in London. She struck a mock outlaw pose and looked at her reflection in the beveled glass. She placed the muzzle to her temple. The cold of the metal surprised her. The resistance of the trigger surprised her. She wondered, again, what was real ... and only the sharpest sliver of sound reached her mind, in answer to her question, before she really knew.

DRIVING THE DEVIL AWAY

Working women were an integral part of immigrant communities in America in the early 1900s, and their work was often as grueling and backbreaking as the work done by their husbands. Daycare existed in those immigrant communities, but it wasn't called daycare. It was called "making-sure-the-children-are-taken-care-of."

For the most part, this meant balancing work schedules. If the father worked the night shift at a mill or factory, his wife's work — in the cigar factory, the silk mill, or taking in washing and ironing at home — was done during the day.

In the close-knit enclaves of immigrants in South Bethlehem, help could always be found to tend to a baby for a few hours or a child for a few days.

In 1923, Joseph and Vilma Kuzma lived in a second-story apartment at 737 Laufer Street with their five-year-old daughter, Mary, and their two-year-old daughter, Irene. They paid a woman in an apartment building across the street to look after the girls while Joe went to work in the Machine Shop at Bethlehem Steel and Vilma went to work in the cigar factory. Vilma prepared lunches for the girls and there was nothing for the neighbor to do but to watch over them.

One day, Stevie Kercsmar, who lived in the next block, saw Joe walking home from work. "Joe," he said, "I have wanted to ask you something. Where do your girls go with those heavy paper bags every morning?"

"Go?" asked Joe, perplexed. "What girls? My girls? They don't go anywhere. Mrs. Mandovitch takes care of them every day. They're with her."

"They're with her all right," jeered Stevie. "They walk with her out of her apartment building soon after you or Vilma take them there. They carry big paper bags. It's almost too much for the little one to drag along. They do this every morning. I see it with my own eyes."

Joe didn't wait to finish the conversation. He hurried to Mrs. Mandovitch's apartment building and collected his daughters. He decided to say nothing until he talked with the girls — at least with Mary, the older daughter.

After supper, Joe raised the question carefully, wanting to hear the information in Mary's own words. "So," he asked casually, "what did you do today at Mrs. Mandovitch's?"

Mary said that Irene had played in her playpen with her toys, and that she had played with her dolls. She said they both took a nap in the afternoon, as they did on most days.

Satisfied, Joe didn't ask any more questions. He didn't want to frighten the children or put ideas in their heads. Stevie, he assumed, was playing a bad joke or had had too much to drink.

A few weeks later, the scene repeated itself, but this time it was Mrs. Gombosi, another neighbor, asking him what his daughters did every morning with the bags they were carrying. The Kuzmas respected and trusted Mrs. Gombosi implicitly. She was a woman of great integrity and there was no chance that she could have been drinking or playing a joke.

Joe marched up to Mrs. Mandovitch's apartment and banged on the door. When she opened it, he asked, visibly angry, "What happens when we bring the children to you in the morning? What do you do with them and where do you go? And don't lie to me. Others have seen them carrying paper bags and I know these people aren't crazy."

Mrs. Mandovitch became coolly indignant. "What happens?" she replied. "I save them from the devil, that's what happens! They fill their bags with rocks from the gravel pits and we walk down to the bridge and over the river. We walk halfway across the bridge and then they throw the rocks down into the river, throw them hard to drive the devil away. Sometimes Irene can't throw so hard and I have to lift her over the railing and hold her out over the river so that she can throw the rocks farther. Every day we drive the devil away!"

Joe's mind was reeling. He was picturing his two-year-old, tiny to begin with, being held out over the bridge railing, 50 feet above the Lehigh River below.

"Drive the devil away?" he bellowed. "I'll drive you away!"

Mrs. Mandovitch pulled back instinctively as Joe lunged to grab her. She shut the door quickly, and as Joe stood there, vibrating with anger, he shouted, "Don't ever come near my children again! Don't come near me or my wife or my home or you will find out what the devil can do!"

Even after he told his wife what had happened and what he said to Mrs. Mandovitch, Joe couldn't stop shaking. His 5'6" frame couldn't contain his rage.

Mrs. Gombosi said that she would watch the children until Joe and Vilma could find someone else reliable enough to be entrusted with their care.

A few weeks later, with their daughters safely in the care of the Jewish family that lived on the floor below them, Joe and Vilma put the river episode behind them. They had not seen Mrs. Mandovitch and there was little chance that they would. It was known that she seldom left her apartment, walks to the river notwithstanding.

Vilma was the first to notice the white grains on their apartment porch. The wind must have blown this here, she thought, and she simply swept the dirt away. A few days later, the unmistakable trail of white granules again bordered the porch. She called Joe outside to look at this oddity.

"Did you spill something?" he asked.

"Of course," she replied sarcastically, "I always spill things in perfectly straight lines."

Joe and Vilma examined the white particles carefully. They looked like sugar or salt, but the Kuzmas were wise enough to not attempt to taste the substance. It might be rat poison, thought Joe. He asked the landlord if he had been placing poison around the building, but the landlord said he had done no such thing.

After the third appearance of the white border, Joe decided to learn for himself where it was coming from. After sending Vilma and the children to bed one night, he sat in his darkened kitchen, holding a heavy wooden club. He saw nothing that first night, although he may have dozed off a bit, and he saw nothing on the second night. He decided to give his investigation one more night.

On the third night, sometime after two in the morning, Joe heard a noise outside, somewhere off the second-floor porch of the apartment. Through the lace kitchen curtains, in the moonlight, he saw the top of a ladder appear against the porch railing. He sat bolt upright to watch what would happen.

In a few moments, a man with a dark cap ascended the ladder and appeared at the railing. Moving noiselessly, the man hoisted himself onto the railing and swung his legs over the side so that he could stand on the porch. He looked from side to side to be certain that no one was looking, and then he reached into his jacket and withdrew a bag and a small glass. He dipped the glass into the bag and drew it out filled with a white substance.

Kneeling down, the man methodically, almost artistically, began to create an edging around the porch, this time in a saw-tooth pattern. Joe watched, more fascinated than afraid. When the mysterious climber was almost finished with his handiwork, Joe quietly opened the door onto the porch and stepped outside, careful to avoid the wooden slats that creaked.

He tiptoed up behind the crouching artist and then, in a loud voice, demanded, "Who are you and what are you doing here?" The man collapsed in a shocked heap on the porch and began to tremble. Holding the club aloft, Joe again asked, "Who are you and why do you do this thing to my home?"

Raising his arms protectively against the possible swing of the club, the black-capped man said, "I am Vincent Mandovitch and you stopped my wife from fighting the devil. So now I must keep the devil within your home so that he does not come to my home."

"What are you talking about?" asked Joe, lowering the club.

"Salt!" shrieked the frightened man, rising but still quaking. "Salt keeps the devil away. The devil will not cross a barrier of salt!"

"You idiot!" laughed Joe. "If you really believe that nonsense, then you've made it so that the devil cannot cross over into my home. You have protected me."

"But the devil is in your house," wailed the little man. "He must be. Because you wouldn't let your children drive the devil away."

By now Joe was more exasperated than angry. "Would your wife have chosen a tool of the devil to fight the devil?" he asked. "No. She chose the children — innocent angels. The devil does not live with innocent angels. The devil does not live here."

Mandovitch looked confused, trying to puzzle out what Joe was saying.

"God is more powerful than the devil," declared Joe, "and God lives here, not the devil. If you dare to come to my home again," said Joe, raising the club in his hands, "there won't be enough left of you to take back to your home in that little bag."

The next day, when he told his wife about Mr. Mandovitch's antics on the porch, Joe told her that they had to begin saving every dollar they could to buy a house, any house, so they could be free from the presence of such lunatics.

"But Joe," said Vilma, "we can never afford a house. We could never save that much."

"Who knows?" mused Joe. "I told Mandovitch that God is more powerful than the devil, and if he is, then he is more powerful than poverty, too."

Six years later, in 1929, Mrs. Gosztonyi, the banker, told Joe to take his money out of the bank. She said the banks were likely to be closing and she didn't want him to lose his money.

"What should I do with it?" asked Joe. "Where do I put it if not in a bank?"

"Buy a house," she advised. "It's what you've been saving for. You have enough to at least buy a small house. It would be the best way to protect and use your money. I know how hard you've worked to save it."

Purchased for $4,800 in 1929, the house at 426 Fillmore Street, built before the Civil War, happily sheltered Joseph and Vilma and their two daughters. In the late 1930s and early '40s, it also housed Mary's husband and their sons for a few years, and later, Irene and her husband and daughter ... for a span of 77 years of continuous residence. The Mandovitches remained in their apartment on Laufer Street, regularly and nervously salting their building, the street, and nearby porches and properties.

ANOTHER LOTTERY

"*B*less me, Father, for I have sinned."

Irma Nagy's voice was almost a whisper as she recited the words, aiming them at the dark blue fabric covering the small window inside the confines of the confessional. She had been sitting in the confessional for twenty minutes, waiting for the priest.

Irma was 38 years old, but like so many women living through the Great Depression, she looked older than her years. Her light brown hair was already streaked with gray, and her hands showed the roughness that comes from working long hours at home and in a factory. Irma and her parents had come to America from Hungary in 1903, when she was ten. In 1911, when she was eighteen, she married Bertalan Nagy, also an immigrant — a good-natured, hard-working man who adored her. That was twenty years ago.

As Irma pulled her old, brown tweed coat more tightly around her narrow body, she stared at the highly varnished mahogany of the confessional and at the ornate carvings around the partition that separated priest from penitent. Her mind groped for words ... words that might help her talk to the priest ... words that might free her from the dreaded obligation she knew she was facing.

"How have you sinned, my child?" It was him. Father Iszak. Irma recognized his voice. But then, she had expected him to be the priest who would hear her confession. He had business with her, and they both knew it.

In response to his rote question, she answered mechanically, "I have said swear words when I've been upset."

"How many times?" asked the invisible priest.

"Four times," replied Irma, making the number up.

"What else, my child?" His voice was low and alluring, almost hypnotic. His voice sounded, thought Irma, the way fine brandy must taste: smooth and honeyed, thick and velvety.

"I have been angry with my children when their play becomes too wild, and I have been angry with my husband," said Irma, stalling for time.

"Why do you become angry with your husband?"

"Oh, just little things. Like when he leaves wet towels on the bathroom floor or when he forgets to bring milk from the store when he comes home from work."

"These are minor things," said Father Iszak gently. "You must control your anger. Children should be indulged at times, and your husband must be respected and honored at all times. He is the head of the family. He is your master in the eyes of God."

Irma was silent. *How*, she wondered, *could you know anything about the stresses of family life in the 1930s? How can you know what it's like to work in a factory where the boss constantly says "Faster! Faster! More! More!" and then come home to making a meal for seven people, bathing and feeding a sick mother, making little Markus take his medicine so that he can breathe better, then washing the dishes and pots and pans, wiping up the floor, and ironing the clothes before you pack six lunches? How could you understand any of this?*

Irma was glad that her fury was all in her head — a head that was throbbing with the pain of worry and anger — glad that she hadn't said anything out loud. After all, she had to be deferential toward Father Iszak. She needed to have him see things her way. She couldn't afford to antagonize him.

"Father," she said meekly, "I will control my anger better in the future. I'm sorry that I don't always understand the pressures that others feel."

"Very wise," replied the priest soothingly. "Such understanding from you ... from any wife and mother ... will go a long way toward making a home harmonious and peaceful." But Irma wasn't really listening. She realized that, by accident, she had introduced an idea, and Father Iszak had just as unintentionally picked it up.

"It is important to understand the situations that others are in, isn't it Father?" she asked.

"Of course," replied the priest, stopping suddenly when he realized how Irma could use these words — his words — against him.

"I'm so glad that you are so understanding, Father," continued a newly focused Irma. "In fact, that is one of the things I hear people saying so often about you: that you are very wise and kind and understanding."

It was Father's Iszak's turn to be silent as he tried to think of how to counter the line of reasoning that he saw heading toward him.

"I realize," said Irma, seizing her momentum, "that you want to speak to me about something, something you want me and my husband to do." Energized and emboldened by her unexpected advantage, Irma came right to the point. "Not only are we seven people crammed into a small house, but even with my work at the factory and Bertalan's work at the steel company, we struggle with money all the time. Week after week, the money goes. We pay the rent and then put some aside for the church. Then we pay the electric bill and put money aside to buy coal. Every day, the children scavenge for as many pieces of coal as they can find along the railroad tracks, but they never find much. There is little money left to buy food. Our table hasn't seen goose or turkey in years, and the children get fruit only when Mr. Palasky is kind enough to put an apple or orange in my bag when I buy cabbage. Mostly, we eat cabbage noodles, pigs' feet in gelatin, and sometimes I make *tarlo repa* 'turnip soup' or *repnocsa* 'turnip pie.'"

"All good food," Father Iszak responded, recalling – involuntarily – the breaded veal cutlets, baked potato with sour cream, cucumber salad, nine-layer Dobos Torte, coffee, and cognac that he had enjoyed at lunch. "All fine and healthy food for which your family should be grateful."

Irma continued to press her advantage. "When the doctor told us that Markus has asthma, what were we to do? Set him outside to die? We buy his medicine before we buy food. And we bought him warm pajamas and an extra blanket. So far, we're fortunate with the other children — Lorant, Andor, and Frici — but they're growing like weeds and we can only let their pants and hems down for so long. None of them has had new shoes or clothes for at least three years." Irma stopped talking. She could think of no more words, but she had said what she needed to say.

Father Iszak hesitated before answering. "I know things are difficult ... difficult for everyone. But Mrs. Nagy, you must know that there are so many others who have nothing at all, who have no jobs in this terrible Depression. You and your husband are at least employed. Why, only last week a woman came to me to say that she thought her husband would try to kill himself, he is so distraught about their poverty. So you see, in comparison to others, you are really well off. You may have to stretch your pennies, but at least you have pennies to start with."

He paused, then continued. "It is a precious and holy part of my priestly life — a sacred responsibility — to help children; even ... at times ... to find homes for babies who have no home. I must remind you, Mrs. Nagy, that our Lord expects us to be charitable. Christ himself told us to welcome strangers in his name, and it was Jesus who welcomed the children to come to him, who said 'of such is the kingdom of God.' "

In the verbal chess game they were playing, the priest silently claimed an intellectual advantage over the uneducated woman seated behind the partition. But Irma was not done fighting.

"We cannot do it, Father. It's that simple," she said. "I refuse. And if Christ is mad at me for what I am saying, then so be it. I know what it is to love, to struggle, and to provide. I know what I can do and what I can't do, and this I cannot do."

Vexation mounted inside the priest. He was not accustomed to being questioned, much less disobeyed. "A baby, Mrs. Nagy," he said cajolingly. "A baby that is truly innocent. A newborn who will take up very little room — it can sleep in a dresser drawer if necessary — a baby that needs the love and care that only a devoted mother like you can provide. Surely there is room in your home ... and in your heart ... for such a baby."

But Irma's determination was stronger than the priest's words. "No, Father. We cannot and will not take the child in. That must be my final answer." Then, with an audacity she didn't know she possessed, Irma added, "If you cannot find a family to take the baby by the time it is born, perhaps it can sleep in a dresser drawer in one of the nicely furnished rooms in the rectory until a family is found." She said the words sweetly, helpfully, almost naïvely, but she knew they had found their mark.

Needing to have the last word, the priest assigned Irma 50 rosaries as penance, far more than she had ever been given before. She didn't care. As she stepped into the bitter cold outside the gray stone Catholic church, pulling her coat collar up around her neck, she felt warm inside. The skies over South Bethlehem were darkening, with the blackness coming much earlier now that it was December, but Irma felt a brightness within her. It wasn't simply that she had prevented the placement of an enormous burden on her family. It also seemed to her that she had stood up for something — something important — although no one ever dared speak of it. As she walked toward her home, she fingered the rosary in her pocket, smiling when she said her Hail Marys.

"Well?" asked Bertalan Nagy anxiously when his wife opened the back door and stepped into their small, snug kitchen. "What happened? How did it go?" he probed, as she shivered and hurried toward the coal stove to warm herself.

"It went the way we needed it to go," replied Irma. "I said no. I said it firmly and said it twice, and he knew I meant it. But I was so nervous. I was shaking all the while I was speaking to him. He's angry, Berti. He's very angry. He gave me 50 rosaries — ten for each of our children and ten for the baby I rejected — as penance."

"What?" shouted Bertalan, all six feet of him rising from the wooden chair where he had been sitting, soaking his aching feet in hot water in the *lavor* 'metal basin.' "No one gets a penance like that! A murderer would get less penance."

"A murderer would get jail," Irma reminded him, chuckling. "I don't care. I really don't. I'll practically sing my Hail Marys, that's how relieved I am. You know, everyone expected us to get the baby. They said it was our turn. We were next on the list that Father Iszak keeps. It was our turn."

"To hell with him and his list," said Bertalan. "I just feel sorry for whoever is next on that piece of paper. Do you know who it is?"

"I think it's the Mosers," Irma answered. "I know that the Demyans and Halaszes were asked before us. It was their turn, but they've each had so much misfortune lately – job losses, Janka's cancer, Ervin's heart attack – that I'm not surprised they didn't say yes, and Father surely must have understood their situations. That makes three refusals. Three flat-out refusals. I'm sure that has never happened before. Father must be very, very mad indeed."

"Let him be mad," growled Bertalan. "If there was any justice in this world, punishment would pour down from Heaven ...."

"Berti!" scolded Irma, shocked. "You mustn't say things like that! He is a priest, a holy man. God will punish you for saying such things!"

"No, God will not punish me. At least not before he punishes fornicators."

"No, Berti! Please! Please don't say such things. You make me afraid!"

"I'm sorry, sweetheart," replied Bertalan. "I didn't mean to upset you. Let's just forget about all of this. Because of your courage, we will not have to add an infant to our burdens. All is well."

"I just hope God forgives me for refusing to take the child," said Irma softly. "Father is trying so hard to place the baby."

"There is nothing to forgive," Bertalan assured her. "God can surely see into your heart. Isn't that what we're told? That God sees us and knows us? He can see that you're a caring and loving woman. He knows that you love children. He knows there is no unkindness in you. And now, let us have an end to this. We're both exhausted from worry as well as from work. Now that this particular fear has passed, let's not go back to it."

"I wonder what the Mosers will say," Irma pondered, not yet abandoning the subject.

"That's their business," replied Bertalan. "What I can't imagine is how Csilla Moser will explain any of this to her husband. He isn't Hungarian, he isn't an immigrant, and he isn't even Catholic. He'll never understand this insanity."

"He's such a nice, kind man," offered Irma. "Who knows? Maybe he'll say yes without having to know anything beyond the fact that there is a baby who needs a home."

With that, Irma began to set the table and get supper ready. The Nagy children, including the pale, coughing Markus, came home from school looking half-frozen — their faces bright red from the biting wind and the sleet that had begun to fall. As she looked at the too-small coats that her children wore, Irma told herself again that she was right to refuse. She stirred the pot of bubbling potato soup on the stove and silently fingered the rosary in her apron pocket.

Two nights later, a few blocks away, in the first-floor apartment occupied by Kenny and Csilla Moser and their three children — including two-month-old baby Katinka, born with a crooked leg — Csilla worried about having another mouth to feed, a worry that had thus far been hers alone. As she fried three little sausages in a pan, not noticing that they were getting darker and smaller as her mind wandered, Csilla pushed errant strands of blonde hair away from her pretty face and considered the various ways she could introduce the topic to her husband.

Kenny Moser was a burly, jovial bear of a man who had a smile for everyone. Kenny was Pennsylvania Dutch, but he was so in love with beautiful Csilla that he happily embraced the Polish and Hungarian customs of her family. When he wasn't working as a crane operator at Bethlehem Steel, he helped his buddy Stan at Stan's auto repair shop. Kenny knew enough about cars to work on simple things like spark plugs and pistons, and the few dollars he earned on nights and weekends at Stan's helped to pay the bills. Kenny hoped that in a month or so Csilla would be able to return to work, to find a job at one factory or another. But he also knew they would probably have to pay more to have someone look after a baby with a crippled leg, a baby who seemed to cry more often than other babies.

Kenny looked down at the baby now, picking her up gently from the brown wicker basket in which she slept. He cooed at her lovingly. She opened her big, bright eyes and smiled at him with a sweet, curled, pink-gummed smile — a smile that might not mean anything, that might simply signal relief from peeing into her cotton diaper — but it was a smile that melted Kenny's heart anyway.

"How's Daddy's little girl?" Kenny murmured at the squirming, tiny bundle in his arms, tucking her soft blanket around her. "Are you giving Daddy a big smile, sweetie? Do you know how much I love you?" As he nestled the baby into the warm crook of his neck, Kenny promised her, "Daddy will take care of you, angel. Daddy will make everything all right. Somehow, everything will be all right."

As Csilla listened to her husband's tender words to their baby, her heart hammered inside of her. How would she ever tell him? How could she explain what it meant for a parish to share the responsibility of taking in babies who had no home? Before she could worry any more, a knock at the kitchen door distracted her.

Kenny placed infant Katinka back into her basket and opened the door. Outside stood Ferenc Geller, one of Kenny's co-workers at the steel mill. Ferenc was welcomed into the kitchen and asked if he would like to have coffee or stay for dinner. He politely declined both offers. He told Kenny that he had to go to his brother's funeral in two days and would have to take a day off from work to do so. Would Kenny cover his shift for him? Without hesitation, Kenny agreed. It would mean working a double shift, but that was all right with him. He worked double shifts whenever he got the chance.

Relieved, Ferenc thanked Kenny and shook his hand.

"I was hoping you'd say yes. That makes everything a lot easier. I'll tell the foreman when I go in tomorrow. He'll be glad the shift is covered. I figured you wouldn't mind making some extra money now, with the new baby."

Csilla's eyes darted fearfully toward Ferenc, but he didn't see her warning look.

"Yeah," said Kenny, "a new baby is an additional expense, although so far little Katinka hasn't cost us much. But I know that because of her leg, we'll have medical expenses in the future."

"I didn't mean Katinka," said Ferenc innocently, unaware that he was introducing a new reality to Kenny. "I was talking about the baby that Father Iszak is asking you to adopt."

Kenny stared at Ferenc as if his words were in a foreign language. When his eyes shot toward Csilla and he saw her stricken, deer-in-the-headlights look, he realized that something important and unknown to him was hanging in the air.

"What baby?" he asked, looking from Ferenc to Csilla and back again. "Whose baby?"

Csilla began to stammer an explanation. "You see, honey," she said slowly, "when there is a baby in the parish with no parents, the priest asks a family to take the baby in as an act of mercy ...."

"No parents?" interrupted Kenny. "What do you mean 'no parents'? What parents in the church have died? What baby is born to no parents? There can be no such thing as having no parents."

Csilla groped for words but found none.

"It's like this," answered Ferenc very directly, forging ahead where Csilla never could have gone. "It's no secret within the church. Almost all of the adults know. They know what goes on. They know what the system is. I think it stinks, and I'll bet everyone in the church agrees with me. They know this is a rotten deal. They know it, but they are afraid to say anything. They are afraid of a God who will strike them dead; a God who will punish them for disobeying the priest."

"But the baby," said Kenny, still not understanding. "What baby? Whose baby? Why us?"

"Whose baby?" Ferenc repeated, laughing. "Whose baby? The priest's, of course! That's whose baby."

Kenny sat down heavily on the wooden kitchen chair as if he was collapsing onto it. Csilla turned off the burner and buried her head in her hands. It was easier to just let Ferenc explain it.

Ferenc pulled up a chair, folded his lanky body into it, and looked unflinchingly at Kenny.

"Father Iszak has two women who work for him at the rectory. You must know them — Ilka and Ilona. They're sisters. They're in their twenties and they've worked for Father Iszak since they were teenagers. Their mother told them it was a service to God to work for the priest."

Kenny nodded mutely. He had seen the young women when he had gone to the rectory to repair the radiator in the library there. Blonde and nice-looking, they seemed timid but kind, and had offered him a cup of coffee. "Yes, I know who you mean. Very pretty, pleasant girls. So, they work at the rectory. So what?"

"Don't you understand, you dumb Dutchman?" asked Ferenc with a smirk. "They don't just clean and do laundry and cook for that hypocrite. They 'do' whatever he asks them to do. I guess they think they have to do whatever he says. Over the years, he's gotten each of them pregnant twice. Now it is Ilka, I think, who is expecting again. Expecting in a few weeks."

"And when these babies are born," asked Kenny, still feeling his way around the bizarre subject, "they're placed with families in the parish? Families who aren't related to these babies?"

"Now you understand!" said Ferenc, smiling and leaning back into the chair.

Csilla couldn't look at her husband and he couldn't bring himself to look at her.

"But what has this to do with us? Why would we be asked to take this baby?"

"As I understand it," answered Ferenc, "Father Iszak has a list of potential families that he thinks could and should take in the babies. He skips the poorest of the families in the parish, of course. And he skips families like mine where there is only an old mother and a few brothers living at home. I also figured out that when baby number three was born — a girl, to Ilona, I think — he had the good sense to ask a priest at a church in Allentown to place the baby there somewhere."

"Why?" asked Kenny. "Why did he do that?"

"You really are a dumb Dutchman, aren't you?" laughed Ferenc. "Think about it. He already had two sons placed in our parish. As the children grew up, what would happen if one of his sons took a fancy to the girl who was his daughter? The young people would have no way of knowing they are brother and sister. So Father Iszak has a plan within a plan. In addition to placing the babies with families that he thinks can care for them, he places them with families that have little contact with each other, that don't live in the same neighborhood. The first boy was given to a family in Hellertown, a family that rarely comes to church. The next boy went to a family in Center Valley that belongs to this parish but attends a church down there, and the third boy — I have been told — is with a family down the street. Little chance that these boys will ever be around each other and notice any resemblance to each other. I'm guessing that they're pretty sure this next baby — his fifth — will also be a boy, or Father wouldn't be trying to place it within this parish. Probably because Ilka is carrying low, and the old women say that means it's a boy."

Kenny sat silently while he took all of this in. He turned to Csilla, who was still standing sentinel at the stove, barely looking at the curled and drying sausages in the frying pan. "And when, exactly, were you planning to tell me about this?"

"Tonight," Csilla whispered, in a barely audible voice.

"I should go," said Ferenc, rising from the table. "Thanks for taking that shift for me, and I'm sorry ... really sorry ... if I broke the news too soon or said too much. But you had to know sometime. And maybe it's better that you heard it from me." With that, Ferenc opened the kitchen door for himself and disappeared into the night.

"I'm so sorry," said Csilla, finding her voice. "I just didn't know how to tell you. I know how absurd it sounds, especially to someone who doesn't understand ... understand our customs and our ways and how the priest has to be obeyed. And I still don't know how I'm going to say no to Father tomorrow. That's when he wants to see me, to ask me to take the baby. I'm to go in for confession at 4:00, and I know that's when he'll ask me."

"Good," said Kenny. "I'm home from work by 4:00 and I'll go with you. He can ask us together, and together we can say no."

Csilla was more stricken by this than by anything else that had been said so far. "But, you can't," she stammered. "You're not even Catholic, you're Lutheran; you aren't even allowed in the church, you...."

"No," laughed Kenny, "I'm not allowed in his church. But I am allowed — no, expected — to raise his bastard child for him? Well, we'll just see about that. We'll see what he has to say tomorrow."

Csilla didn't want to argue with her husband, and she knew she'd never convince him not to accompany her to confession. What she couldn't fathom was his smile, his humming a cheery tune, and what was apparently his absence of worry. Maybe it's something about being Pennsylvania Dutch, she thought.

The next afternoon, when Father Iszak entered the rear of the church where the confessionals were located, he was surprised to find both Csilla and her husband standing there. He thought momentarily of reminding Mr. Moser that he was not allowed, as a non-Catholic, to participate in confession. Before the priest could say anything, Kenny Moser spoke up. In a calm and pleasant tone, he said, "I know what it is you wish to discuss with my wife, and I think that, perhaps, this is a subject that is better discussed with a husband and wife together."

Before Father Iszak could interrupt or re-direct the conversation, Kenny continued.

"I understand that there is a baby coming that will need to be placed with a family. I'm sorry for the child — more sorry than I can say … for reasons that I will not say — but it is impossible for my wife and me to take the child in. This is no reflection on the child, of course, and on the terrible, terrible circumstances into which this poor, truly innocent baby will be born. But we cannot even consider providing a home for this baby who is, after all, the son or daughter of an actual mother and father who should be responsible for him or her."

"But there are extenuating circumstances," interjected Father Iszak, "that make caring for the child by its parents quite impossible. Quite impossible. However," the priest went on, reciting one of his most often-used assertions, "it is one of the hallmarks of our Christian faith that, in love and charity, we reach out to each other in times of hardship, and we open our hearts and our homes to those in need, especially to … ah, as you have said … those who are truly innocent, like this baby whose imminent birth has been brought to my attention."

"Brought to your attention, eh?" Kenny goaded the priest, mischievously. "Perhaps it was brought to your attention seven or eight months ago? Perhaps to give you time to think of where the baby might be placed?"

Father Iszak's face blazed red, and he began to draw himself up indignantly, but Kenny Moser continued fearlessly.

"Believe it or not, I understand what it is to help others. I grew up in a family that always gave food to any poor souls who came knocking at our door, as I'm sure you do as well, Father. I'm sure that you often … perhaps daily? … share your food with the hungry. You do that, don't you? But that isn't the subject we're talking about, is it?"

Clearly enjoying the enormous discomfort he was causing, Kenny continued relentlessly, never seeing Csilla's open-mouthed shock as she listened to him.

"I want to be helpful, Father. I really do. And I understand that this is not the first baby who has needed such placement and who, apparently, has no parents whatsoever, strange as that may seem. So I'll tell you what I'm going to do. Now, as my friend Ferenc always says, I'm just a dumb Dutchman. I'm not clever in the ways of the world, and I'm certainly not as highly educated as you are. Why, I guess I should consider myself privileged and honored to even be allowed in your presence, uneducated and unpolished as I am."

Father Iszak's dark eyes narrowed into slits that could barely hide the fury and outrage he felt. And behind those feelings, something ... yes ... something very much like panic was rising within him.

"My brother Marlon works at the *Bethlehem Globe-Times*," explained Kenny, "and he knows the reporters there. He says they're always looking for a good human interest story. Well, this is a human interest story if ever I heard of one. I'm sure one of the reporters would be interested in writing about the astonishing fact that five children born in the parish — to invisible parents, no less — have been placed with compassionate families that are barely able to feed another mouth. And such a story will have great power. What a few people in the parish can't do, many people in the community can do. When this story appears, when the reporter does his research, I'm sure many people will be glad to contribute money to help feed and clothe these poor children. Perhaps a family will offer to adopt this next baby. The more publicity we get, the better."

"Ah ... I appreciate your ideas and your enthusiasm, Mr. Moser," said Father Iszak hurriedly. "But I don't think that will be necessary. We have been blessed thus far in placing the ... the ... unfortunate children, and I have no doubt we will be able to do so now. And we don't want to draw attention to their plight, do we, Mr. Moser? Surely you wouldn't want them to be identified ... have them feel they had been abandoned or that they were somehow less wanted than other children?"

"Do you mean have them feel these hurts more than they inevitably will? When they learn the truth, as they surely will someday? When they figure out that whoever fathered them didn't love them, didn't care enough to keep them and be responsible for them? Is that what you mean?"

Father Iszak rose from the brocade armchair in which he sat. "I think we have discussed this sufficiently, Mr. Moser. I appreciate the consideration which you and your wife have given to this situation, and I ask that you think about it no more. Please do nothing more about this matter. Please." The priest stared penetratingly at Kenny Moser for a long moment.

"I think I understand," said Kenny, rising from his chair and extending his arm toward his wife, signaling that they were ready to leave. "But I want you to know that I'm prepared to make all of this public whenever you wish me to do so, whenever you think it would help the children." Kenny couldn't control the impulse to curve his mouth into a denigrating smile which the priest could hardly fail to decipher.

"Thank you," said Father Iszak icily. "I will let you know if I ever require your assistance."

"Another thing," said Kenny, not willing to release his prey until he had shaken and played with him a bit longer, as a fox harries a helpless rabbit. "Because you must know these parents personally, perhaps you could speak with them about responsible behavior. You know — the kind of behavior that Jesus speaks of in the Bible. The idea that people, especially women, are not to be used simply for sexual pleasure. That they are to be loved and treated with respect. That men should not create children they cannot support and be true fathers for. I'm sure your Catholic teachings on these matters are the same as those in our Lutheran church, are they not? Perhaps you can use your influence with these parents to stop these pregnancies from happening. Isn't that your real obligation in this matter? To make sure there will be no more babies who need to be placed?"

Kenny didn't wait for an answer, thus sparing himself from seeing the pure hate emanating from Father Iszak's eyes; eyes that followed him and Csilla as they walked down the long center aisle of the church, toward the arched front doors.

When they stepped into the cold, indigo twilight, Csilla reached up and drew her husband toward her to kiss him warmly. "My dumb Dutchman," she laughed, linking her arm in his as they walked home.

"I wonder who's next on his list," mused Kenny.

"I think it is the Bernats," answered Csilla sorrowfully.

At 5:00 p.m. the next day, petite, frightened Gizi Bernat sat in the confessional, twisting her embroidered handkerchief in her hands as anxiety overwhelmed her. She heard the outer door shut, signaling the priest's presence. Closing her eyes, she silently and desperately beseeched God to be with her. Then she spoke. "Bless me, Father, for I have sinned."

LOSING GRANDPOP

*I*n the early and mid-1900s, the Bethlehem City Market at the corner of Third and Adams Streets was a hub within which the South Bethlehem community gathered. Bustling with people of all ages and nationalities, the market offered fresh and colorful produce from scores of vendors and farmers. It also offered breads, cakes, and specialties such as kiffles, strudel, and palacinta from many skilled bakers, fresh fish from a vendor whose display anchored the southeast corner of the market, homemade and imported cheeses, and a variety of fresh meats from butchers who came from local and more distant towns.

At the break of dawn on every Saturday morning, my grandfather walked to the market to do the weekly shopping, carrying with him a sturdy, brown wicker basket, in which he would place his purchases. At those impossibly early hours, the farmers and vendors were already established in their stalls, selling their goods to hundreds of people like Grandpop, who wanted to be there to get the first and freshest of foods.

After he came home with his basket filled, Grandpop would have breakfast, linger over his coffee, and chat with my grandmother and my parents. Around 8:00 or 9:00 a.m., when I was awake and had been dressed for the day and given breakfast, he would hold my hand and walk down to the market again, with me in tow.

Grandpop's forays with me began in my infancy, when he would walk around South Bethlehem, pushing me in a baby carriage or stroller. My parents enjoyed recalling the time that they wheeled my stroller down Fourth Street to go to Archond's Ice Cream Parlor. When they came to the corner of Fourth and Polk Streets, where Zelko's Bar was located, my little arm shot up into the air and I pointed at the door to Zelko's, announcing in my tot's voice, "Petzel!" They immediately understood that Grandpop had taken me into Zelko's and I had learned that this was a place where I would get a pretzel.

Grandpop was my first and best friend. Before my birth, he had been just as attentive to my older cousins, Louis and Robert Hassay (his first grandchildren), who lovingly called him Dayda. He walked them around the South Side too, and treated them to sodas and pretzels.

My outings with Grandpop continued when I was big enough to patter alongside him, his strong hand firmly holding my little fist. He walked slowly enough to accommodate a toddler's shorter stride, and together we went everywhere in South Bethlehem: bakeries and barber shops, haberdasheries and hardware stores. Going to the market with Grandpop was simply how every Saturday began.

One Saturday, in summer of 1949, when I was two-and-a-half years old, Mom dressed me in a cotton shirt and coveralls and off Grandpop and I went to the market. On his second visit to the market each Saturday, having completed his basic shopping earlier, Grandpop concentrated on socializing with his neighbors and buddies. They would light their pipes or cigars and cluster and chat as the crowds bustled around them. That tableau unfolded on this Saturday near Riccaboni's produce stand.

The stands at the market were square or rectangular arrangements, with an open center from which the vendors called to the crowd — "Fresh strawberries! Get your strawberries here!" — and where they would take money and make change. Produce was piled high on the counters surrounding that open center, and it spilled over onto wide metal shelves that projected outward from the stalls. Those shelves were just high enough for a toddler to walk under and become completely hidden in the world under the stalls.

I walked under the shelves whenever I spotted crates with animals in them. I was afraid of chickens, so I never approached crates with those clawed, beaked inhabitants. But the rabbits! That was a different matter. I loved to touch the soft fur of the bunnies that were occasionally brought to the market in wooden crates. Too young to know the fate awaiting them, I simply loved to pet them through the slats of the crates, talk to them, and rub my nose against their twitching noses.

On this particular Saturday, a vendor near Riccaboni's had brought crates of rabbits, all stacked in the center of a stall. Under the shelf I went, letting go of Grandpop's hand, to pet the wonderful, furry creatures. I must have been fascinated with the rabbits for a long while, because when I came out from under the shelf Grandpop wasn't there … none of the old men were there. I looked up and around but didn't see Grandpop anywhere.

I walked away from the stall and kept looking up at the sea of people towering over me. I looked all around at a veritable forest of legs surrounding me. No Grandpop. I knew the market well enough to navigate it and I did so that morning. I didn't know the names of many vendors, but I knew where things were. I walked past Riccaboni's toward Joe Phillips's meat counter; no Grandpop. I walked back toward the fish stand; no Grandpop. I walked toward the place where Grammy bought farmer's cheese. No Grandpop. I walked all the way across the market to the stand where we always bought sausage from Peter Heinrich. No Grandpop. No Grandpop anywhere. I looked back at the bustling market and must have understood that there was little chance that I'd find Grandpop in that crowd. Mr. Heinrich's butcher's stand was near the wooden doors that led out onto Adams Street. I walked through those big, open doors and into the sunshine. My little mind must have reasoned that there was nothing left to do but to walk home … but I was so worried about Grandpop being lost!

I walked to the nearby corner of Adams and Mechanic Streets, looked both ways as I had been taught, and crossed Mechanic Street when no cars were coming. Next came the railroad tracks. Grandpop often walked me down to the railroad tracks that cut across Fillmore Street so that I could wave to the engineer — who always waved back — as the train chugged past. I liked doing that. I knew that you could only cross the tracks when the gates were up, not when they were down. The gates were up on this morning, and with no train in sight, I crossed the tracks and walked toward Fourth Street. I had been taught to know my address, but I didn't know the names of these streets. I simply knew the route between our house and certain locations, including the market, from my repeated outings with Grandpop and my parents.

At the corner of Fourth and Adams, I turned left and headed toward home. I didn't know anything about 'left' or 'right,' I simply knew the way home. At the intersection with Webster Street, and again at the intersections with Taylor and Polk Streets, I stopped and looked carefully in every direction before stepping off the curb and crossing the street. At the intersection of Fourth and Fillmore Streets, I knew I had to walk up the street to go home. Crossing Fourth Street seemed to be a much bigger thing — it was a wider street — than any of the other crossings had been, and I was especially careful to look in all directions before I set off to cross Fourth Street. Once I was on the other side, where the gas station was located, I knew that home was straight up the street. I walked up the hill and was soon standing at the green-painted, iron gate at the side of our house.

I was too small to reach the squeeze-latch of the gate, and I would not have had the strength to open it anyway. So I did what came naturally: I tugged back and forth on the gate, making it rattle, and I yelled, "Mommy! Mommmeeee!" Instantly, the wooden screen door at the side of the house opened and my mother came out and walked toward me, looking at me questioningly. She came to the gate and looked up and down the street. "Where's Grandpop?" she asked, looking down at me.

"He's lost," I answered woefully. "I lost him!"

Mom opened the gate and scooped me up.

"How did you get home?" she asked, with some hint of fear in her voice.

"I walked," I replied, matter-of-factly, with no hint of anything in my voice.

For some reason she started hugging me tightly and kissing my face, muttering something about thanking God.

After touching my hands, arms, legs, and feet, and looking at my face and assuring herself that all the parts were there, Mom picked me up again and took me into the house. She sat me down at the kitchen table and asked me what had happened. I said that I had gone under the stands to pet the rabbits and when I came out, Grandpop was gone. "I lost him," I said broken-heartedly. Then I told her that I walked home and that I had looked both ways when I crossed the streets and the railroad tracks. When I mentioned the railroad tracks, Mom hugged me again and started to cry. She hadn't thought about the railroad tracks. First, I lost Grandpop and now I made Mommy cry. This was not a good day for me.

Mom instantly knew that Grandpop must be frantically searching for me, sick with worry and grief. But there was no point in going to look for him; there would be no way of knowing where he was. My father wasn't at home; he had gone to work on the day shift that day. But my grandmother was at home, and as soon as she learned what happened, she devised a way to torment her husband for his carelessness.

Mom comforted me and assured me that Grandpop was probably looking for me and would soon be home. I was taken into the parlor and seated on the sofa to look at my picture books. After an hour or so, Grandpop came home, looking — as my mother always recalled in the years that followed — far older than he had looked when he left that morning. In the endless telling of this story, which cemented it in my mind and memory over the years, Mom would recall that my grandmother did not tell Grandpop that I was home, safe and sound. Instead, she asked him where I was. When he agonizingly told her that I was lost, she berated him ruthlessly for losing me. When Mom heard her doing this, she immediately came downstairs and told Grandpop that I was home and that I was all right.

When I heard his voice, I ran to Grandpop. He picked me up and gave me the biggest, tightest, longest hug he ever gave me. We settled down on the sofa together but I didn't understand why he was crying. Then I remembered — he had been lost! He must have been so scared! I clambered onto his lap and snuggled my face into his neck and told him that I was sorry I lost him and that I would never, ever, ever lose him again. He hugged and kissed me and then he turned on the big brown wooden radio in the corner of the parlor — the one with the fabric front through which the music and voices came out — and we sat and listened to polka music.

I could not know it at the time — and I would have been far too young to understand it even if it had been explained to me — but on that summer Saturday I encountered two of life's largest lessons for the first time: the bottomless heartache of losing someone you love and the inexpressible bliss of finding someone you love.

THERESA

*F*ifty years before Cheers became the bar where "everybody knows your name," Theresa's Fillmore Street Restaurant in South Bethlehem had the same sort of family and neighborhood atmosphere, not only in the bar (where Theresa's husband, Steve, presided) but also in the kitchen, where Theresa ruled.

I only saw Theresa dressed up on one occasion — "dressed up" meaning she was wearing a nice dress, with decent shoes, stockings, and with her hair neatly combed. That occasion was her son's funeral. Every other time I saw her she was in a well-worn house-dress that was covered with a white bib apron bearing the stains of the kitchen, and she invariably wore an old pair of men's shoes, un-laced, spread open, and clomping as she walked. Her dark hair, liberally streaked with gray, was pulled back and knotted in a small bun at the nape of her neck. Loose strands of her hair fell from her forehead and at the sides of her face.

On any given night, Theresa's kitchen was filled with dozens of aromas of wonderful food: roasted turkey, fried chicken, sweet potatoes, breaded veal sizzling in butter in a skillet, brown sugar-glazed ham baking in the oven, fresh-baked bread, the pungent smell of pork cracklings in biscuits, and the aromas of chocolate, cherries, and apples in various desserts. The kitchen was also filled with men sitting around a large wooden table, on well-worn wooden chairs. These men worked in the foundries at Bethlehem Steel. They did backbreaking, filthy, dangerous work all day, every day. Most of the men lived at Theresa's, above the restaurant, in small, sparsely furnished rooms that she rented to them on a monthly basis. All of the conversations were in Windish or Hungarian or broken English. And always ... always ... working feverishly in the kitchen was the small, frail figure of Marika — a woman around Theresa's age, who did anything and everything Theresa ordered her to do.

Marika was almost blind. Her glasses had lenses that were soda-bottle thick, and those lenses were always smudged with grease and fingerprints. She didn't have time to clean them. Marika washed dishes, pots, and pans in tubs filled with steaming, soapy water. She rinsed them in equally hot water from the spigot — water so hot that its steam filled the kitchen and drifted ceiling-ward. When she wasn't doing the endless piles of dishes that accumulated in the sink, Marika was washing clothes in an old ringer washer, soaking the whites in bluing solution, starching the white shirts worn daily by Theresa's husband and son, and ironing … constantly ironing … pressing those starched shirts perfectly, and ironing table-cloths, napkins, Theresa's aprons and dresses, and the bedding from the boarders' rooms upstairs. Marika also cleaned vegetables, peeled potatoes, and did whatever cooking and baking Theresa ordered her to do.

All the while, Marika meekly tolerated the endless stream of expletives and abuses that I heard Theresa hurl at her almost mindlessly. In English and Windish, she called Marika a moron, a bitch, a good-for-nothing lazy dog, and anything else she could think of. At some point, I suppose, Marika stopped hearing the abuse or she stopped caring about it. With no education and no special skills, Marika knew that Theresa's was one place where she could work and earn whatever pay Theresa felt like giving to her. So she worked. Endless hours each day, seven days a week, month after month, year after year. Marika rarely had a day off and never had a vacation. When she was finally too old and frail to even stand, Marika was placed in the Northampton County home for the aged at Gracedale. There, she didn't have to work, people brought food to her, her clothes were washed for her, and no one called her ugly names. The last years of Marika's life were the best years of her life — years of peace and rest.

Theresa's waitresses often didn't fare much better than Marika. During an armed robbery, in which Theresa was knocked to the floor, her waitress, Julia, was pistol-whipped and shot in the back, with the bullet penetrating her lung. Bleeding profusely and struggling to get to the pay phone, Julia took a dime from the counter to call the police. After Julia's hospitalization, Theresa informed her that, after five decades, her services were no longer needed.

It is a strange, human characteristic that compassion and cruelty are often found in the same person. So it was with Theresa.

There were people Theresa liked; my grandmother was one of them. Theresa could be kind when she chose to be. But the callous streak in her, most obvious in her treatment of Marika, could be seen even in her treatment of her son, Billy.

Bill was Theresa's son from her first marriage. I have no doubt that she loved him. Bill was movie-star handsome and had a white-collar job in Bethlehem Steel's main office building. At night, he helped Steve at the bar. My grandmother told me that all Bill ever really wanted was to be a farmer. As a child, he had fallen in love with farming and that was the life he wanted. Theresa could have bought him any farm or acreage that he would have desired. But her son was not going to be a farmer. That would be beneath him. Beneath her. He had to go to college. And he did. He had to work in an office. And he did. He had to marry a woman with money. That he did not do.

For many years, Bill had one special girlfriend, a very pretty blonde with a warm smile and a sweet disposition. It was obvious that she cared for Bill as much as he cared for her. My parents and I would occasionally see them and talk with them when they were shopping or out to dinner. But Theresa's iron will extended to the son she loved, and in the same way that Bill never did the farming he wanted to do, he never married the woman he apparently loved. He never lived the life he wanted to live. What Bill did do was drink. The availability of all that liquor in the bar made it very easy for Bill to numb himself with alcohol. His drinking took its toll. By the time he was in his late thirties, Bill was overweight and red-faced. His death came swiftly when he was 45.

Theresa seemed unable to believe that anything like death could happen to her Billy. On the day of Bill's funeral, Theresa turned to my mother as we left the church to go to the cemetery. Theresa looked at the quiet crowd assembled on the sidewalk in front of the church and she said to my mother, in Windish, "Ge schin znauty kau un mew za kurvo."

Translated: "I want to know which one he had for a whore." "Shto ye?" — Which one is it? — Theresa asked my mother. Mom gestured toward Bill's lady friend, beautifully coiffed, impeccably dressed, wearing a pale beige mink coat, and sobbing uncontrollably. Leaning against a telephone pole in front of the church, she was crying as if her heart had been ripped from her. It would have pained any human being to hear those sobs. Mom started to tell Theresa her name, but Theresa sniffed her contempt, turned away, and lumbered down the church steps. The parting crowd silently made way for her as she headed toward the empty funeral limousine reserved for family members.

There were many key places in the lives of South Bethlehem's immigrants — churches, the City Market, the Steel. Theresa's Restaurant — *Treza's* Restaurant — was one of those landmark places. A place where everybody knew your name.

GHOST

*I*n 1973, St. John's Windish Lutheran Church sponsored the first of several trips to Slovenia. Travelers could visit with relatives they knew and meet some they never knew. They could see where their ancestors came from and visit cemeteries with gravestones bearing engravings dating back to the seventeenth century.

A special feature of this trip was the presence of the church choir, which gave concerts in several cities. At one of those concerts, a very elderly woman, bent with age, sat in the front pew of the church in Murska Sobota. She was wrapped in a black shawl against the evening breeze coming through the open windows, and she listened to the soaring, inspiring music with rapt attention. She also stared, spellbound, at a member of the choir, Ron Hari. As the concert proceeded, she couldn't take her eyes away from the young man, and she began to weep, silently but helplessly.

When the concert ended, attendees mingled with choir members, thanking them for their concert and for coming to their city. The old woman approached Ron cautiously, still not taking her eyes from his face. She gathered the nerve to speak to him. In hesitant words, she thanked him for the beautiful music and for coming all the way from America. Ron looked at her, smiled, and took the small, frail hand she offered him. He could tell that her eyes, now clouded with age and wet with tears, were once the color of the sapphire sky above the Slovenian Alps. Her heart-shaped face and still-rosy cheeks must have made her the village beauty many decades ago. Her snowy white hair, pinned up in braids, was still thick and wavy. When she was young, mused Ron, her hair must have cascaded down her back or been tied with ribbons and flowers. In her limited English, the woman began to speak to Ron, and in his limited Slovenian, he attempted to answer her.

"I am, how you say, sorry," she said, trilling the 'r's, "that I look so hard at you. I no want you be mad with me."

"Oh, that's all right," Ron quickly assured her, squeezing her small hand in his. "I don't mind at all that you looked at me."

Sensing that her English would not suffice for the message she wished to share, the old woman looked around for someone to help her. She caught the eye of a church member who is fluent in both English and Slovenian. That church member, Mary, came over to translate in both languages.

After the woman spoke to her intently, Mary turned to Ron to say, "She is sorry if she stared at you. She had no wish to offend you. It's just that you look exactly like someone she knew many, many years ago, someone she has not seen for decades."

"Who was he?" Ron asked, for Mary to translate.

The tears ran swiftly down the old woman's cheeks as she answered. Mary said, "He was her sweetheart, someone she loved very much … someone who loved her very much. He wanted to marry her, but there was no work for him here and he moved to America, following his brothers to Pennsylvania, to Bethlehem. He did not know how to write, just as she did not know how to write, and so they lost touch and she never saw him again."

The woman looked expectantly, searchingly at Ron.

"I hope she found someone else to love," said Ron, sympathetically.

Again, Mary translated and then answered. "No, she never married. She could never love anyone else. Her heart was always with him. It still is."

"What was his name?" Ron asked.

The old woman understood his question and she answered directly. "Hari," she said, again trilling the 'r.' "Istvan Hari."

Astonishment washed over Ron's countenance, draining the color from his face. The hairs stood up on the back of his neck.

Seeing Ron's amazement, the old woman asked, hopefully, "You know?"

Ron answered softly, "He was my grandfather."

Neither of them spoke for a long moment and then they embraced, both of them allowing the tears to flow freely.

In time, the old woman lifted her face from Ron's shoulder and looked up into his eyes. She reached up to stroke his cheek and touch his hair. Then, slowly and in perfect English, as if she had been rehearsing the words for a lifetime, she said, lovingly, "My boy. *My* boy."

THE ODDS

"There she is again," thought Phil Watkins, "first in line, as usual." Phil was a bus driver for Carriage Line Tours, and every week, Monday through Friday, he drove a bus route from Triangle, New Jersey, to Atlantic City.

As he pulled the big white and maroon bus into the terminal in Triangle, he saw the short, elderly woman at her usual place in the front of the line to board the bus. Dressed always in black, dark brown, or navy blue, she looked as if she was in perpetual mourning. Neatly groomed, she didn't look poor, like some of the other regulars on the Atlantic City route, but she certainly didn't look prosperous, either. She had short, wavy gray hair, and Phil guessed that she was in her seventies.

As always, she took her place in the front passenger seat of the bus. As always, she sat alone. Only rarely, when the bus was crowded, did she have to tolerate someone sitting next to her for the two-hour drive to Atlantic City.

As he pulled away from the terminal, when all of the people with tickets had boarded, Phil thought again about the old woman sitting four feet away from him. He didn't know why he was curious about her; he simply was.

Phil was 58 and retired from the postal service. Driving a bus gave him some extra income. It also gave him something to do, something to occupy his time now that his wife was gone. She died of breast cancer when she was 55, and Phil missed her every day. They hadn't been a demonstrative, lovey-dovey couple, but they were each other's best friends and rock-solid allies. Their children — a daughter and a son and their spouses — lived in California, so Phil didn't have the pleasure of having family nearby. Maybe that's why he was occasionally curious about his passengers — where they came from, what they did for a living, and what their life stories were.

In his mirror, Phil could see the old lady, staring out the window as she always did. She took the bus to Atlantic City two or three times each week. Unlike most of the other passengers, she never brought a magazine or a newspaper to read. She never came with a friend. When they got onto the Atlantic City Expressway, like clockwork, she would open the black zippered purse in her lap and take out a sandwich she brought from home. Carefully unwrapping the sandwich, she would eat half, and just as carefully, re-wrap the remainder for the trip home. A few crackers or pieces of candy completed her meal. She never brought soda, water, or anything else to drink. "Probably doesn't want to have to go to the bathroom as soon as she gets off the bus," mused Phil.

As they rolled along the Expressway, Phil took a chance and threw a comment her way: "Not much traffic today. We should make good time." The old woman looked up at him, startled that he was speaking to her, but she didn't reply. When they got to Atlantic City, the casino greeter boarded the bus while Phil stood outside. After the greeter swiped everyone's comp card and exited the bus, Phil helped people to disembark. As always, the old woman was first off the bus. "Have a good day," Phil said cheerily. Once again, she looked at him and said nothing. When Phil brought the bus back to the boarding area six hours later, he assisted the passengers onto the bus. He had a modest greeting for most of them and often joked with the regulars about whether they had left their money at the casino or were taking the casino's money home. He tipped his hat to the old woman as she boarded and said that he hoped she had a good day.

That routine repeated itself three days later, when the old woman again made the trip. Phil tried to engage her in conversation several times. He arbitrarily decided that if she didn't say anything to him by the end of the day, he would simply stop trying. That morning, when he helped her to board the bus, he said, "My name is Phil. What is your name?" She looked at him suspiciously and said nothing. Having decided that his overtures were a waste of time, he said nothing to her on the ride down to Atlantic City and paid no special attention to her as the passengers exited the bus. The ride home, in the darkening evening, was quiet as well. As he helped people off the bus in Triangle, he noticed that the old woman wasn't the first one to leave. She was the last one off the bus. She stopped at the bottom of the bus steps and looked up at Phil. "Betty," she said. "My name is Betty." Then she walked off into the darkness.

Phil greeted Betty by name every time she boarded the bus. It didn't matter, somehow, if she didn't respond to the occasional comments he made about the weather or traffic or the casinos. Once in a while she would nod in agreement or offer a brief sentence in response to his observations. Mostly, her thoughts were about the day she would spend at the casino: What slot machines would she go to first? Would she play anything other than a penny machine? Should she try one of the mega-line machines? How would she parcel out the money she had brought to spend?

Betty was not a crazy gambler. She knew her limits. In her bedroom, she kept a small, leather clutch purse and always had $500 in that purse. That was money to pay bills. When her monthly Social Security check arrived, along with the widow's pension she got from the Veteran's Administration — she got no pension for her 52 years of work in the textile factory — she would first put enough money in the purse to reach that $500 level. That was more than enough to pay her bills. In another, smaller purse, she would place $150 each month. That accumulated amount would cover her various taxes when they came due. Downstairs, in the living room, behind the Bible in the corner curio cabinet, there was a small vase with irises and daffodils painted on it. In that vase, Betty kept money to buy food and household supplies. Money to put into church envelopes also came out of that vase. In the kitchen, in the cookie jar on top of the refrigerator, Betty kept her playing money. This was the money she used when she played bingo or went to Atlantic City. If the cookie jar was empty, she didn't play bingo and she didn't go to Atlantic City. There had been months when the cookie jar was empty by the end of the first week of the month. When that happened, Betty stayed at home and watched TV or knitted. She was nothing if not disciplined.

On this particular day, Betty was thinking long and hard about what she would play and what she would bet. Everything depended, of course, on how the machines treated her. If she won, she could afford to play a more costly machine or play, perhaps, a two-cent or even nickel machine. The possibilities intrigued her and she reviewed them again and again in her mind.

When they arrived in Atlantic City, Betty was the first one off the bus and she hurried into the casino. She didn't like to waste time getting started. She looked at some of the newer slot machines near the entrance. She hadn't tried them yet but they were crowded. She didn't like crowds. She walked around the casino, waiting for that urge, that inner prompting that sometimes directed her toward one machine or another.

After a few moments of looking around the casino, her gaze returned to the penny machines that featured bars, bells, coin symbols, and one, two, or three sevens, some of which had stars behind them. Five columns offered plenty of room for winning combinations.

Betty started conservatively. Thirty lines at a penny a line; 30 cents for each press of the Play button. She started well:

One line gave Betty 400 credits, another gave her 20 credits, another gave her 2,000 credits, and various other combinations on the 30-line screen gave Betty another 600 credits ... 3020 credits in all, or $30.20.

Betty hadn't had a start like that in months, maybe in a year. She had played $2.10 in pennies in the machine and now had $30.20 in credits. After she hit 400 additional credits with her next 30-cent bet, she doubled her bet to 60 cents. She paused. The machine felt like a winner, but you never know. It can turn on you, she thought, and the credits could evaporate quickly. She decided on one more bet. That 60 cents yielded only 50 credits so she decided to cash out and look for another machine.

She tried a few more bar-and-sevens machines and added to her small winnings. By the time she decided to take a break and sit on a bench on the Boardwalk for a while, she had $27.50 in her purse — in addition to the remainder of the money she had brought from home. As usual, she made up her mind to hold onto the vouchers and cash them in before she left to board the bus. She had a system. She didn't spend voucher money unless it was $5.00 or less.

The sun was warm, as it usually is in early autumn, and people still crowded the Boardwalk and the beach, trying to make summer last as long as possible. The sun felt good on Betty's face and she closed her eyes. On days like today, something very much like contentment came over her. The sun seemed to warm her heart, and her soul. She could feel herself smiling ... smiling as she used to smile so, so long ago. After an hour or so she decided to walk to another casino, somehow testing whether or not her luck would follow her.

She stepped from the bright sunshine and ocean views into the neon brightness of the casino interior. There, it was never night or day, just ringing bells, dazzling light displays, and vivid colors everywhere. Betty found herself walking toward the always-busy machines featuring animated woodland creatures — machines she rarely played because they were, for her, too addictive. She knew she could easily be lured into playing longer than she should, hoping for a bonus game. But as she arrived at the row of woodland machines, a player stood up and left. Was that a sign? She quickly sat down, her heart pounding a little faster.

She started conservatively – 30 lines at a penny a line. She won enough to keep playing, her winnings roughly replacing the coins she spent on each spin. Suddenly, a bonus game appeared on the screen. Betty's heart started racing. She knew that the big winnings on bonus games usually went to players who had multiple coins in, sometimes the maximum — $3.00 per spin. But occasionally, rarely, a 30-cent player could get a good bonus. The odds were not in her favor with a 30-cent bet, but you never knew. She watched the cartoon animals spin the wheels. Betty watched in amazement as the first reel, then the second, then the third came up as WILD. This would be a huge win! The fourth reel came up with three Wilds and two images of a bear cub, a high-paying symbol, and then — amazingly — the fifth reel came up as WILD. Betty's eyes widened, and her heart pounded as if it would burst. She rubbed the screen face of the machine and whispered "thank you, thank you, thank you" again and again.

Betty felt someone patting her shoulder and heard whoops and cheers behind her. As the bonus numbers tallied up at the top of the screen, she searched for the small-font numbers near the center that would tell her what she won. But her eyes were blurred. Then she realized she had tears in her eyes. She looked toward the top of the machine and laughed as the numbers kept going higher and higher — $75, $120, $180, $230, $400, and finally, $780. The other players in her row congratulated her and said they hoped some of her luck would come their way too. She stared at the number for a long while when the tallying stopped. 78000 credits. She had never won that much at one time. Only rarely had she ever scored a five-figure hit. Her hand was shaking as she reached for the Repeat Bet button. With the money she already had in the machine, her total was $803. She decided to play the three dollars and cash out $800. That three dollars, generating some wins, lasted another fifteen minutes. That gave Betty time to calm down, relish her amazing luck, and to enjoy the sheer pleasure of watching the reels spin in their unpredictable patterns. When she had exactly $800 in the machine, she pushed COLLECT with an odd combination of triumph and humility.

Betty tucked the paper voucher into the bill compartment of her wallet and carefully closed her purse, double-wrapping its straps around her arms. She had $20 more that she was willing to spend that day from the money she brought from home, and she took her time choosing her next machine. She decided to play a circus-themed machine, with its variety of bonus games. There, too, she was lucky. Playing only one penny per line, Betty won at least a few coins on almost every spin. Then she hit a streak of bonus games that added $15.00 to her winnings. She felt as though she was in some magical place, not unlike the forest in which the bear cub appeared.

Betty checked her watch: 4:00 p.m. The bus would be there at five. She decided to call it a day and walked to the cashier's window to proudly turn in her vouchers. "Any special way?" the cashier asked perfunctorily. Betty hadn't thought about it. Then she said, "Hundreds, please," knowing she was unlikely to ever break a hundred-dollar bill for gambling. The $800, she decided, would be emergency money; money to be used if something broke or needed repair around the house. And maybe, just maybe, she would use some of it for new curtains for the living room — the white, crisscross, sheer ruffled ones she always wanted. Yes, that was something she would treat herself to.

As she descended on the escalator and headed for the bus lounge, Betty decided to also treat herself to a bottle of soda from the vending machine. Feeling wealthy, she even bought a pack of cookies from another machine. Then she sat down to enjoy her soda, cookies, and her own smile.

She was surprised to see Phil, the bus driver, walking toward her. "Did you have a good day?" he asked, smiling. She was so surprised to see him that she didn't answer, and instead, asked him why he was there so early. "I thought you had to come only ten minutes before departure."

"That's the schedule," said Phil, "but I had to bring the bus tools up here for one of our guys who was having some problems with his bus and didn't have a tool box. I'm parked over on the street where they're doing construction and I'll bring the bus up when it's almost five, and I can get my tools back. So, how was your day?"

Betty's eyes grew teary again. "I won $800," she told him in a whisper, leaning toward him so that no one else could hear. "I never won that much before. Never. And I had thirty cents in. Do you know what the odds are of getting a hit like that with only thirty cents in? I am so happy ... so happy that I won."

"Good for you!" said Phil, beaming. "I'm glad that you won too, and that's quite a hit! You must be a lucky person."

Betty grew quiet and stared into the middle distance beyond Phil.

"Not really. I wouldn't say that. It's just that sometimes the odds ...."

"Are you from Triangle?" Phil asked, abandoning the luck theme for the moment.

"No," answered Betty, "I'm from Bethlehem, in Pennsylvania. It's about an hour drive from Triangle. I grew up in Bethlehem and lived there, on the South Side, until about five years ago."

"What made you move?"

"My son, Joey, wanted me to live with him and his wife. I didn't want to do that. Sometimes three generations in a house doesn't work so well. But I could see the sense in being near him, especially as I got older. So

I sold my half-double house in Bethlehem and bought a smaller half-double in Triangle. It's all right. It's big enough for me and not too big for me to take care of."

"Your son must be happy to have you closer too," suggested Phil.

"Well, he was," said Betty. "But two years after I moved, they told Joey he had leukemia. They said there was a good chance that he would make it, and he got so much chemotherapy that I thought he'd die from the treatments. But he went into remission and we were all happy. But he was so weak. About a year later, it was back and there wasn't much more they could do. He died a year and a half ago."

"I'm so sorry," said Phil, gently. "Was he your only child?"

"The only one who lived. I had twins. Joey and his brother, Manny, Jr. They were premature and both of them were very small. Manny died the day after he was born. They didn't have the fancy equipment then that they have now. Maybe if Manny had been born now he would have made it. Maybe."

As she stroked the soda bottle in her hand, something made Betty talk about herself and remember things she hadn't thought about in a long time.

"My parents came over from what was Yugoslavia. My father worked in the steel mill. Most of the men worked there. It was hard, dirty work but he earned enough to feed his family. But when he was thirty-five he had a heart attack and died. Just like that. Suddenly. One day my mother was a wife, and the next day she was a widow. She did odd jobs around the neighborhood, but the Depression made things very tough. I had to quit school at fourteen to go to work to help with the bills and help raise my younger brother and sister. I didn't mind. Most of my friends did the same thing. In those days it was unusual if you *didn't* have to quit school.

"In 1938, when my brother was sixteen, he was delivering groceries, trying to earn a few cents, and he was driving his friend's car. It was wintertime and there was a lot of snow and ice on the ground. My sister wanted to go to her friend's house and my brother didn't want her to walk in all that snow. He said he'd drive her to her friend's house when he delivered the groceries. The car skidded down Buchanan Street on the ice just when the freight train was coming on the tracks. The car stopped on the tracks but the train couldn't stop in time. They must have died instantly. Just one minute earlier and they could have gotten out of the car. Minutes later and the train would have been gone. My brother was sixteen and my sister was fifteen. The undertaker wouldn't let my mother see them. He just kept saying that everything was all right and their bodies were whole. Maybe he was lying, maybe not. My mother kind of died then too. She kept saying that you should never bury your children; they should never go before you do. She said it was something you couldn't understand unless you went through it. She was right. I couldn't understand what she went through until Joey died.

"In 1939, I met Manny. He was a neighbor of some people in our church and he came with them to our grape festival. That was a celebration we had every October. Good food, wine and beer, lots of music and dancing. It was always a good time. Manny asked me to dance and I agreed. I liked him right from the start. He was Mexican. There were lots of Mexicans in Bethlehem then. They came to work at the Steel and they had a big, tight-knit community.

"We went out a few times and we both knew, somehow, that we would be together. Manny may have been Mexican, but he was Catholic and that was the important thing. My mother said that if we could be happy together, God bless us. We were married on April 23, 1940. By summer I was pregnant. The twins were born on our first anniversary the next April. April 23. What are the odds? We named the first one Manny, Jr. after his father and the second one Joseph, after my father. We buried the baby, Manny, Jr., in the same plot where my father, brother, and sister were buried. It seemed easier, somehow, to have him be with family.

"Manny kept working at the Steel, but he wasn't doing what they called an essential job so he was drafted in 1943. He was sent to Europe and trained as a medic. He actually liked his work. When he wrote to me, he said that he knew he was doing something important, something that meant a lot to those guys. He even said that when he got home he might try to get more training and do some kind of medical work as a full-time job. I think he meant it.

"He was in Italy, at Anzio. The outfit he was with came under heavy fire. He and the other medics made several runs to bring back the guys who had been hit. They got them all back. Manny made one last run to bring back a sergeant who got hit in the legs. Manny tried to stay down and drag him, but it was easier to hoist the sergeant over his shoulder and carry him. Manny's buddy told me he ran like hell, even with carrying the weight of the sergeant. He was almost at the trench when he was shot in the back. He died instantly. Every guy in that outfit survived that day, all except Manny. I guess the odds just weren't with him.

"I am so sorry for your losses," said Phil. "All of them. My God, what you've been through. I've only lost my wife and that nearly killed me. I can't imagine ...."

"A loss is a loss," replied Betty. "One or many. Every one of them hurts. And you never get used to the hurt. It's not like the second or third or fourth death hurts less than the first. Maybe it would be better that way. But that's not how it works. I cried as hard for Joey as I did for little Manny, and Joey at least had a life ... had a chance to live, get married, and have children. But it hurts the same."

Phil checked his watch and was relieved to see that it was time to bring the bus around to his appointed lane. Betty, too, was glad to have an end to the reminiscing, although she felt strangely comforted by having told Phil her story.

On the ride home, Betty enjoyed looking at the dense trees on either side of the Atlantic City Expressway and seeing the occasional deer foraging in the grass. The setting sun bathed the sky and trees in a warm, rosy glow, and Betty closed her eyes and allowed herself to picture that bonus game again and again, the reels spinning WILD, WILD, WILD and then that last, fifth WILD. She knew this was a daydream she would enjoy replaying in her memory again and again. What are the odds, she wondered, of ever having another day as good as this one?

When she disembarked from the bus in Triangle, Phil clasped her hand and asked if she thought her lucky streak would continue.

"Maybe. Maybe not. You never know."

"See you here in the morning?"

"Maybe. You never know. You just never know."

GO, WHITE!

"Go, white!" The crowd in the college gymnasium cheered for the women's basketball team. Team members were wearing the white uniforms signifying the home team. "Go, white!" the crowd thundered again. The shout ricocheted off the walls as the home team charged down the court. The players scored a two-pointer, got a rebound, and then made a three-point shot from almost the half-court line to go ahead 50-48. "Go, white!"

Thirty-two-year-old Edgar added his cheers to the roars of the crowd. He never cheered until he heard others shout. He never wanted to be conspicuous. Careful to sit by himself and not intrude on anyone else's space, Edgar nevertheless enjoyed sitting close enough to people to feel as though he was part of the crowd. Shy and wary by nature, Edgar didn't enjoy contact with people, but he liked being part of the group. "Go, white!" he yelled, thereby doubling the number of words he had spoken out loud that day.

For the past two years, Edgar had been walking from his apartment in South Bethlehem to the college gymnasium on the north side of the city to attend the basketball games. He had discovered the women's basketball games accidentally when he showed up at the gym one night expecting the men's team to be playing. Since then, he hadn't missed one home game for the women's team. Attending the games gave him something to do, allowing him to be with people without having to actually interact with anyone.

Edgar did not attend away games. His travels were limited to the distances he could walk and the bus routes that took him to and from Westgate Mall and Elizabeth Avenue. He never went farther than that. In his lifetime, Edgar had never gone beyond a two-mile radius from center city Bethlehem. He hadn't needed to. South Bethlehem was a place where you could walk to work, to church, to stores, banks, to a dozen or more eating places, movie theatres, even to the hospital. Edgar had never been to Allentown or Easton. He didn't like the idea of going beyond the streets and neighborhoods familiar to him.

Edgar lived alone in an efficiency apartment in a subsidized-housing building on Third Street. Like the other residents of the building, he was a single man with a limited income. Occasionally he returned a nod from one of the men as they passed in the hallway, but there seemed to be an unspoken agreement that this was a place to live, not a place to develop friendships. He didn't know the names of any of the men in the building and no one knew his name. He liked it that way.

During the day, Edgar worked at St. Anthony's Roman Catholic Church and the nearby St. Anthony's School. He cleaned the church and the rectory during the day, when school was in session, and he cleaned the school in late afternoons and on Saturdays. He also did minor repairs, replacements, and refurbishing. Edgar enjoyed his work. He liked polishing the pews in the church, and he didn't mind cleaning the bathrooms or washing the windows. It was a solitary job and he liked it that way. On most days, unless he saw the priest, Father Michael, or Mrs. Kilpatrick, the cook at the rectory, he didn't have to speak to anyone.

Edgar had dropped out of school in twelfth grade, three months before graduation. He didn't like being with the other students in class all day, and he recoiled from the pressure of taking tests, answering questions, and proving that he had learned something. What his timidity disguised was the fact that Edgar learned easily and thoroughly. Edgar was smart. He could do algebra problems in his head. He loved history, and after he read them, the lines of poetry taught in Mrs. Heller's English class were fixed in his mind. Those lines often came to him randomly, and he enjoyed remembering portions of *Invictus, Leaves of Grass*, and *A Shropshire Lad*. He had most of the poems from the latter volume memorized, and he contentedly recited them in his head. In fact, the vast majority of Edgar's conversations occurred in his head — conversations he had with himself, in which he contemplated things he couldn't talk about with anyone.

Edgar's primary reason for quitting school was the death of his mother. Edgar loved his mother with his whole heart, and he did not mind tending to her in the last year of her life, when she fought a losing battle with cancer. Edgar and his mother lived rent-free in a small home owned by St. Anthony's parish in South Bethlehem. His mother worked as a waitress and earned a modest income — enough to feed and clothe herself and her son, but certainly not enough to afford rent or a mortgage. Edgar was twelve years old when he learned why they paid no rent for their home and learned the true story of his father.

His mother had only told him that his father died before he was born. In some ways, that was true. Edgar's father was a handsome young priest who had been assigned to St. Anthony's. He fell in love with a pretty eighteen-year-old girl in the parish, and she was completely smitten with him. They knew that theirs was an impossible situation, but their irresistible attraction to each other, their blossoming love, and their easy access to the guest bedroom in the rectory had doomed them. Neither the priest nor the girl, Katalin, knew anything about biology, but both had heard the old adage that "you can't become pregnant the first time." They learned, about two months later, that that particular maxim was false.

The young priest was swiftly dispatched to Rome, and presumably, de-frocked or reassigned to another parish or sent to another country. Katalin never knew what happened to him. She never heard from him again. But she saw him — saw him every day in the gray-green eyes of her son, in his auburn hair, and, as the boy grew, in that lopsided smile that clutched at her heart every time she looked at him. In her heart, Katalin knew how much she loved the boy's father and she knew that he loved her too.

But Katalin did not have time to think about love. At age eighteen, she was left alone to cope with a baby and with the towering rage and condemnation of her parents. They were cold, self-righteous Austrian immigrants for whom the idea of human frailty was unthinkable. They attended Mass every day and went to confession every week. But now, as they told her relentlessly before they evicted her and stopped speaking to her, she had condemned them to shame in this life and eternal damnation in the next, and they regretted that she was ever born.

All of this Edgar learned one day when his mother was at work and he had come home from elementary school with a stomach-ache. Edgar often had what the school nurse called a "nervous stomach." He had gone upstairs to lie down and then heard the back door open. He recognized the voice of his Aunt Helen, his mother's sister. He didn't like Aunt Helen. He thought she was sometimes nasty to his mother, and he knew she was a gossip. She had a habit of reminding his mother that she had more money, nicer clothes, and a nicer house than they did, "... and that's what you get for what you did, Katalin." Aunt Helen's visits always left Edgar's mother with a sadness in her eyes that he could do nothing to erase, and that tore at his child's heart.

On this day, Aunt Helen was obviously talking to someone she had brought to the house. Edgar crept down the stairs quietly, not wanting his aunt to see that he was at home.

"My sister has a beautiful Hummel figurine and I want you to see it," said Aunt Helen loudly. "I know she won't mind; she never minds when I just come in. Ah, here it is — look how pretty this is. And my sister found it on the dollar table at the St. Joe's bazaar. Imagine! A dollar! Not that she can even afford one dollar, but she bought it and I can't say I blame her. It's probably the nicest thing she owns. But she made her bed and now she has to lie in it.

"She let that priest do filthy things to her and that's what she got — a child. A bastard. Of course, no man would want a woman, even a pretty one like Katalin *used* to be, once she was damaged goods, ruined by the filthy things that priest did to her. That's why our mother and father haven't seen or spoken to her since the boy was born. This has been such a burden to them! That's why she lives here. The parish lets her live here free because of what the priest did to her. I guess they thought they owed her something, though I don't see it that way. She was old enough to know better. She let him do those filthy things to her. She let him! And because of what he did, she lives on charity. I would be so ashamed. But as I always tell her, she made her bed ...."

With that, Aunt Helen and her friend left the house. Edgar heard the screen door slam shut behind them. He felt sick to his stomach all over again. It was too much for a youngster to take in, too much for him to understand, but it explained so much. It explained why Aunt Helen talked to his mother about their parents but he had never seen them; why his mother kept to herself, often lowering her head when people from the church walked by; why she seemed to actually shield him from contact with others. It explained why some church members didn't allow their children to play with him. It explained so much. Edgar understood, intuitively, that he could never tell his mother what he now knew, but the thoughts in his head began to swirl incessantly.

After he overheard what his Aunt Helen said, Edgar's life changed. At age twelve, he felt marked, weak, and helpless. He had been powerless to protect the mother he loved. At times, he felt as though it was he who had doomed his mother to poverty and shame by the fact of being born. *I'm the reason she's damaged and ruined,* he thought, his aunt's words coming back to him. Edgar wanted to fight someone, hurt someone, get vengeance for what had been done to his mother, but he couldn't think of who he could fight or who he could hurt to redeem his mother and to make his own pain go away.

Hate began to seep into Edgar's young soul that day — hate for his Aunt Helen who knew this terrible thing and used it as a weapon to humiliate and degrade his mother, hate for the priest who "did filthy things" to her, hate for the parish that made her feel poor and indebted, hate for the grandparents who abandoned his mother and him, and hate for himself because he couldn't protect his mother, couldn't defend her, couldn't guard her against whatever the priest had done to her. *If only I had been there*, Edgar kept thinking to himself, too young to recognize the impossibility of preventing his own conception. And when his Aunt Helen's words reverberated in his mind, like a mocking chorus —"She let him do it; she let him do it; she let him do it." — Edgar almost hated his mother for her submission to whatever the priest did to her.

Katalin noticed the changes in her son, but she assumed it was the unpredictable tides of adolescence flowing into the corners of his mind and personality. She made a point of hugging him more often and telling him how much she loved him. It seemed to her that he hugged her more tightly in return, as if trying to convey something to her. She loved him so much! Sometimes she was tempted to tell him the truth about his father, tell him how much she loved his father and that his father had loved her. She wanted to assure Edgar that she loved him so much that having him was worth any and all criticism that had descended upon her. But she never found the courage to explain that to him. She didn't want him to be ashamed of her. That she could not bear.

Katalin was 37 years old when she died. Her parents did not attend her funeral. When she died, Edgar felt a grief that was beyond tears. But it was not a clean grief, the kind that heals from the inside out, like a clean wound. It was a grief tinged with guilt, because for the second time, Edgar could not save his mother.

By the time his mother died, the contradictions within Edgar had taken root: the desire to protect and the compulsion to hurt; a craving to be with people and a distrust of them; most of all, the need to love and be loved contrasted with a nameless wrath that could not seem to find its purpose or its target.

After Katalin's death, the parish decided that it had paid its due to her and no longer needed to provide a home for her son. Unless he could pay rent, which he had no way of doing, Edgar had to leave the house. He had no choice but to quit school. Father Michael offered Edgar a job as custodian of the parish, a job he could keep for as long as he wished. At age eighteen, Edgar began the job that he assumed would be his for life. The custodian's job paid very little, but it met his needs, financial and otherwise.

The children at St. Anthony's School were typical grade-schoolers, energetic and effusive. One day, Edgar watched them play at recess. He didn't mean to stare at them, but he was captivated by the scene of joyful, childhood fun. When some of the children noticed him staring, their demeanor changed. They became fearful of the quiet man who never spoke, and they stopped their play. Edgar had never had that effect on anyone before. He rather liked the idea that he could make people uneasy, although he certainly didn't want to frighten children. He knew too well what it was to be a frightened child. But from then on, from time to time, Edgar would test his stare on select people. Although this distanced him even further from others, Edgar felt a kind of satisfaction from knowing that he could seem threatening or intimidating, that he was not powerless. He valued the sense of control he felt when he made people uneasy. It was the only way he could feel strong. Sometimes he thought, *If only I could have frightened away the priest who hurt my mother.* And less often, *If only I could have frightened my mother into staying away from the priest.*

Edgar often read the writing on blackboards when he came in to clean the classrooms in late afternoon. He was fascinated by the nouns and verbs of foreign languages, and he wrote some of them down to read and repeat later, when he was in his room for the night. He also enjoyed the quotes from books that were sometimes written on Sister Ann's blackboard. These, too, he sometimes wrote down. And occasionally he took a book from the library, careful to return it in a day or two.

One day, on Sister Margaret's blackboard, he saw the pronouncement that, "There are three primary words for Love in the Greek language — Agape, Eros, Philia." Edgar pronounced each of the words carefully, out loud, because he knew no one could hear him. "Ah-gah-pay" he said slowly, pronouncing the word correctly but placing the emphasis on the last syllable. Next, he tried "eh-rose," coming close to the exact sound. His "philia" was flawless.

I wonder, he thought to himself, before he erased the words from the blackboard, *how many words there are for 'lonely'.*

By the time he began going to the college basketball games, Edgar had become accustomed to his identity as a recluse, contented with the silence in which he usually lived, and empowered by his ability to create an air of menace when he chose to.

When the women's basketball season began, Edgar noticed a new girl on the team. The scoreboard said that #12 was named Garcetti. Edgar watched her closely — he didn't know why — throughout the first half of the game. She was a good shooter but she was a team player, setting her teammates up for shots and feeding them the ball. At halftime, Edgar picked up a program left behind by people who'd left the gym. The program told him that #12's first name was Tawny. Tawny Garcetti. He decided the name suited her. With her lithe body and her golden brown hair swept back into a bouncing pony tail, she looked like a Tawny. The program told him that she was a senior, and a transfer from the University of Bridgeport. The program said that she was an education major, was from Bernardsville, New Jersey, and was 5'7". *Just a few inches shorter than I am,* he thought.

During the second half of the game, Edgar's eyes were riveted on #12. He saw that she had well-shaped legs, athletic but feminine — legs that looked smooth and silky to the touch. She had a rounded backside and small breasts that looked feminine without looking sexy. Edgar didn't think girls should look sexy. He thought her breasts might be the shape and size of halves of oranges.

At the next home game, Edgar cheered the team, but he cheered especially for Tawny Garcetti. A few games later, he was bold enough to yell, "Go, 12!" It excited him to do that.

Edgar's life began to revolve around the women's basketball games, and thoughts of Tawny began to fill his otherwise empty days and empty life. For the next three months, Edgar attended every home game, feeling more and more connected to Tawny, more a part of her life as she now was of his.

While cleaning the rectory one day, Edgar spotted Tawny's picture looking up from the sports section of the local newspaper — a newspaper Father Michael had left in the living room. Edgar took the photo back to his room and taped it to the wall abutting his bed. Tawny's face was the first thing he saw in the morning and the last thing he saw before turning out his light. He studied her face, memorizing its contours, almost feeling its softness.

Edgar sometimes talked to Tawny's picture, telling her things he never told anyone else. *I know it's unusual,* he thought, *but it's harmless and I like talking to her.* It felt to Edgar as though Tawny was, in a way, living with him, and he felt far less lonely. And less angry. The newspapers at the rectory yielded two more photos of Tawny over the next few weeks: one in a team shot and the other a formal head shot. Edgar taped these to the wall, too, and placed a sheet of plastic wrap over the photos so that he wouldn't soil or damage them when he touched and kissed them.

When the team won the conference semi-finals on their home court, fans mobbed the floor, screaming and shouting, throwing confetti, and patting the jubilant girls and their coaches on the back. Edgar allowed himself to be swept along with the crowd. He reached out ... as everyone else was reaching out ... and actually touched the bare arm of #12. Her skin was hot and sweaty and soft. He fleetingly wondered if she had felt something in his touch, like Jesus did when the sick woman touched him.

Three weeks later, having not seen Tawny since basketball season ended, Edgar found himself walking to the campus on his day off. He sat down on a bench near the library. No one questioned him, no one bothered him. Edgar did this for the next three Fridays, taking a book with him so that he would look more natural sitting near the library. On the fifth of Edgar's Friday excursions to the campus, he spotted her. Tawny was walking toward him with a group of friends. Edgar's heart raced. It was really her. She was wearing tan jeans and a dark blue sleeveless sweater. She was laughing a silvery, tinkling laugh and her honey-colored hair, hanging half-way down her back, glistened in the sunshine. Tawny and her friends walked past Edgar and headed toward a building that he saw marked as College Center.

Driven by the same overpowering urge that had drawn him to the campus each Friday, Edgar rose from the bench and walked toward that same building. Inside, he saw some students sitting in a lounge area, a few standing in front of a bulletin board, and others gathered in clusters laughing and talking. But he didn't see Tawny.

Edgar spotted the Bistro sign and assumed that it was a place to eat. Tentatively, with his heart pounding, he walked through the open doors. He spotted Tawny and her friends sitting at a table, having sodas and pizza. Edgar glanced around. Miscellaneous people were in line to buy food. Edgar got a soda and brought it to the cashier. He was further out of his comfort zone than he had ever been, yet it seemed to Edgar that he was moving with destiny. He had walked into Tawny's world just as if he had stepped onto a stage. With as much courage as he had ever mustered, and trying to look as if he belonged there, he strolled into the dining area and sat at a table next to Tawny's. He opened his book and pretended to read.

Edgar enjoyed hearing the girlish chatter of Tawny and her friends. Their laughter sounded musical to him, and he felt at home somehow as he heard the descriptions of school-work and exams that the girls exchanged so easily and naturally. Then he heard something important.

"I'm so relieved that I've had two offers," he heard Tawny say. "I know how tough it is to get a teaching job."

"Which one are you gonna take?" the red-haired girl asked her.

"I don't know yet," Tawny replied. "Part of me wants to live somewhere new, and part of me wants to stay closer to my family, at least for a while. I think I'd feel more secure. So I'm leaning toward Whitehouse Station. That's close enough that I can see my family anytime I want. Yeah, I think I'll take the job in Whitehouse Station." Edgar wrote the name down in his book so he wouldn't forget it.

On his walk home to his apartment, Edgar kept repeating the name Whitehouse Station, wondering where it was. That night, Edgar could not sleep. He thought about Tawny's being a senior: *In another month, she'll be gone and I'll never see her again. She'll be out in the world where bad things could happen to her.*

The next day, he looked up Whitehouse Station in the atlas in St. Anthony's library. It was in New Jersey. In Hunterdon County. *She'll be close*, he thought, *but not close enough.*

Two days later, Edgar told Father Michael that he wanted to move to New Jersey to be near some friends he had made. He asked if Father Michael knew of any custodial jobs at churches near Whitehouse Station. Stunned, Father Michael said that he would make inquiries.

When Father Michael told him that two parishes in Flemington needed custodial help, Edgar felt certain that something or someone was opening the way for him.

In early June, after he attended commencement ceremonies to watch Tawny graduate, Edgar packed his few belongings and took the bus to Clinton, New Jersey. The priest from St. Emeric's came to the bus stop to pick him up and take him to the rooms provided for him at the church — rooms formerly used for visiting missionaries.

Before he left Bethlehem, Edgar walked to two places: his mother's grave at Fountain Hill Cemetery and the college's placement office. With a fantasy-fueled bravery, Edgar explained to the administrative assistant in the office that he was Tawny Garcetti's cousin. He said that she told him she would be teaching in Whitehouse Station, and she wanted him to send her teaching materials, but he had lost the address of where she would be living. Would the placement office have her address? Of course, replied the assistant, saying that recent grads usually provide addresses so that contacts from prospective employers can be forwarded to them. "Great system," said Edgar, smiling. The assistant wrote the address down for Edgar: Apartment C-3, Finty Crest Apartments, 118 Morgan Road, Whitehouse Station, NJ. "Thanks!" Edgar said with a cheery smile, wishing the helpful woman a nice day.

Settled in his new job in Flemington, Edgar purchased a used car from an elderly member of St. Emeric's. Edgar had been bold enough to ask the old gent if he would consider selling his car after he heard the man say that he would soon give up driving. The car gave Edgar the means to drive to Whitehouse Station and locate Finty Crest Apartments.

Every week that summer, on many evenings and on his day off, Edgar drove to Whitehouse Station and sat in his car, about a half-block away from Finty Crest Apartments. Finally, on a Friday in late July, Edgar saw a station wagon pull up and he saw Tawny and some other young people get out. Edgar pulled up closer, to a parking space that was nearer to the station wagon. The young people began to unload the rear of the vehicle, extracting such things as plants, lamps, and the other makings of a first apartment. They were laughing and joking. Edgar was glad that Tawny seemed so happy, and he was glad to be part of her happiness.

About an hour later, when most of the young people piled back into the station wagon and drove away, Tawny remained on the sidewalk, her arms wrapped around a young man who bent down to give her a long, lingering kiss. Tawny smiled at him and he kissed her again, sliding his hands down from her waist and pressing her body into his. *She let him do that*, thought Edgar. *She let him*. They stood there for a long while, holding each other, looking into each other's eyes, and whispering to each other. Then, arm in arm, they returned to Tawny's apartment building.

Edgar couldn't breathe. He couldn't count or name the feelings exploding inside him. His brain was on fire. His eyes and throat burned.

He felt as if he was suffocating with rage. Edgar sat for a long while, clutching the steering wheel with white knuckles. Then he got out of his car and walked toward the apartment building. He knocked on the door marked Harry Roth, Manager. "Come in!" barked a masculine voice from inside the office.

"There are no vacancies, sorry," said Mr. Roth immediately. "School's starting soon, folks are back from summer vacations, and all my apartments are taken."

"I'm not looking for an apartment," replied Edgar, calmly. "I'm looking for a job. I'm a custodian and I can do minor repairs and fix-it jobs and I'd like to work in this area."

A look of puzzlement came over Harry Roth's face, then a smile. "Now isn't that strange? My maintenance guy left last week. Moved to Florida. I was just going to put an ad in the paper. What's your background? What can you do?"

Edgar answered the questions confidently, embellishing the descriptions a bit. He was vaguely aware of ... but not able to analyze or verbalize ... how the larger and larger, outflowing, expanding circles of his increasing boldness were allowing him to create smaller and smaller, contracting, narrowing circles drawing him nearer to his Tawny. He never thought he would get this close to her. *Eight months ago, I didn't even know her.*

Harry Roth led Edgar down to the basement and showed him the sparse rooms that came with the job. "A hundred-fifty bucks a week and this apartment, if you could call it that, with utilities," he said.

Edgar looked at the kitchenette area with its old stove, a brown-stained sink, a small refrigerator, and in the corner, an old table with two chairs. Off to the side of the kitchen was a small bathroom with a sink, toilet, and stand-alone shower. The middle room had a single mattress on an iron bedframe, a small dresser, and an upholstered chair that had seen better days. On the far side of that middle room was a brown plaid sofa, a coffee table, and a table on which sat a portable TV. Beyond the middle room was a large, empty, concrete-sided room that had been used for storage. Some metal shelving remained along one wall, and hooks on the walls and ceiling allowed for a variety of uses. Like the other rooms, it had no windows, and like the middle room, it had no exit except through the door that led from the kitchen into the basement hallway.

As he looked around those three rooms, Edgar relaxed into his convictions — his identity. He was no longer enraged, no longer suffocating, no longer tormented by images of filthy things. He drew power and determination — a strength that was physical as well as mental — from having found his destiny ... his purpose in life. *I'll watch over her*, he vowed. *I'll protect her. No one will ever hurt her.*

"Nice and quiet down here," said Edgar, turning to Harry Roth. "I like that. I don't like noise. Never did. This will be fine. It will do just fine," he said, as he shook Roth's hand and agreed to come to work on Monday.

"I know you're disappointed," said Tawny into the telephone receiver in her apartment, "I'm disappointed, too. School starts in a couple of weeks and I know how busy I'll be after that, so I was really looking forward to going to New Hope with you today." ... "I'm gonna miss you, too, Suzy-girl. I'm sorry you're leaving tomorrow." ... "Yeah, Mark is away all week with his parents in Ocean City, and I miss him. But you'll never guess! Before he left he told me that he was planning on giving me a special gift at Christmas — a gift in a small box that would come with a question — but he decided to give it to me next month for my birthday instead! Can you believe it? I am sooooo excited!!!" ... "Of course you'll be a bridesmaid!" ... "Yeah, it would have been fun to go shopping today, but the new maintenance guy called and said he has to fix the air-conditioning controls in my apartment. He said I have to be here so he can show me how they work." ... "No, I don't know how long it will take. Hey, I gotta go! That's the doorbell. Must be the maintenance guy. I guess this really is good-bye. Always remember: Go, white!"

INTERSECTIONS

*I*n the late 1950s, when Jimmy Petrides announced that he was selling his hot dog shop, disappointment rippled through South Bethlehem. Jimmy's was the go-to place for cheese steaks, fries, and hot dogs when you wanted a quick lunch or didn't want to cook dinner after a hard day at work. Everybody ate at Jimmy's. Lehigh students sat at the white Formica counter next to steelworkers, teenagers, and shop clerks. The irresistible mixture of smells propelled through the fan at the front of the shop drew people through that rickety old screen door like a magnet: mounds of fresh chipped steak sizzling on the grill; sliced onions turning brown and adding their pungent tang to the air; French fries crackling in the deep fryer; and the special sauces for hot dogs and steak sandwiches that added a sweet, tomato-based scent to the aroma of 'good grease' that drifted into the atmosphere in every direction. Jimmy's was a busy, successful business. But fifty years of standing at the grill had taken their toll on Jimmy's back, and he knew it was time for him to retire.

Within a few weeks the shop had a new sign out front: "Elsa's." The same hot dogs and cheese steaks were on the menu, but the décor certainly changed. The only decorations at Jimmy's had been the red tin soda signs and the blackboard on which menu items and their prices had been listed. Now, the half-dozen tables in the shop were covered with red-checkered cloths, and each table had a slim milk-glass vase with bright plastic flowers. The menu was also expanded with the addition of a "soup of the day" and several "platters of the day." No change was more visible and dramatic, however, than the change in proprietors. Jimmy was a short, skinny, black-haired Greek in his sixties. Elsa was a big, blonde, buxom German woman in her late thirties. She had a fondness for bright-colored, flowered dresses, a laugh that rolled out in waves, and a tendency to hug everyone to her rounded bosom. Once she knew your name, she never forgot it. If she knew you liked spaetzle, she'd make some just for you so you could "eat and enjoy!" In her heavy accent, she asked repeatedly if the food was all right and if she could get anything else for you. Elsa was like an overpowering force of nature, and she enjoyed feeding people as much as she enjoyed talking and laughing with them.

Our family came to know Elsa well. In addition to accommodating our weekly stop for cheese steaks, she soon encouraged us to come down for specially made platters of Weiner schnitzel, sauerbraten, and many other dishes that never made it to the official menu. She would serve us and then sit and talk with us, leaving the grill and counter service to her young helper, Stella.

Elsa told us that she had left Germany in 1946 to come to America. After years of helping her cousin at his restaurant in Brooklyn, she decided to buy her own small place. That's what brought her to Bethlehem. She said that her cousin knew Jimmy Petrides from their childhood days in New York and they had kept in touch. "Their lives intersected," said Elsa, pronouncing the last word carefully and emphasizing every syllable, "and then Jimmy's life intersected with mine through my cousin. That's how things happen. That's how it is meant to be. Life is all about intersections."

She asked us about Bethlehem and the many nationalities that populated the South Side. She told us about the picturesque German countryside of her childhood, and about the warm family life that she had shared with her parents and sisters. Elsa's use of English was a work-in-progress, but she eagerly told us about her life. "We never got much money, but we was happy because we got lots of love. And we eat good!" As time passed, Elsa revealed more about her life in Germany. She told us that she had just started to work in a fabric shop in Berlin when the war began. She said that in those first years, the news of the war meant little to her and her roommates who were simply trying to make ends meet while still sending money to their families.

"The war did not seem real to us," she said. "Seem to be happening somewhere else."

I could almost see the thoughts passing through my WWII-veteran father's mind: *Yes, the war begun by your Fuehrer happened "somewhere else" for a long time.* But I could also see his instantaneous recognition that saying anything like that to Elsa would be as pointless as it would be cruel, and there was no part of Dad that could ever be cruel to anyone. He said nothing more and changed the subject. Elsa didn't speak about the war again for many months.

One day, as we sat at a table in her restaurant and finished our dinners, Elsa told us about a young man she had met and fallen in love with in 1944. He, too, worked in a shop, and they talked about maybe being married when the chaos of the war would be over. "Then, everything changed," she said, quietly. "It all changed when the Russians came. It was horrible, what they did ...." She didn't finish the sentence. She stared into that middle distance between memory and reality and was silent for several moments. When her eyes began to fill with tears, she stood up and left the table, wiping her eyes with her apron, and walked back to the kitchen. When she returned to the table a few minutes later, she continued her narrative.

"Sometimes it helps to think about it, to talk about it, to know that it is in the past, that it is all over. And sometimes ... sometimes ... it just brings the nightmares back," she said softly, not looking at us but staring fixedly at the pressed glass salt and pepper shakers on the table, as if that focused staring was helping her to remember and to deal with the memories.

"It was 1945 and the war was all around us," she continued. "Nothing was normal anymore. We was afraid all the time. You hurried from your home or apartment to places you had to go and you hurried back, hoping to stay alive. You didn't want to even look at anyone or say something to anyone. You just wanted to go home and close the door behind you. But when the Russian soldiers came, there was no hiding; there was no escape. They came into our building looking for rooms to sleep in. They found us ... found women ... found me. They kept us there for weeks. They forced themselves on us. What is the word? Rape?" she asked, rolling and extending the 'r.' Mom nodded in the affirmative, not saying anything. "I never say that word before," Elsa continued. "That's what they do to us. Raping us again and again. Again and again. When some left, more came, and the rapes went on day and night." Elsa paused for a moment. We said nothing. There was nothing to say. Needing to finish her story, she went on.

"It felt like they was making war on us, on our bodies," she said angrily. "It would have been better if they cut our throats or shot us. One barely finished and another piled on. The hours and days went on with no end. And the smells! Sickening! I could smell their sweat and their liquor and their piss. And I smelled my own blood. I passed out many times, and every time I woke up, I could feel one of them laying on top of me, almost suffocating me, hammering into me down there. I begged. I prayed. I cried. I screamed that I would kill them but they just laughed or they beat me. Two of the girls died. But I was so angry, I refused to die. I refused to die because of them. Then they left. There was terrible noise outside, like bombs, and then they was all gone. I must have passed out again and I woke up in a hospital. A nurse told me I lost a lot of blood. I remember nothing about those next days, but I remember so many of their faces. Their faces come back to me in the night. I never forget their faces." We sat silently for a while and then embraced Elsa before we left to walk home.

About five years after Elsa bought Jimmy's, my mother learned that a shoemaker had opened a shop a few blocks away from our house. She heard that this shoemaker did shoe restyling, something that our friend Mr. Zavacky preferred not to do. Mom loved fashionable shoes and high heels, but she often had to have those chic shoes cut out or re-sewn to accommodate her misshapen toes. She decided to try this new shoemaker, and sent me there with a pair of beautiful, green leather high heels. I almost couldn't find the shop. It was the size of a small shed, and was tucked under the house above it. There was barely room for a small counter and a shelf to hold the cobbler's tools.

The new shoemaker was a huge, muscular man with thick, jet black hair falling over his perspiring forehead and onto his bushy eyebrows. He didn't make eye contact and used few words. The words he did speak sounded like a low, heavily accented rumble. He held Mom's soft, leather shoes in his big hands and turned them over and over. I saw that he had thumbs on both hands but that other fingers on his hands were missing at least one joint and part of his left hand was cut away. "These very fine shoes," he said in a gruff voice. "Very fine leather."

I asked if he could cut an opening for the toes and sew a small seam around the openings. He said that he could do so but that it would take time. I said that would be all right; there was no hurry. When he finished the shoes, they looked exquisite. Although we still took all of our shoe repair work to Mr. Zavacky, I was sometimes told to take special re-styling needs to this shoemaker who seemed to have no name.

One day, I brought him a pair of pale gold high heels that Mom wanted to have re-sewn. Again, he praised the quality of the leather and offered ideas about how the shoes might be re-styled. I asked him how he had learned to do such fine work on shoes.

"I worked for the ballet. I made many shoes for the dancers."

"Where?"

"In Moscow."

As if reading my thoughts, as I glanced at his disfigured hands, he said, "That was before the war."

"You didn't go back to work at the ballet?"

"I didn't go back to Russia."

I knew better than to ask any more questions. I thanked him for his suggestions about the gold leather shoes and I left them there for his expert craftsmanship. I retrieved the shoes three weeks later, marveling at how the shoemaker's damaged hands could create such intricate stitching.

A few months later, I was at Elsa's to get take-out for Saturday supper. I was there when he walked through the door. The shoemaker. It was obviously his first visit to Elsa's and he looked around for the menu sign as he took a bulky, black leather coin purse from his pocket. He was reading the menu when Elsa came out from the kitchen. He turned to face her and she looked up at him. They both froze. Each of them seemed to be studying the other's face. Their eyes were searching, intent, as if trying to uncover mysteries or messages in each other's face. Neither of them moved even a fraction of an inch. A combination of curiosity and confusion seemed to infuse their expressions. I didn't dare move or disturb them. No one came into the restaurant. The frozen moment seemed to last forever. Then the shoemaker tipped his hat respectfully to Elsa, bowed ever so slightly, and left the shop without saying anything or buying anything. Elsa stared after him for a long moment and then wordlessly returned to the kitchen, forgetting entirely about my order. I left too, sensing that on this night I should not bother Elsa about food.

When I took another pair of Mom's shoes to the shoemaker's a few days later, the little shop was empty. No explanation was posted on the door, no new shop address was given. I peered through the smudged glass in the front door and saw the shabby wooden counter with its worn-off paint and the small tool shelf behind it — empty, bare, abandoned. A few weeks later, there was a For Sale sign on Elsa's front door. She told us that she was moving to a new location in North Bethlehem. More room, she said. Bigger kitchen. More people. "Better intersection," she said, "much better intersection." Elsa maintained her restaurant at its new location until she died. We visited her there frequently, but she never spoke to us of the war again.

THE STEEL

*I*t would be difficult to imagine a city more identified with an industry than Bethlehem, Pennsylvania, was with Bethlehem Steel. Immigrants who lived in South Bethlehem and the coal regions ("up the line" as steelworkers said) dominated work in the foundries. Management and white-collar workers came from — or moved to — North and West Bethlehem, and in later years, to Saucon Valley. Bethlehem grade-schoolers learned how steel is made and described the process on homemade poster board diagrams. Many South Bethlehem bedrooms never knew what it was to be dark. The rose-orange glow from the blast furnaces illuminated the rooms softly until sunrise. Before unionization, immigrants worked in brutal, almost inhumane conditions in the plant; conditions so perilous that in 1909 alone, 21 of 9,184 plant workers died of work-related injuries and 927 were critically injured, triggering the failed 1910 strike and a federal investigation that condemned the company's working conditions. The steel plant's largely immigrant employees worked 12-hour shifts for less than 10 cents an hour. They could get one day off every two weeks if they worked back-to-back 12-hour shifts before that day off. There were no vacations and no pensions, even after decades of work. After the union was in place, steelworkers got better wages and reliable benefits. They bought homes and cars and sent their children to college. They entered the middle class and provided a foundation for decades of broad economic growth and strength throughout the region. They also got lung cancer, silicosis, throat cancer, emphysema, interstitial lung disease, asthma, and permanent orthopedic injuries and disabilities. As befits a giant behemoth, Bethlehem Steel took a long time a-dying. It flailed and thrashed and bellowed as its 12-mile length shuddered with the impossibility, first, of failure, and later, of survival. Millions of words have been written about The Steel: its glory and its guilt.

Perhaps the truest of these words were that, "Bethlehem Steel built America" and, in its demise, "There is enough blame to go around for everyone."

I

"You should see the floor at the Ingot Mould. It looks like an orchard!" My father made this strange announcement when he came home from work on his first day back after a 116-day strike in 1959. He explained that many workers ate fruit at lunch, and those who ate oranges often spit the seeds onto the dirt floor of the foundry. Over the course of 116 undisturbed days, in the warmth of the foundry and with rain coming in from cracks in the roof slats, the seeds had the time and conditions in which to germinate. Scores of knee-high seedlings and hundreds of smaller plants awaited the returning men like a fantasy garden. Many of the foundry workers gently removed the plants and took them home to try to keep them growing.

Talk of the strike dominated dinnertime conversation that day. "It was tough to be out of work that long," said Dad, "but at least it wasn't like 1941." In response to my questions, he said that in 1941, mounted police wielding clubs were brought in to quell the strikers. Pictures of the confrontations were front-page news. "What did the men want?" I asked. "The right to organize," he replied. "In earlier years, the demands were 10 minutes to eat in a 10-hour shift, eight-hour shifts for six-day work weeks, and a private place to go to the bathroom — even a wall behind which the men could 'go.' The company called the demands extreme and unacceptable." At the time of the 1959 strike, six of the ten highest paid executives in America were Bethlehem Steel employees, and Bethlehem's chairman, A.B. Homer, was the highest paid executive in the country. "All that money ... all that authority," mused Dad, "and they aren't even on track. They aren't modernizing. They aren't planning for the future. And the union is just as bad, asking for protections that will kill our ability to compete or grow. We'll pay for this someday. We'll all pay."

II

My father seldom lectured or 'taught lessons.' I learned from him by example. On most days, having gotten up at 5:00 a.m. and been on his way to work by 5:30, he would be home by 3:30 p.m. and asleep on the sofa, exhausted, by 3:45. He would sleep soundly until dinnertime at 5:00 or 5:30. But one day when he came home from work, he was too angry to be tired. On that day, this easygoing and good-natured man vibrated with anger, and his anger was tinged with humiliation, something I'd never seen in him before.

"You won't believe what happened today," he finally said. "I saw it; I heard it, and I still don't believe it." He said that a new assistant superintendent had been assigned to the Ingot Mould foundry and the new boss's first order was that all work should be stopped. Stopping work in the foundry was virtually unheard of. It not only affected production but safety as well. Having no alternative, the men ceased their work as the order went from one corner of the foundry to another. Even the crane operators, including Dad, were ordered to descend to the floor. The next order, as bizarre as the first, was for all of the men to line up in a single line across the plant floor. There were 50-80 men in the foundry at the time. Looking at each other in silent speculation, they lined up as instructed. In time, the new boss appeared and began his tour at the far end of the line. No one knew what was being said until the new boss approached.

One by one he ordered the men to repeat these words: "*I am nothing. I do not matter here. I can always be replaced. I am only a number in a book.*" If someone hesitated, in anger or surprise, the order was barked out again. Soon the refrain was heard ten, twenty, thirty, and more times. "*I am nothing. I do not matter here. I can always be replaced. I am only a number in a book.*" "*I am nothing. I do not matter here. I can always be replaced. I am only a number in a book.*" The men heard the words spoken by their co-workers before the new boss stood in front of them.

"I wanted to punch him in the mouth and tell him to go to hell and just walk out," said Dad, rage still in his voice. "I wanted to do that more than I have ever wanted to do anything else in my life. I felt my body shaking with anger. I felt sick to my stomach. No one should ever be forced to say something like that. No human being should be told that they're nothing, that they don't matter. Then I thought of you and sending you to college," he said, looking at me. "I knew that, if I walked out, I'd never find another job that would pay enough to send you to college. That's what I thought about, that's what I focused on: sending you to college. If this is what it takes, this is what it takes, I told myself. By the time he stood in front of me, I said the words but I spit them out. He opened his mouth to say something but he hesitated and didn't say anything. He just moved on." It seemed to drain Dad just to tell us about it.

Then he looked at me intently and said something I never forgot: "If you ever have a job in which other people report to you — a job where you're the boss or you're in charge in any way — never, never, never humiliate or mistreat those who are under you. Never treat anyone, especially a subordinate, with anything other than respect. Never do to anyone what that ignorant sonofabitch did to us today. Never treat a man or a woman as less than a human being who is absolutely equal to you. Not only is it wrong to do what he did to us today, but he hurt himself by doing it. No one in that shop will ever do anything extra for him. They'll never give him their best. They will never forget what he did to them. They will never forget. I will never forget. And he's too arrogant to even realize what he's done." Then Dad went to the sofa where, for the first time, he could not sleep.

III

In 1989, when I worked for United Way, I had the chance to visit the Ingot Mould foundry to make a presentation about the annual campaign. My being there was a special privilege, given because I was "Henny's kid." My Dad had died two years earlier, on September 8th, nineteen days after he turned 65. His heart attack was swift and merciful, sparing him from more of the chemotherapy and radiation targeted to his lung cancer. He had survived throat cancer eight years before and saw no reason why he couldn't beat lung cancer. The heart attack must have surprised him before it silenced him.

I was fascinated by the cavernous foundry, near the Emery Street gate, that I had heard so much about. Sunshine pouring through slats in the walls created shafts of light that illuminated iridescent black particles suspended in mid-air; millions of sprinklings of blue-black confetti, making the atmosphere seem like the devil's version of New Year's Eve. Soon, my white hard hat was covered with the miniature flakes. It was impossible to rub them off. A stroke of the finger simply turned them into a greasy smear on the helmet. *So this is what Dad breathed into his throat and lungs for forty-four years,* I thought. Then I remembered a time when he and the other men tried to clean up the Ingot Mould foundry.

Dad had come home and told us that the Ingot Mould was about to get something like a make-over. The reason for this almost comical attempt was an announced visit by "the top brass." At the very least, an assortment of vice presidents would be coming on a drive-through tour of the foundry, and perhaps, the workers were told, the chairman himself would come. The men were ordered to clean the place up as much as possible and assure safe passageways across the foundry floor, near the equipment and near the deep 'pits' integral to making the moulds for ingots. The men in the foundry were proud that their area had been selected for such a visit, and in addition to doing their regular work, they tackled the clean-up energetically. Supplies were organized and centralized, tools were cleaned and stored, the floor was swept repeatedly, the showers and latrines were scrubbed spotless, rough edges of work benches were sanded smooth, the windows of the small plant office were shined, and sturdy wooden paths through the foundry were constructed for the expected visitors. Dad gave us progress reports on the work every day. The men's palpable pride in the new look of the Ingot Mould exceeded their pride in being selected for the VIP visit.

"Well, how did it go?" we asked eagerly when Dad came home on the day of the big visit. "Never happened," he said. "The Super came around and said that the tour was canceled. Someone decided that the foundry was too dirty and dangerous for the vice presidents, much less the chairman, to visit. The Super said they told him that exposing the vice presidents to the Ingot Mould might harm them. Then he told us to get back to work."

"After doing all that clean-up, how did the guys react?" Mom asked. "They laughed and got back to work," Dad replied, matter-of-factly. "Johnny said he was glad he didn't wear his tuxedo and Kozicky said he hoped the vice presidents didn't trip and hurt themselves on the thick carpeting in Martin Tower."

IV

In the 1970s, I wrote an article about the chairman/CEO of Bethlehem Steel for the alumni magazine of the college at which I worked. When the article was published, the chairman invited me to his office for lunch. The director of media relations at Bethlehem Steel had told me that such articles almost never made it through the review process with no changes, but mine had because the chairman liked it. I said that the chairman knew me and perhaps that made a difference.

The chairman had always been gracious and friendly to me, and I had never seen him exhibit any trace of arrogance or snobbery. In fact, he always asked about my father and said, "Men like your father are the heart of this company, not me and not the people in this office building." The chairman and his wife had invited me to their home for dinner and for parties on various occasions and had always been cordial and welcoming. But this was the first time I had visited the chairman's office.

It looked as I expected it would — polished, professional, and furnished in exquisite taste. Before we began our conversation, a doorbell rang. I turned instinctively toward the large door to the chairman's office. It didn't open and the chairman didn't rise from his desk. The doorbell sound chimed again. He reached for an ornate carved box on his desk, lifted the lid, and withdrew a telephone receiver. My surprise showed in my face. He smiled at my reaction and concluded the brief call. After talking for a while about the article I had written, and about various college and community matters, the chairman suggested that we have lunch. I rose to go toward the massive door with its I-beam handles, assuming we would be eating in a company dining room. Instead, he gestured toward the large, polished conference table in his office. He said that the vice president for public affairs had asked to join us for lunch. A uniformed waitress appeared and handed us printed menus on heavy card stock. She also described some offerings the chef was recommending for that day. Another uniformed waitress appeared and prepared place settings for us with linen, china, and silverware. I looked at the center of the long table. There, a collection of Steuben crystal otters with ruby eyes cavorted casually, as if their natural habitat was the office of the Chairman/CEO of Bethlehem Steel Corporation. I smiled. "What are you smiling about?" the chairman asked perceptively. "The Ingot Mould foundry," I replied. "I'm thinking about the men who eat their lunch in the Ingot Mould foundry and about the orange trees that once grew there."

V

After my introduction to Bethlehem Steel's vice president for public affairs and its director of media relations, they regularly invited me to the company's Martin Tower headquarters for lunch. Over time, they each became valued friends to me. Our lunches were informal, giving us a chance to talk about the company, the college, and the community. We were often joined by other members of the public affairs staff and we frequently talked about writing, public relations, and professional interests.

One day, after we placed our lunch trays on a table in the dining room, one of the executives asked me what was new at the college. I told him that we had just begun a long-range planning process, and that those of us on the college's executive staff were serving as the long-range planning committee as well. "I'm finding it a bit frustrating," I said. "We seem to be spending so much time deciding on process and on how we'll tackle planning issues. I'm anxious to get on with the work itself, but we seem to be stuck on so many of these procedural matters. How do you do planning here? Is it a top-down or bottom-up process or is it customized according to area?" There was silence around the table as I waited for an answer. Thinking that my question had not been clear, I explained it. "What I mean is, do you have defined procedures for doing short- and long-term planning or does the process depend on the department or the circumstances and issues at hand?" Again, silence, but now interspersed with some embarrassed chuckles. I tried it again. "I guess I'm not phrasing my question clearly–" One of the staff members stopped me before I could continue. "There's nothing wrong with what you asked," he said. "It's clear enough. And we're not laughing at the question. We're laughing because your fledgling planning process at the college, with its frustrating start and its many decisions to be made, is light years ahead of anything we do here. I'll say it for all of us. We don't plan. We used to talk about planning but we don't even do that anymore. We don't plan."

V I

I remember my father and grandfather coming home from work with heavy hearts on three occasions. Once, in mid-summer, Grandpop came home to say that a co-worker who was a good friend had died of heat stroke in the plant that afternoon. "Hell," Grandpop said. "That's what it feels like in there in summer. Just like hell must feel. It's a wonder more don't die of the fire in the air and the fires in the furnace." On another day he came home shaken and grief-stricken. A friend had fallen into a vat of molten metal. "He slipped," Grandpop said. "He just slipped. They said it happened so fast. He must have been gone before his screaming started." With my child's logic, and patting Grandpop's hand to comfort him, I said, "He can't be all gone because they have to bury him." "When something like this happens," explained my grandmother, "they give the family a block of metal from the vat to bury. And they do not use the rest of that metal." My grandfather looked up at her and uttered the only cynical comment I ever heard him make: "Of course they don't." Years later, after Grandpop died, Dad came home one day with the news that a friend of the family had been killed when he was splashed and covered with molten metal, trapped in a corner with no way to escape the 2500-degree wave of liquid metal crashing down upon him. I remembered Grandpop's words from a decade before: "He must have been gone before his screaming started." Dad couldn't talk about the incident beyond telling us that it happened. I couldn't forget it. I thought about that image when the drive-through tour of the Ingot Mould foundry was canceled. I never mentioned the incident to Dad and he never spoke about it again. But I couldn't forget it. I still can't. "He must have been gone before his screaming started."

MORECZ-NINA

She looked like every photo or film image you ever saw of an elderly, foreign, farm woman. I never saw her without an apron and a babushka — a triangular, flowered scarf tied under the chin and worn by women from Siberia to Slovenia. I also never saw her without a warm, wide smile that made her eyes shrink into small slits and crinkle her skin from the corners of her eyes all the way down to her chin. Her skin was a warm, tan, honey color all year long — a legacy of long hours and days spent working in the sun in her garden — and she had a perpetual rosy bloom in her cheeks.

She was my grandmother's close friend, Mrs. Theresa Morecz, and she lived in Hellertown, a small town that abutted the eastern edge of South Bethlehem. When you passed the Ingot Mould foundry and the Coke Works of Bethlehem Steel and came to Crest Avenue, you were in Hellertown. Once surrounded by working farms, Hellertown was home to many immigrant families that had moved there from South Bethlehem. There was something of a permeable membrane between Hellertown and Bethlehem, and many people worked in one and lived in the other. When my Dad was a youngster, his family lived on Crest Avenue and he said that sometimes it felt as though they lived in Bethlehem, sometimes as if they lived in Hellertown.

Mrs. Morecz lived in a two-story red brick home on Whitaker Street. She would take the bus to Bethlehem to visit my grandmother, or one of her sons would drive her, and Dad would drive my grandmother to Hellertown so that she could visit Mrs. Morecz. I always tagged along. Mrs. Morecz, who told me to call her Morecz-nina from the time I could talk, was the most loving person imaginable. Her arms could cuddle a child in an embrace that was pure comfort. When I was very young, two or three years old, I would curl into her lap while she and my grandmother talked over coffee or wine, and she would hold me and rock me with a practiced, timeless rhythm. You could fall asleep in Morecz-nina's arms in perfect peace. Her tiny dining room and living room were filled with vases of fresh flowers from her garden and decorated with doilies and lace curtains that she had crocheted. Her kitchen was always warm and smelled of freshly brewed coffee and just-baked cake.

As I grew older, Morecz-nina encouraged me to explore her flower beds and vegetable gardens. Being avid and gifted gardeners was something she and my grandmother had in common. But in contrast to the welcome offered by Morecz-nina's garden, my grandmother's garden was off-limits to everyone. Once, when I was a toddler, I plucked a flower from Gram's garden to give to my mother — her daughter. You would have thought that I had stolen money from the church collection plate. Even at two, I knew that I had caused a major uproar, and touching the flowers in her garden became like touching the sides of the coal stove — after you did it once, you learned to never do it again.

There were no such restrictions when I went to Morecz-nina's house. She took my hand and walked me around her gardens, and in Windish or broken English, told me the names of the flowers, when they grew, and how they grew. She told me how the ants crawling all over the peony buds were necessary because they ate away the sugary coating that held the buds closed, thus allowing the huge, beautiful blossoms to open. She taught me that some flowers would come back next year and some would die and not come back at all. When my face crumpled up with sadness at this news, she consoled me by saying that this was nature's way, and that death was part of life — part of God's cycle for all living things. Morecz-nina could look at leaves and know if the coming winter would be harsh, and she could look at a tree and know if it was sick before it showed any signs of failing. She was completely in tune with nature and nature's seasons. When we walked through her vegetable garden, she told me about the seasons for onions and snap peas and red-leaf lettuce. She let me pick and taste anything, and the sun-warmed tomatoes from the vines in her garden had a taste that no tomato has equaled since. In my child-sized denim overalls, I would sit down in the soft soil of the vegetable garden at the side of her house and have my fill of juicy tomatoes, sprigs of tender endive, and stalks of slim, spring garlic.

Morecz-nina showed me how potatoes, beets, and other vegetables could be kept in the root cellar, and the shelves of that lower cellar were lined with scores of glass quart jars filled with green tomatoes, peppers, cabbage, cucumbers, applesauce, and jellies that she had canned and put away for the winter. My favorite of these were the Mason jars of green peppers filled with white, raw cabbage, as crisp and pungent in February as when she canned them in September. Morecz-nina knew how much I loved sunshine pickles, made when cucumbers were allowed to ripen in vinegar, water, dill, and spices, inside a glass jar placed in a sunny location. On summertime visits I was always given a jar of sunshine pickles to take home. Pickle sandwiches were my own specialty — a slice of bread wrapped around one of Morecz-nina's dill-infused sunshine pickles, with a sprig of dill still clinging to it. People came from all over to buy the foods she jarred and preserved. She almost couldn't keep up with the demand. Not only were her peppers, tomatoes, and cucumbers delicious, they were also a bargain. She charged 25 cents per jar, which was a bargain even in the 1950s and '60s.

Outside the back door of Morecz-nina's house, on a small concrete patio, a wooden, bench-style swing hung down from a slatted canopy covered by a trumpet vine. While Grammy and Morecz-nina visited in the house, I'd lie on my back on that swing, pushing it back and forth by pressing my foot on the concrete. I'd look up through the maze of bright orange trumpet flowers, and watch the sun and the blue sky play hide-and-seek with the dark green leaves of the vine as I rocked back and forth. At my Aunt Mary's and Uncle Louis's house on Morton Street, there was also a large, wooden two-seater swing in the backyard, one with the bench seats facing each other. There, I would stand in the middle of the swing and push it from side to side, as high and as fast as I could, my head thrown back, eyes closed, imagining I was on a trapeze in the circus or at the controls in the cockpit of a plane, like the ones Daddy flew in the war. If I swung high enough and fast enough, I could pretend to be anything or anybody. It was the same at Morecz-nina's house, although you couldn't go fast on that front-to-back swing. Something about a swing, especially the swings at a playground that would let you fly up almost parallel to the ground — faster and higher, faster and higher — opened the doors to imagining that anything was possible. Swinging high and fast and with my eyes closed, I was Ginger Rogers dancing with Fred Astaire; I was a cowgirl riding a blue-black horse with the wind whipping his mane into my face; I was a sailor trimming the sails to go faster in the wind. Something about speed and height and being off the ground propelled my imagination as well as my body. I loved going on swings and always headed for the swing at Morecz-nina's.

When I'd climb down from the swing, I would play with the dog ... the mongrel of the moment which was invariably tied to the dog-house nearby, and then I'd explore the gardens, gently lifting ladybugs onto my fingertips, letting fuzzy caterpillars crawl on my arm, and peeling back the petals of a flower to look deep inside at the colors and shapes within.

One day, I left the confines of Morecz-nina's property and walked across the gravel road at the side of her house and down to the railroad tracks nearby. No train was coming from either direction so I crossed the tracks and walked into the tall grasses and prickly shrubs on the other side, drawn by the sight of fuchsia-colored flowers growing on tall stems. Then, a short distance away, I saw it — a sparkling, beautiful creek; water burbling and flowing quickly, brown rocks glistening in the sun under the shallow water, tadpoles scooting into marshy grasses at the side of the creek. I felt like Columbus discovering the new world. I later learned that it was Saucon Creek. I simply never knew that a creek was so close to Morecz-nina's house. It couldn't have been more than twenty or thirty feet across at its widest, but to me it looked like the Mississippi and I felt like Huckleberry Finn. I took off my shoes, socks, and dress, and waded into the creek in my undershirt and panties. I was five or six years old at the time and this was the neatest adventure I'd ever had. I touched the velvety mosses on the rocks in the creek, I gasped as fish (small but real fish!) swam by, and I carefully caught tadpoles ... not sure what I would do with them, but glad for my trophies just the same.

The water was so clear that I could easily see changes in its depth and make my way across the creek and down long stretches of it in both directions. When an inner prompting told me that a significant amount of time must have gone by, I made my way back to the embankment where I had left my dress, socks, and shoes. I dried my legs by rolling in the grass and I dressed and hurried back to the house, hoping that my grandmother hadn't missed me and gone on the warpath. She and Morecz-nina were still talking in the house, so I quietly helped myself to some kiffles and sat down in the parlor, giving no signal that I had just become a genuine explorer. Of course, I never told my parents about exploring in the creek or even walking down the railroad tracks. I may have been only five, but I wasn't stupid. From then on, year after year, weather permitting, whenever I went to Morecz-nina's, I wore shorts or slacks that I could roll up or take off, and almost every visit found me leaving the house quickly to go to 'my' creek and go exploring. Sometimes I was a big game hunter looking for crocodiles; sometimes I was a pirate looking for hidden treasure, and sometimes I was simply Huck or Tom Sawyer, hiding from Injun Joe.

In the years when our family had troubles that permeated every corner of our lives, my two refuges were school, where I would have been happy to stay for 24 hours a day, and Morecz-nina's house, where I would always find hugs, kisses, cookies, and the escape of exploring the creek and its environs. Much later, in my college years, when I first read and fell in love with Dylan Thomas's poem "Fern Hill," those Saucon Creek days came alive again in meaning and memory: *"In the sun that is young once only/Time let me play and be/Golden in the mercy of his means ... in the pebbles of the holy streams."*

Mrs. Morecz had the kind of hard and demanding life that was common for many immigrants and their families in the early twentieth century. Hard work to earn a living was accompanied by hard work at home. Days began before sunrise and ended only when the fire in the coal stove burned out and the ironing was finished and the housework for the day was done. As years turned into decades, Mrs. Morecz carried on with her mothering and housekeeping and cooking and gardening and canning and preserving. The love and goodness in her overcame any sadness or difficulties in her life, and she was blessed many times over by the love of her sons, their wives, and her grandchildren.

Always in tune with the cycles of nature, Mrs. Morecz could feel the change of seasons and the coming of the end in her own body. One day, her friend Lena Skrilecz phoned Mrs. Morecz to ask how she was and to talk for a while. They chatted amiably on the phone, and Mrs. Skrilecz told Mrs. Morecz that she would come to visit her the next day. "That won't happen," said Mrs. Morecz, calmly. "Tomorrow I will be dead." Taken aback, Mrs. Skrilecz couldn't believe what she heard, and she chided her friend for saying such a thing. But on the next day, Christmas day, as naturally and simply as a leaf releasing itself from a tree when winter beckons, Mrs. Morecz passed away. She left this life, left the gardens she had loved and tended, left the family she loved and that loved her; she left in her own time and way, in the season that she always knew would come and of which she was never afraid. The world suddenly seemed far emptier without Morecz-nina, but to me ... when the next spring came ... the trees, the gardens, and the heavens themselves seemed fuller.

TREASURES

*B*ela Volkov read the announcement in the morning paper with interest. It said that Bethlehem's 250th Anniversary Committee was inviting city residents to bring "personal treasures," mementos of their families' homelands, to be part of an extended anniversary exhibit. For a city that had so many immigrant groups in its DNA, this was a natural and creative way to pay tribute to the many cultures that had become part of its life.

Within days, the Committee's headquarters was inundated by a spectacular assortment of ethnic treasures. Polish women brought intricately embroidered dresses and beribboned vests. Hungarian headdresses and handmade Italian boots were added to the guitars, sombreros and hand-carved castanets contributed by Mexicans and other Latinos. Assured that their treasures would be carefully labeled, shown, and returned to them, citizens contributed generously to the exhibit, proud that their families' mementos would be displayed during the celebration.

As he sat in his home on Hillside Avenue in South Bethlehem, Bela thought about the family stories that were part of his small treasure. His mother, Marina, had been a teenage servant in no less auspicious a place than the Winter Palace in St. Petersburg. With some education and a gracious manner, she had become a favorite of Czarina Alexandra.

In the summer of 1917, with Czar Nicholas having abdicated his power, the family was told it would be moved to Tobolsk. If the Czarina had any suspicion that this journey would end in tragedy, she gave no such sign to the servants and certainly not to her daughters and young son. But she knew that she and her husband and children were likely to be exiled, to England she hoped, and she was unlikely to ever see the Winter Palace or its people again. As she gathered the clothing and accoutrements for their journey, the Czarina impulsively took a jeweled evening purse from a bureau. Marina, who had so deftly repaired the gold embroidery on the purse, was helping the Czarina's personal maid, Anna Demidova, with the packing. In a gesture of gratitude and farewell, the Czarina gave Marina the purse. The young servant realized that she would never see the Czarina or her family again, and as tears formed in her eyes, she impetuously embraced the Czarina, who briefly wrapped her arms around Marina and kissed her forehead.

Marina and many of the servants left the palace soon after the royal family left, sensing that their association with the Czar and Czarina would do them no good in the midst of the revolution. Marina traveled with a family heading south and then west, away from St. Petersburg and Moscow, away from the worst of the fighting. Taken in by various farm families in exchange for work in the kitchen and fields, Marina made her way westward. Always, always, she kept the evening purse carefully wrapped in cotton and hidden in her bodice. It never left her.

In one farm village, Marina met a tall young man whose ambition to leave Russia matched her own. Alexii Volkov had saved enough money to travel to America. On July 16, 1918, Marina and her new husband boarded a ship in the port of Danzig and set sail for the new world. Marina had no way of knowing that on the same day, as night fell, more than a thousand miles away, in Yekaterinburg, the Czar and Czarina, their children, and their servants, including Anna Demidova, were being herded into the basement of Ipatiev House to be assassinated. By the time the shots rang out in rapid bursts in that basement, Marina and Alexii could barely see the shoreline behind them.

Alexii found work in the steel mill in Bethlehem. In May of 1921, Bela was born, and soon after, his sisters Olga and Tatiana. They were teenagers when Marina finally told them the story of her life in Russia and her work at the Winter Palace. She brought the cotton-wrapped parcel to the dining room table and opened it gingerly. The purse was beautiful. Made of a bronze-brown satin, it had a gold clasp imbedded with diamonds and pearls and it bore an ornate letter H embroidered in fine, gold threads and embellished with pearls and imperial topaz. "That is not really an H," said Marina. "That's the way the letter N is written in the

Russian alphabet. The N is for Nicholas. Many of the family's personal items bore the Czar's initial."

The children were allowed to touch and handle the purse, and they marveled over its beauty. Marina proudly pointed out where she had repaired the torn gold threads in the embroidery.

"What is it worth?" Bela asked.

"It is worth more than all of the money in the world to me," Marina answered. "And it should be worth that to you too."

With his parents and sisters now dead, the purse belonged to Bela. He appreciated its importance as well as its beauty, and he knew that the story of its journey to America would be fascinating to anyone. He was proud of the purse, and proud of his mother's story. But he also knew that there could be no absolute certainty that it wouldn't be lost or stolen. Insurance was meaningless. If a policy paid him money, where would he go to buy another brown satin purse that had belonged to Czarina Alexandra? Bela sat in his chair for a long time, glancing at the story in the newspaper, then looking at the purse in his hands. Finally, he stood up and walked to the kitchen table. He folded the white cotton around the purse as carefully as his mother had, and placed the small bundle back into the plastic bag where it was kept. He returned the purse to its place in the china cabinet, next to his mother's silverware. He was content with his decision.

Across town, on West Broad Street, Celeste McGillis read the same story about the 250th Anniversary Committee's request. She, too, had some thinking to do. Her great-great-great-grandmother, Berthe, had lived in Vetheuile in France and was a friend of Claude and Camille Monet. Camille's frail health had worsened after the birth of her second child, and it was Berthe who cared for her. She made Camille broth and fresh eggs, said to be good for those with tuberculosis. Monet loved his wife, and even painted her on her deathbed. But he had relied on Berthe for the constancy of care-taking that Camille needed. Two years after Camille died, Monet left Vetheuile. Before he went away, he gave Berthe a painting he had done of Camille in her youth, showing her in a garden with the sun shining brightly on her lavender dress and on the flowers around her. Berthe never saw Claude Monet again. But she kept the painting as a remembrance of her friend, Camille. The painting came to America with Berthe's son, Etienne, and found its way into his great-grandson's simple home in Bethlehem. The painting had been evaluated and authenticated, but there had never been any thought of selling it, despite the entreaties of the appraiser from Christie's. The painting hung on the wall of this simple home, appearing to the casual observer to be nothing more than a giclee print.

After thinking about the possibilities for a long while — the joy of sharing the painting, the pride of owning it, the burden of insuring it — Celeste folded the newspaper and threw it in the trashcan. The painting was where it belonged: in Berthe's family's home.

Along with hundreds of other city residents, Bela and Celeste attended the opening festivities for the 250th Anniversary exhibition. They marveled at the variety of handicrafts, lavish clothing, jewelry, religious icons, and musical instruments assembled for the homeland treasures exhibition. It was true — each family, each culture, each homeland has treasures and stories to tell.

When the representative of the 250th Anniversary Committee concluded his remarks at the exhibition's opening, he said, "Many riches surround us here. Many memories of homes and countries far away. We will value and cherish these items ... these memories and symbols ... always. With such an abundant and remarkable display, I am certain that there isn't one corner of the city that has any more treasure to offer."

Sitting on opposite sides of the hall, Bela and Celeste both smiled.

Part II

Sweet Revenge

Stronger than lover's love is lover's hate.
Incurable, in each, the wounds they make.
Euripedes
Medea

Revenge proves its own executioner.
John Ford
The Broken Heart

SWEET REVENGE

*F*anny Austerlitz looked like her name, which was unfortunate. Hopelessly heavy-set, she had poker straight black hair that refused to hold a curl. Adding to the homeliness of Fanny's appearance were two front teeth that overlapped almost as much as they protruded, giving her something of the look of a simpleton, although she was far from that. Born in Vienna in 1936, Fanny had come to America, to South Bethlehem, with her parents when they left Austria in 1938. Blessedly, she had no trace of her parents' heavy accent. The trifecta of being heavy, homely, and too smart was enough of a burden to the shy grade-schooler. She didn't need the additional millstone of an accent to attract the derision of the bullies in her class. Fanny winced sympathetically when she heard the ridicule harpooned at the awkward pronunciations of those kids whose families spoke Windish, Italian, Hungarian, Polish, or other languages at home — kids for whom English was still a foreign language.

Even in grade school, Fanny understood, as all children understand, her strengths and shortcomings and where she ranked in the unwritten pecking order of the classroom. She knew that she was one of the two smartest students in the class, the other one being Graydon Sinclair. He was as skinny as Fanny was chubby, and he was just as homely, hiding behind thick horn-rimmed glasses, and being careful not to let anyone in the class know that his father was a professor at Lehigh University. That would only cement his nerdy image among the working class kids at Central Elementary School. Like Graydon, Fanny was careful not to say or do anything to draw attention to herself or trigger any mockery from other kids in the class. At recess, Fanny and Graydon often sat together and talked about their interests or their school work, a respite that both found enjoyable. Fanny was an only child. Her mother was 45 and her father was 60 when she was born. She was the light of their lives, their much hoped-for and long awaited blessing. Whatever confidence Fanny had, came from their praise, love, and encouragement. They would both pass away by the time she turned twenty, thus depriving her of that singular source of unconditional love and support.

When Fanny entered junior high school, she was inexplicably befriended by her polar opposite: a popular, bubbly blonde named Bambinella Angelina Santa Maria. Bambi, as she called herself, had attended Holy Infancy Elementary School. For reasons no one could fathom, Bambi chose to bestow her time and attention on painfully shy Fanny. In the schoolyard, there were two theories for this strange choice by Bambi. When the boys talked about this odd combination, they observed that Bambi was the prettiest girl in the school but hardly the brightest, while Fanny was whip smart and a straight-A student. They assumed that Bambi needed Fanny's help with homework and test preparation. The girls were less generous. They were convinced that homely Fanny was the perfect physical foil for the beauteous Bambi. If Bambi had to be seen with someone, they reasoned, she would choose someone whose homeliness set off her own good looks.

The universal hierarchy of the various grade schools transferred itself seamlessly to junior high. The prettiest girls in the class, with Bambi heading that coterie, were at the top of the social pyramid. Almost equal to them were the boys who were athletic, cute, confident, or in some cases, all three. Everyone else seemed to form an accepted middle grouping that had made its peace with being second-tier popular. The big change in the hierarchy was Fanny's ascension, courtesy of Bambi, to that heady ranking of the most popular kids. No one made fun of her anymore, and some of the popular students actually sought her advice and opinions. Fanny was still shy, and she knew she was still homely, but she was no longer isolated. And she made a point of always talking to Graydon Sinclair and the scattering of other kids at the bottom of the social ladder.

Fanny's response to Bambi's attentions was to give her instant and profound devotion. She didn't question Bambi's motives, didn't pay attention to schoolyard chatter. The most popular girl in the school was her friend and she was blessed beyond comprehension. Bambi and Fanny walked to class together, ate their lunches together, and sat together in study halls. They discovered, to their delight, that they even had birthdays in the same month — the month of June, 'their' month. Bambi's popularity and vivaciousness were like a glow that extended to and enveloped Fanny, and Fanny found her identity within that light.

Even in the tender years of junior high school, Bambi's fickle nature was evident. She teased and toyed with the boys in her classes. She led them on shamelessly and dropped them heartlessly. Such behavior only made her seem more desirable to the boys and never seemed to tarnish her in Fanny's eyes. When they moved on to high school, Bambi would make three dates for a Saturday night and would choose a fourth boy to actually have the privilege of taking her to the movies. Fanny explained it all, to herself and to others, as Bambi's way of playing the field and preventing any young man from thinking he had sole claim on her. No matter how shameless or hurtful Bambi's behavior was, Fanny explained it, excused it, or ignored it. Her devotion to her friend was absolute.

After graduation from high school, Fanny got a job at Goodman's Wholesale Candies and Cigarettes in South Bethlehem. In 1954, jobs were valuable and not to be taken for granted. Fanny's father knew Abe Goodman, the owner of the business, and Fanny was grateful for that connection. She knew she was smart enough and diligent enough to do any work that was required of her, but she was glad she did not have to endure the anxiety of an interview. Despite the ease she felt around her best friend, Fanny was still very shy and reserved. She was not inclined to promote herself or be aggressive in any way. Bambi, with her good looks, outgoing nature, and flirtatious charm, quickly landed a customer service job with a local utility company. To their delight, Bambi and Fanny worked within a block of each other on West Fourth Street in Bethlehem, and they had lunch together almost daily, whether it was a brown bag lunch at Goodman's or the treat of lunch at the nearby Archond's Ice Cream Parlor or the Royal Restaurant.

While Fanny was diligently and quickly learning all the aspects of Abe Goodman's business, and how she could most effectively assist him, Bambi was assessing other possibilities at her workplace. She was well suited to her assignment in customer service and she was pleasant and attentive to those who had questions or problems. She genuinely enjoyed her job. The office manager, Stephen Haynes, had complimented Bambi on her good work several times. Stephen was thirty years old, married, a college graduate, and an up-and-coming manager in the company. Very professional and well-spoken, he had that unusual combination of natural authority and a sensitivity toward his employees, which easily earned their loyalty. Stephen Haynes was well liked and much respected by his employees and his supervisors. Having made her assessment of possibilities within the office, it wasn't long before Bambi was turning her wily eye toward her boss, Mr. Haynes. It took only a few months of her skilled manipulation before he found it necessary to take Bambi to lunch at least once a week. Fanny understood and didn't mind. Such meetings were necessary for Bambi's work.

Bambi's weekly lunches with her boss led to occasional after-work drinks and eventually to dinner. For several months, Stephen Haynes maintained at least a quasi-professional approach to their time together, asking Bambi's opinion of office procedures and giving her additional customer service-related assignments. By the time he kissed Bambi, after driving her home from their fifth dinner together, he knew that he was lost. He could think of no more fake assignments or work-related questions. He told her that he was in love with her and would leave his wife for her if only she would marry him. But by that time, Bambi's interest had waned. She spared him any further angst by telling him that she had no interest in him whatsoever and never would. Stephen's confusion was like a mental and emotional paralysis. It felt as though he had walked into an invisible but immovable wall. Within two weeks, however, he focused his thoughts sufficiently to tell Bambi that the company no longer needed someone in customer service. To her credit, she shrugged off the dismissal and wished her co-workers well. Bambi told Fanny that she had left her job — that she had simply grown tired of the repetitive nature of her work and could see no future with the company. That part, at least, was true.

Within a month, Bambi got a job as a secretary in the Bethlehem Police Department, courtesy of a policeman who had walked her home one evening when she told him she was afraid of walking alone in the dark. He had stayed at her apartment until it was no longer dark and she was no longer afraid. Bambi began to date Officer McCourt and he often stayed to make sure she wasn't alone in the dark. He thought that if she worked as a secretary in the police department, he would be able to see her more often. Officer McCourt was 25, single, handsome, and as extroverted as Bambi.

Fanny was delighted that Bambi had found a new job so quickly, and she taught Bambi some office procedures and gave her useful suggestions about basic office management. When Fanny had begun her work at Goodman's, she worked behind the counter at the front of the store. In only a few weeks, Abe Goodman, who was a very savvy and insightful man, recognized that Fanny was smart enough to run the business end of the store, while his gregariousness was better suited to greeting and waiting on customers. Fanny kept the books, paid bills, sent invoices, managed the inventory, and even came up with effective ideas for purchasing and sales. Abe was in his element schmoozing the customers and sales people, and with the combination of Abe's and Fanny's skills, the business thrived. There was much that Fanny could teach Bambi that would help her in her new job.

What Fanny couldn't teach Bambi was common sense, restraint, and good judgment. Bambi found that she had a weakness for uniforms and black leather boots. She liked Mike McCourt and she appreciated his attentiveness to her. But she refused to date only Mike. For the most part, she was discreet about the number of officers who were helping her with her fear of the dark. Most were single, some were married. All seemed besotted with her but were too manly to let their feelings show around the police station. Thus, the number of Bambi's helpful friends on the police force remained a secret for far longer than could be reasonably expected.

When one of the motorcycle cops who occasionally dated Bambi saw a married colleague leaving her building at 6:00 a.m., he understood the situation. The fact that his sister was the woman to whom his colleague was married made the situation unacceptable. The police chief told Bambi that her position was being eliminated and he gave her two weeks' severance pay. She never dated a policeman again, and after several weeks, even the most persistent of them stopped calling her.

A series of dead-end jobs followed for Bambi, and when she couldn't pay the rent, she borrowed the money from Fanny or stayed at Fanny's apartment. This pattern continued for almost five years. While Bambi drifted from job to job and man to man, Fanny found a solid sense of satisfaction in her work at Goodman's. She liked being there. She didn't earn a big salary, but her parents had left her enough to provide a nice income stream from savings bonds, CDs, and Treasury Notes. Fanny lived simply but comfortably in an apartment in a large Victorian mansion in Fountain Hill. On her way home from work, she often stopped at the library to choose a book or two for her evening reading. She usually stopped at the Royal Restaurant for dinner and started reading while she waited for her meal. For Fanny, life was quiet, peaceful, and good, and by the time she was in her early thirties, she had formed the startling opinion that her life was actually much better than Bambi's. Fanny remained devoted to her friend and saw her a few times a week, but she no longer envied Bambi, and she knew that she was no longer thought of as "the one who is always with Bambi."

A few weeks before Christmas in 1968, Bambi took a job as a sales clerk at a department store in Allentown, working in the perfume and cosmetics area. The atmosphere seemed to suit her, and for the first time in a long while, she was not surrounded by or distracted by men. The fact that most of her customers were women was a pleasant change. Over the years, Bambi had become skilled and effective at the use of make-up, and she found genuine satisfaction in helping her customers to look prettier with the simple application of rouge, mascara, and other cosmetics. She loved to do "make-overs" and she became the sales person to whom many customers came for advice and assistance.

That winter, Bambi met Jack, a teacher from Easton, and after several months of dating, he proposed. Bambi, for the first time in her life, said "yes" ... even though she had still never felt that sensation she heard people describe as love. She tried to ignore the fact that, with Jack, she never even felt lust, a sensation to which she had become very accustomed in prior relationships. But Jack was a teacher ... a well-educated, professional man. Thinking that she had nothing to offer beyond her prettiness — "I only graduated from high school, I never went to college, and I'm only a sales clerk." — Bambi concluded that Jack was as fine a man as she would ever find. Bambi's fiancé planned a two-month honeymoon for them in Hawaii, to coincide with his summer vacation. Jack made a down payment on a small house in Easton, and at his insistence, Bambi quit her sales job in the cosmetics department. Jack said that he wanted to be the provider in their marriage, and he assured her that she would never have to work again. He even said that, when they had children, Bambi could hire someone to help her around the house. Head over heels in love with her, Jack would have given or promised Bambi anything she wanted. But as her wedding day approached, Bambi felt a tightening in her stomach, a sense of being trapped, being confined in a life she wasn't sure she wanted. She also, for perhaps the first time, did not want to be unfair to the man in her life, did not want him to marry someone who did not really love him. Two weeks before the wedding, she told Jack that she couldn't marry him. She said she was sorry, and this time, she meant it.

While Bambi was navigating the hairpin turns of her changing feelings and desires, life continued in agreeable and comfortable predictability for Fanny. One of the salesmen who came to Goodman's regularly was a stocky, balding man named Carl Schneider. He represented Gutekunst Candy Company, and Goodman's sold a lot of Gutekunst candies. Although he was by nature shy and reserved, Carl always made a point of visiting with Fanny, as well as with Abe Goodman, when he came to the store. He complimented Fanny on the way she handled all of their business transactions, and he told her interesting things about Gutekunst Candy and his travels as a salesman for the company. Despite her satisfaction with her life just as it was, Fanny found herself looking forward to Carl's visits and thinking about him when she knew he would be coming to the store. One day, the possibility that she hadn't been willing to think about occurred — Carl asked if she had time to have lunch with him. Abe told them to enjoy their lunch and take their time.

Fanny had never been on a date and wasn't sure this counted as one, but she knew she enjoyed Carl's company. She took special and unexpected pleasure in being seated, in her regular booth at the Royal Restaurant, with a man. Carl was a gentleman and he was smart. He was also obviously very diligent about his job. Fanny recognized that he was not handsome, even in a friend-of-the-leading-man way. He was balding and portly. But Fanny had studied her own image in the mirror too often to have any illusions about her looks. She did find herself fussing over her appearance a bit more on the days when Carl was expected to come to the store. She wore some jewelry, put lipstick on, and even had her hair cut in a more flattering style at Josephine Harris's Beauty Salon, abandoning her heavy bangs and allowing Josephine to give her a shorter, almost pixie haircut. Fanny wondered if all of this fussing about appearance was part of the animal courting rituals she had read about in one of those hundreds of books she had taken home from the library. When she saw Carl come into the store with an obviously new and better quality suit, with his hair trimmed and with a bright red tie, she smiled to herself and decided that, yes, they must be acting out a pattern that was deep in the nature of all living creatures. Whatever it was, it was working. Fanny's lunches with Carl became a regular part of his bi-monthly visits.

A year after their lunches began, Carl surprised Fanny by saying that he had decided to stay in Bethlehem overnight and had taken a room at Hotel Bethlehem. He would be pleased to take her to dinner if she was available. This, Fanny knew, counted as a date even if all of those lunches hadn't. Fanny felt the kind of giddy pleasure that is usually the province of newly-dating teenagers. Abe Goodman understood what was happening and told Fanny to go home early that day. He also told her to go to Alice Kay's Dress Shop, or even Essie's or Natalie Nadele's on the North Side, and buy herself the prettiest dress she could find. He pressed some folded money into her hand and said that he didn't want any arguments. For the second time in the day, Fanny felt her heart swell.

Carl took Fanny to the chic restaurant in the Hotel Traylor in Allentown. Fanny looked beautiful in the way that only a woman with a happy heart can look beautiful. Abe's generosity had allowed her to buy a very expensive dress: a steel blue shantung silk cocktail dress that drew attention to its quality, cut, and style ... and didn't need a model to do it justice. She also bought an evening purse and patent leather high heels that emphasized her surprisingly shapely legs. Her mother's double-strand pearls and matching pearl earrings added the final touch of elegance to her appearance. When Fanny caught sight of herself in the restaurant mirrors, reflecting the soft lighting from the ceiling and the candlelight from the tables, she could scarcely believe that she was looking at her own image.

Fanny was so nervous that she wasn't sure she would be able to eat. She told herself that she would simply be talking with Carl — the same Carl who came to the store to sell candy. As they began to relax, Carl admitted to his nervousness and Fanny acknowledged her own butterflies. "It has always been a problem for me," she said. "I am basically shy and often frightened of things that others seem to take in their stride."

After Fanny and Carl enjoyed their dinners, the Hotel's pianist began to play popular tunes, as well as familiar standards from the 1930s and '40s. Carl could not escape the need to ask Fanny to dance. She agreed, but quickly confessed, "I really don't know how to dance." With relief, Carl conceded that he, too, was a novice at dancing. As they laughed and walked onto the dance floor, the vocalist began to sing, "*What a difference a day makes, twenty-four little hours ....*" Fanny thought that no song had ever captured someone's feelings as much as those lyrics captured hers. She closed her eyes, as she rested her chin on Carl's broad shoulder. *If I never go out again in my life,* thought Fanny, *I won't mind. I'll be content with tonight.*

After dinner, Carl and Fanny strolled and window-shopped on Hamilton Street, relaxing more and more in each other's company. When he drove her home, Carl kissed Fanny respectfully on the cheek and said that he hoped she would go to dinner with him again. "I think you are a very nice lady," he said, his face reddening. Fanny said that she thought he was a fine man and she would be pleased to have dinner with him anytime. Before she fell asleep that night, Fanny replayed the now-familiar song lyrics in her mind and she smiled as she hummed the tune: "*It's heaven when you ... find romance on your menu ... what a difference a day makes, and that difference is you.*"

After that, Carl made a point of staying in Bethlehem for two or three nights whenever he came to Goodman's. Thus began an old-fashioned courtship in a sexually adventurous era. Movie dates, after-work walks around the downtown areas of Bethlehem, evenings of dining and dancing, and quiet conversations formed the structure within which Fanny and Carl came to know each other as the months passed by. After each of their dates, Carl escorted Fanny back to her apartment, and departed after he kissed her gently on the cheek, preserving the unusual and somehow arousing chastity of their courtship.

Carl took Fanny to the Havilland Inn to enjoy jazz, and he made a point of taking her to the places where orchestras, such as those of Matt Gillespie and Parke Frankenfield, provided music for listening and dancing. Knowing how much she liked the song, Carl was bold enough on several occasions to ask the orchestra to play "What a Difference a Day Makes."

One evening, as they sat with their after-dinner coffees at the Maples Restaurant, Fanny told Carl about her parents and how she had lost them at an early age, with her father dying when she was nineteen and her mother dying the next year. She also confided that her extended family — aunts, uncles, and cousins who had remained in Austria when her parents emigrated in 1938 – disappeared in the horrors of the war, presumably in the camps of the Holocaust. In a voice that was almost a whisper, Fanny told Carl that she had tried to contact the people whose addresses she knew. But she had never received a response, never had an answer from anyone as to what happened to her family. All of this, she said, made her feel the loss of her parents more keenly, underscoring how alone she really was in the world.

"Perhaps that's why I so often feel frightened, even of little things," she said. "Bambi and Abe," she continued, "are all I have. They're the only people who are close to me ... the only ones who care about me."

"And me," said Carl, taking her hand and clasping it tightly. "I care about you. Very much. As long as you allow me to be part of your life, you will never be alone in this world, and you need never be frightened."

Fanny knew at that moment that she loved Carl, that she needed him, wanted him, and trusted him. These were feelings she had never hoped to experience, and they flooded her with a warmth and joy that were inexpressible. That night when they stood at her apartment door, as

Carl turned his head to the side to kiss her cheek, Fanny turned her face toward him, placed her hand behind his neck, and pulled him toward her. She kissed him ardently on the mouth, not pulling away when he touched her lips with his tongue and for a brief second allowed his desire rather than his caution to guide his actions. The heat that blazed through her body told Fanny that this, indeed, was what love and desire must feel like. Realizing that they were in new and unpredictable territory, Fanny and Carl ended their kiss hastily and said their good-nights.

Several months later, when Carl returned to Pennsylvania from a sales trip to Maryland, he took Fanny to dinner at Hotel Traylor, where they had had their first date. After a leisurely dinner, Carl ordered a dessert of cherries jubilee for them to share. When the waiter approached their table with the chafing dish, he placed a gold-rimmed porcelain plate in front of Fanny. On that plate was a white orchid trimmed with lavender lace and gold cording. Next to the orchid was a small, white jewelry box that could only be holding a ring. Carl smiled impishly as Fanny picked up the box, staring at it with genuine shock.

Carl took her hand and said, "I never thought I would fall in love. I never thought I would marry. I thought those things only happened for other men. But with you I have found real love. If you will marry me, I will spend the rest of my life trying to make you happy." Carl's voice grew husky as he continued. "Fanny, will you do me the honor of becoming my wife?"

By then, Fanny had tears in her eyes and she let them fall as she said, "Yes. Yes, of course I will marry you. I love you so much, and I would be honored to be your wife." They kissed and almost forgot about the ring until Carl noticed that Fanny was still holding the small, white velvet box in her hand, unopened. She opened the box and he placed the beautiful three-stone ring on Fanny's finger. Carl hadn't hesitated to spend a significant amount for the ring, and it sparkled dazzlingly in the candlelight at the table. Any ring would have pleased Fanny, but she recognized that the size of the diamonds in the ring and their incredible beauty represented an extra measure of being loved, valued, and desired. She had never expected to be so fortunate or feel so ecstatic. When she looked at Carl, gratitude as well as love emanated from her eyes.

Carl and Fanny knew that a large or fancy wedding would not be right for them. Their ages — he was 37 and she was 35 — as well as the differences in their faiths — Lutheran and Jewish — called for simplicity. They were married by the Mayor of Bethlehem at City Hall on July 20, 1971. Fanny wore an ivory silk suit and a matching pillbox hat with an ivory veil. She carried a small bouquet of red roses. Carl wore a navy blue suit and a red tie, and his beaming joy made him look almost handsome. Bambi was the maid of honor for her friend, and Carl had asked Abe to be his best man. Abe hosted a dinner for the little group at Hotel Bethlehem, and the day was a complete joy to both Fanny and Carl. Fanny didn't throw her bouquet; she simply handed it to Bambi, saying, "I wish for you the same love and happiness that I have found." Bambi had no explanation for the tears that flowed unexpectedly down her cheeks or the emptiness that suddenly seemed to open like a chasm in her heart.

Carl had made arrangements for them to spend their honeymoon at Buck Hill Falls Inn in the Pocono Mountains, and their suitcases were packed and ready for their departure the next day. But on this, their wedding day, they returned to Fanny's apartment for their wedding night. The fact that they were equally nervous and ill at ease about what would or would not happen on this night seemed to make that apprehension easier to bear. Carl even joked by saying, "This is one night when I wish I was Cary Grant." Fanny chuckled and replied, "If you were Cary Grant, I would be even more nervous ... and I'm nervous enough as it is."

At Carl's suggestion, Fanny went to the bedroom and bathroom first, to prepare for bedtime. As she brushed her teeth, she debated about washing her lipstick off, but decided to keep it on. Somehow she felt more confident with that touch of crimson on her lips. A few weeks earlier, Fanny had stopped at the Le-Roy Shop to look at lingerie. Until now, Fanny had never owned anything she would call lingerie. She had underwear and pajamas, plain and simple. Her brassieres were functional. They were white cotton, in the same style, with the exception of two black bras, same style, to wear under dark dresses. Her cotton panties were full coverage, in basic white, beige, and black. Fanny's most exotic piece of clothing was a garter belt, a necessity for keeping stockings on if you didn't want to be bothered with a girdle. At the Le-Roy Shop, Fanny couldn't quite bring herself to buy a lacy bra or a fancy pair of panties, but with this night in mind, she did buy a pale blue nightgown with white lace trim around the neckline. The smocked bodice of the nightgown was embroidered with small satin rosebuds, and Fanny felt very feminine in her new nightie. She even bought a pair of pale blue slippers to match the nightgown. When Fanny finished her bedtime preparations, she called out to Carl.

"I'm finished in the bathroom and I'm in the bedroom. Take your time. Please don't hurry."

Carl understood, and he was in no mood to hurry. Carl had had sex with women three times in his life. The first two experiences happened when he was in the Navy during the Korean War. On a shore leave, his buddies had taken him to a place where the women at the bar would willingly take a sailor upstairs. Carl had been so flustered that he was glad that the petite brunette who took him upstairs could only say, "Johnny like me?" After that first experience, Carl had returned to the bar on his next leave, and he was almost as nervous the second time he went upstairs as he was during the first visit. His third sexual experience happened long before he met Fanny, when he had been on a sales trip to New York City and had stopped at a bar and grille for dinner. A woman at the bar talked to him, listened attentively to his descriptions of his work, and allowed him to buy her a beer. After he had had too many beers, she took him to her apartment two blocks away. He had been too groggy to push her away when she unzipped his trousers, and after she touched him he was too aroused to push her away. In each of these encounters, the women had been far more experienced than Carl, and they had done all of the initiating and maneuvering. After a certain point of arousal, Carl's body seemed to know what to do and shifted into automatic, but Carl felt more like a bystander than a prime mover of the action. Apart from these three episodes, Carl had simply attended to his needs himself. His three sexual encounters seemed to Carl to be very feeble qualifications for his wedding night, but he reminded himself that they were three more than Fanny had known.

Carl, too, had purchased new nightwear, a pair of navy and gray-striped pajamas still bearing the fold marks of the package from which he had taken them. New leather slippers completed his ensemble, and as he entered the bedroom, he fleetingly wondered if he should have covered up with a robe.

As it turned out, Carl's pajamas were in no danger of being seen that night. After a few awkward moments of clinging to the opposite sides of the mattress, facing away from each other, Fanny and Carl laughed at their nervousness and relaxed into the love that linked them. After Carl turned off the bedside lamp, Fanny nestled herself into his embrace and told him that she was content to let this part of their life evolve as it would. With undeniable relief, Carl told her that he loved and desired her, but with the momentous day they'd just had, perhaps simply sleeping now would be best. Before they fell asleep, Fanny half-murmured, half-sang to Carl, "*What a difference a day makes ....*"

Three nights later, after they enjoyed wine with their dinner at the Inn and danced to the music of the Guy Lombardo orchestra, Fanny and Carl retired to their hotel room, and with no nervousness, consummated their marriage. Carl did what he thought Cary Grant would do, and Fanny's fears of pain and failure receded under Carl's gentle and patient caresses. By the time their honeymoon ended, they were enjoying real passion in their lovemaking, with Carl becoming more confident and Fanny more relaxed. They still dressed and undressed separately, in privacy, and Fanny was too shy and inhibited to have the lights on when they made love, or to look at Carl's nakedness, but she blissfully surrendered to his explorations of her body. The ecstasy that they both felt was, perhaps, the biggest surprise for each of them — a kind of bonus to their love that found them smiling at each other, frequently and bashfully, as if they now had a secret that no one else could ever know.

A few months after their honeymoon, the newlyweds purchased a split-level red brick home in Fountain Hill. They kept most of Fanny's furniture and decorative items because of their sentimental value as well as their usefulness, but they enjoyed shopping for additional furnishings and accessories for their home. Carl was happy to have a small garden in which to plant tomatoes and peppers, and Fanny began to do more cooking now that she had a husband for whom to prepare meals. As time passed, Fanny and Carl enjoyed a profound contentment with each other and an ever-deepening love. Fanny felt a special warmth and pleasure when Carl held her hand as they walked or when he placed his arm around her as they sat to watch television. For Carl, there was an almost palpable satisfaction in coming through the door and announcing, "Honey, I'm home!" This ritual made Carl feel as though he really belonged — to this home, this woman, this life. It made him feel as if he was, indeed, living the American dream of family life.

Carl's work involved so much travel that it was just as easy for him to commute from Bethlehem as from the Gutekunst Candy headquarters. Carl and Fanny spent two-week summer vacations in Cape May, and as they entered their forties, their lives were settled and serene. Carl and Fanny were genuinely happy with each other, and secure and fulfilled in their marriage.

As Bambi moved through her forties, she was showing the wear and tear of too many relationships and too many disappointments. She tried to hold back the clock, but her prettiness had left her long ago, replaced by a kind of dullness in her kohl-rimmed eyes and a forced smile that was neither warm nor natural. Her attempts to keep her long blonde curls and blue-shadowed eyes backfired by making her look dated and slightly ridiculous. Bambi worked hard at keeping her figure. Her breasts, with the aid of push-up bras, still pointed toward Canada, and she showed off her slim waist and rounded backside in tight jeans and mini-skirts. She could still turn heads in a barroom, but her best days were behind her and she knew it.

Bambi was the only subject on which Carl and Fanny disagreed. Carl had never taken to Bambi and couldn't understand why Fanny was so devoted to her. Fanny had explained the length of their friendship and what it had meant to her to have Bambi befriend her in her teens. Carl understood all of that, but he also saw Bambi's less admirable characteristics, to which Fanny maintained a blind eye. Fanny still invited Bambi to dinner and spent time with her as often as she could, but she did so knowing that Carl was uncomfortable around her dearest friend. To abandon that friendship, however, would have been disloyal, and Fanny ranked loyalty as the highest virtue.

When Carl traveled, Fanny continued to help in Goodman's store. Abe hired an accountant who took over some of Fanny's work and Fanny had a manageable and pleasant span of responsibilities doing the purchasing, maintaining inventory, and overseeing invoices and payments. In weeks when Carl made day trips from home, Fanny scaled back her work at Goodman's or did some of that work from home. Thus, the Schneiders' work and home lives blended in ways that were comfortable and fulfilling for both of them. Consideration and thoughtfulness came naturally to Carl and Fanny, and each of them found genuine joy in making the other happy. Two incomes allowed them to save money toward what they planned as an early retirement. "In a few years," Carl often said, "I'll be home every day and sitting on the patio and asking you to bring me iced tea. You'll get tired of my being around all the time!" Fanny would just as predictably assure him that what she looked forward to most was their being together every day when they retired. For almost twenty years, Carl and Fanny enjoyed the kind of happiness that comes to few couples — the kind that is rooted in mutual respect and a deep pleasure in each other's company.

In the year that Bambi and Fanny turned fifty-four, Fanny saw Bambi walking past Goodman's in early April. She called her friend into the store and embraced her warmly. She reminded Bambi of their upcoming June birthdays. She suggested that they spend a day together — shopping, enjoying lunch, seeing a movie. "It will be a girls' day out," Fanny promised, "and it will be special because I haven't seen you for so long." There was an unmistakable hesitation in Bambi's voice as she considered the offer. Finally, she agreed and a date was set.

When Fanny saw her friend at the restaurant where they had agreed to meet, she thought that Bambi had aged even in the two months since she had last seen her. It seemed clear to Fanny that the day might not be filled with smiles and memories as she had planned.

It didn't take long for Bambi to admit that the past year had been unusually difficult for her. She told Fanny that she had met someone, who for the first time in her life, she really loved ... someone she hadn't told Fanny about: a man named Randy who worked for the same insurance company Bambi worked for.

"Randy said that he loved me," Bambi avowed, as if saying it could make it true. "But Randy was married."

Again? thought Fanny, silently wondering why Bambi could never understand that there were territories into which decent people simply did not venture.

"Randy said that he would leave his wife, that he never really loved her, not in the way he loved me," Bambi continued. "I know he meant it. I believed him. I know ... I still know ... what he felt for me and what we had together. I could picture our life together. I wanted to be married to him more than I have ever wanted anything."

Bambi confessed that even Randy's delays did not arouse suspicion in her. His reasons sounded plausible to her. He wanted to wait until his son graduated from college. He wanted to stay with his wife until their granddaughter was baptized. Bambi understood all of that. She never doubted Randy's love or his promises.

Bambi told Fanny that she kissed Randy with absolute love every time he left their bed to go home to his wife. She welcomed him with love every time he came to her apartment for their mid-day trysts. Fanny was stunned when Bambi told her that, at Randy's suggestion, she had quit her job to stay at home for him, to be available for him, to make love to him whenever he wanted to come to her apartment.

"In the past year, though," Bambi said softly, "when I wasn't working, I used up my savings. Randy gave me money once in a while, and he often brought food to the apartment." But Bambi admitted that her bank account had eroded to nothing within the past twelve months. Bambi paused for a long moment as she steadied herself to continue her story.

"Two weeks ago, just as I was getting up the courage to push Randy for a definite date for his divorce and our marriage, I saw him walking on Main Street with Laurie, a girl who works in the same department that Randy and I worked in at the insurance company. Laurie is about twenty or twenty-one years old."

Again, Bambi paused as if she was trying to comprehend how anyone could be only twenty or twenty-one. Then Fanny realized that Bambi was also pausing because the next part of her story must be almost unbearable to think about ... much less talk about. Bambi's forehead, already lined by middle age, now furrowed itself more deeply as she frowned from the almost physical pain of remembering.

"I knew they were probably out on business or heading somewhere to talk business." Again, Bambi paused, and Fanny felt a deep, visceral sympathy for her friend, for the agony that seemed to be crushing Bambi's very soul. Fanny knew intuitively that the next part of Bambi's story would be as painful to hear as it was to relay.

"For some reason ... I don't know why ... I followed them." With something like determination in her voice, Bambi went on. "I followed them into a restaurant, and I slid into the booth next to the one they took. They couldn't see me because the booths have those frosted glass partitions between them. You can hear sound through the top and bottom of the partitions, but you can't see anything."

A cold, bitter tone crept into Bambi's voice, a tone that Fanny found almost frightening — as frightening as the hardness that she saw in her friend's eyes and expression.

"I leaned my head against the partition," Bambi said, almost hissing the words, "and I heard Randy say the same things to Laurie that he had said to me. Things he had still been saying to me a few days before I saw him with her. I heard him say that he would leave his wife for her, that he never loved his wife. And then ... then ... I heard something I'll never forget — never be *able* to forget. Laurie asked him what ever happened to the 'older woman' who used to work in the office. 'The one with the long bleached blonde hair and the silly name.' 'Bambi?' he asked. 'Yes, that one,' she said.

"Randy said, 'I saw her for a while. To be perfectly blunt, when a guy isn't getting any at home, he has to look for it somewhere else, and Bambi is so long in the tooth that she was happy to give me what I needed. But she means nothing to me. Never did. Never will. Not like you do, honey.'"

Fanny instinctively recoiled from the brutality of these words, and she reached across the table to grasp Bambi's hand. She was shocked to find that it was ice cold to the touch. She saw that the same iciness seemed to have glazed over Bambi's face.

"I don't know how I managed to get up from the table," Bambi continued. "I couldn't even think about interrupting them or embarrassing Randy. All I could think of was getting out of there, getting to the door and getting out. I couldn't even see right. The tears in my eyes blurred everything. I practically ran back to the apartment and I cried for hours. I cried so hard that I couldn't breathe, couldn't catch my breath. You know, the kind of crying that has you gasping, as if you'll never be able to stop crying. I thought of killing Randy. I really did. I thought of killing myself. But then I realized that I was already dead. My body might still be alive, but everything inside me was dead. When Randy came to the apartment that night, he could see that I had been crying. All he said was, 'What's with you? Watching some soap opera?' I told him that I had been at the restaurant, in the booth next to the one where he and Laurie had been seated, and I heard everything they said. For a second he seemed stunned, but then he said, 'I guess that's the way it goes.' Then ... you'll never believe this ..." Bambi went on, actually chuckling. "He said, 'I don't suppose you'd want to have a farewell roll in the hay? For old times' sake?' I told him to do it to himself ... but I said it differently ... and I closed the door. Then I started to cry again. I think I cried for days."

Bambi told Fanny that a week after overhearing Randy and Laurie at the restaurant, she was served with an eviction notice. She had only a few days left to find another place to live. And she had to find work, but she had no way to explain being unemployed for a year and she knew it would be hard to find a job.

Fanny stopped her in mid-sentence. "You'll come to live with us," she said. "That's what friends are for and we've been friends for forty-two years. Imagine that. More than forty years of friendship. I won't take no for an answer. If you live with us, you'll be able to put your life back together. You'll find a job; you'll get back on your feet, and until then you won't have anything to worry about."

Bambi stared at Fanny with disbelief. Then she squeezed Fanny's hands. Her tears and gratitude were genuine. She felt an overwhelming relief and realized that she hadn't even considered the possibility of living with Fanny. She had come to lunch because she needed to be with someone she could trust. This offer of help was an unexpected and incomprehensible extra blessing.

Carl was not pleased when Fanny told him about her offer, when she told him that Bambi would be moving into their guest room. But he understood the desperate circumstances that Fanny had described. Fanny, of course, didn't tell him anything about Randy or the year of unemployment that had led to Bambi's impoverishment. She simply said that Bambi had lost her job and then had too many medical expenses to shoulder.

Bambi moved in with Fanny and Carl, and for a few weeks life in the house was peaceful, if sometimes strained. Carl seemed to notice every fault and failing of Bambi's, from her too-short skirts and too-tight tops to her talking when they watched TV. More often than not, he held his tongue and reminded himself that Bambi had been through a rough time and needed some friendship and care-taking. Sometimes, when he was exasperated with her mindless chatter or sloppy habits, he vented with Fanny as they got ready for bed. "I don't know how you can stand her," he'd say. "You must have the patience of a saint as well as the heart of an angel."

When Carl was away on his sales trips, Fanny and Bambi got along very well, and Fanny was actually glad to have Bambi's company on evenings when she would otherwise have been alone. Fanny would talk about what had happened at Goodman's that day, and she would listen encouragingly to Bambi's descriptions of her search for a job — a search that was usually fruitless.

When Carl was at home, a different atmosphere seemed to prevail, marked by the uneasiness that comes when three people are sharing a space and a life meant for two.

Dinner seemed to be the most stressful time of the day. Instead of the easy conversation that Fanny and Carl had savored for many years, a strained silence often hovered over the dinner table.

Bambi's gushing comments about new shades of eyeshadow reinforced for Carl just how shallow she was, and the fact that she never offered to help Fanny with preparing dinner or cleaning up afterward ("Oh, I'm just so clumsy in a kitchen!") grated on him even more.

Once, over dessert, in something of a desperate attempt to create conversation, Fanny began to talk about the emerging political campaigns. Even the local elections, she said, had taken on a negativism and nastiness that she found troublesome. "That isn't what this country is about, is it?" Fanny offered, looking at Bambi and hoping to engage her in a substantive discussion.

"Hmm?" Bambi queried, obviously not having heard what Fanny said or perhaps not having understood it.

Fanny repeated her observation, explaining it with references to the negative advertising being done by various candidates.

"Oh, I don't even know who's running," admitted Bambi casually. "I've never even voted in an election. I don't care who wins, really, and I don't see what difference it makes."

With that, Carl rose from the table and excused himself, before he would be tempted to say something about citizenship and responsibility and the privilege of voting. *But she probably wouldn't even understand any of that,* he thought to himself, as he headed for the den that served as his office.

As the weeks and months passed, a kind of unspoken routine evolved in the Schneider home. Bambi and Fanny conversed as pleasantly as ever when they were alone, and Carl invariably excused himself from the dinner table as soon as he was done eating, citing the need to do work in the den.

When Christmas came — which Fanny and Carl celebrated as a secular holiday, with no reference to their distinct faith traditions — any feelings of irritation or frustration seemed to be suspended or forgotten. The Schneiders and Bambi had fun decorating their small and fragrant Douglas-Fir tree, and they shared memories of the holidays in their childhoods.

On Christmas morning, Bambi surprised Fanny with the gift of a beautiful indigo silk scarf and gave Carl a dark green wool vest with cable stitching. Knowing that Bambi's income from her sporadic part-time jobs was very limited, Carl and Fanny were genuinely touched by her thoughtfulness and generosity. They surprised Bambi with the gift of a small television for her room, a gift that was more strategic than generous on Carl's part. He wanted to be alone with Fanny in the living room when they watched TV at night, as he had been before Bambi's arrival, and he hoped that Bambi would take the hint and remain in her room more often.

Carl gave Fanny several gift certificates and a beautiful pearl and diamond bracelet, which she immediately declared was far too lavish a present. Fanny gave Carl pajamas, two cashmere sweaters, and a large envelope, at which he stared inquisitively for a moment before opening it. Inside the envelope was a letter from Dwyer Travel, informing him that he was the recipient of a week-long, all-inclusive vacation for two at a mountain resort in West Virginia. As surprise and elation animated Carl's face, Fanny jokingly said, "I assume I'm the person you'll be taking with you on vacation!"

"Of course, sweetheart," replied Carl, as he leafed through the brochures enclosed with the letter, already picturing himself fishing in the clear mountain streams near the resort.

"On the other hand," cooed Bambi mischievously, "you just never know who he might decide to take." She quickly added a laugh to show that she was just teasing.

That night at dinner, Bambi asked Carl how he had come to work for Gutekunst Candy. What had led him to that company and to that job? Carl was as flattered by the question as he was surprised by it, and he took real satisfaction in explaining how he had researched several companies before deciding to apply to Gutekunst for employment. He recounted the effective training he had been given and the steady promotions — in terms of sales territories and accounts — that he had earned.

"But it must be so hard to sell things," declared Bambi, "so exhausting to try to convince people to buy something. I'm sure I could never do it."

"Of course you could," Carl assured her, warming to the subject. "Sales is a matter of understanding how to create a win-win situation, how to convince your customer that he or she will benefit from the transaction, that they have something to gain by it, something they couldn't get anywhere else, perhaps something they might never find again. You just have to frame your whole strategy in terms of giving the customer what he wants and needs, even if it's something he doesn't yet know he wants or needs. You have to create that need in him, make him desire what you have to sell. If you do that, you're sure to succeed."

Fanny sat at the table smiling, looking from Carl to Bambi, marveling at their civil and even friendly conversation, and feeling happier than she had felt in months. The husband she loved and the friend she loved seemed to have made peace with each other, however temporarily. The atmosphere at the dinner table that night was not only peaceful, it was actually pleasant. Fanny whispered a prayer of thanks — to whatever God was listening — for this respite from tension and this glimmer of hope that Carl and Bambi might learn to co-exist in peace with each other. Fanny felt certain that God heard her prayer.

After that break-through dinner conversation, Bambi often asked Carl about his work, especially when he returned home from a sales trip, and she asked him about his growing-up years, his family, and his interests. She was interested in anything and everything about Carl. Fanny was surprised at the freedom that this rapprochement between Carl and Bambi gave her to putter around the house and catch up with things she wanted to do. She no longer felt as though she had to be a referee when Carl and Bambi were together or that she had to be Carl's companion every minute of the evening to buffer him from Bambi. The peacefulness in the house would have been gift enough; the laughter and friendliness that she heard in Carl's and Bambi's voices was an added blessing.

One day, as Bambi helped Carl in his workshop, sanding a bench that he wanted to repaint, she suddenly asked him why he and Fanny never had children. She said that she thought he would have been a wonderful father. Carl admitted that he'd always wanted children, but Fanny had simply never become pregnant.

"You could have adopted," Bambi suggested, cannily.

"I mentioned that several times," replied Carl, "but Fanny was reluctant to have only one child, because she knew how lonely it is to be an only child. And she thought we were both getting too old to manage well with two or more children, especially with my traveling. She thought it wouldn't really be fair to them."

"I think you could have managed very well," affirmed Bambi. "I think you could do anything, and I think you deserved to have children: a son to carry on your name, a son you could take fishing and to baseball games, and a little girl you could have pampered and spoiled ... a little girl who would have called you Papa and wrapped you around her little finger. I know I would have wanted to give you children." Bambi made sure she saw the wistful look in Carl's eyes before she changed the subject.

Carl noticed the changes before Fanny did. Bambi came to the breakfast table in her robe and wasn't always careful about completely closing that robe. She often left her bathroom door ajar when she took her bath. She smiled and laughed at Carl's slightest joke. Carl couldn't imagine that she was attempting to be alluring, but he was confused and uncomfortable nevertheless. And he knew that Bambi was a closed subject with Fanny, so he had no way of discussing these disturbing actions with the one person to whom he might have confided his suspicions. Meanwhile, Bambi's fascination with Carl's work and opinions continued, and Fanny continued to be grateful for their growing friendship.

In the natural world, many spiders have a built-in mechanism for survival and self-protection. If an insect that would be dangerous to a spider lands on its web — an insect that would be perilous or even fatal to the spider — that insect vibrates at a frequency too high or too low for the spider to detect along the silken filaments of its web. Thus, the spider is not drawn to something that would be dangerous to it. Neither Fanny nor Carl were as fortunate as the spiders. Neither had any such self-protective mechanism. Trusting and naïve, they were drawn openly and innocently toward every vibration in their relationships with Bambi.

Winter melted into spring and Fanny remained unaware of the changing nuances in Bambi's behavior. For her part, Bambi was so skilled and stealthy in her stalking that her web seemed to be spun with invisible threads. When June came around, Fanny promised Bambi a special joint birthday celebration. "We haven't done that since our fiftieth birthdays!" she said. Fanny planned to mark their 55th birthdays with a large cake decorated with 25 candles for each of them, plus five for both them — 55 in total. "A birthday split" she called it. But the split that surfaced on that fateful day was not one she saw coming.

When Carl told Fanny that he wanted a divorce and that he and Bambi would be getting married, the words blurred in her ears. She couldn't hear him ... couldn't quite understand him. Carl knew that her reaction would be delayed and volcanic. He had the foresight to have an attorney available for her, at his expense, and to leave the house with Bambi, their clothes already packed, before Fanny could put the candles on the cake.

"You won't understand this," he said. "I'm not sure I understand it myself. I just know that I never felt like this. A man doesn't get many chances for real passion in life, a chance to have it all, and I have to take this chance." In another second, Carl and Bambi were at the front door with their suitcases. Bambi looked back at Fanny and waved a limp good-bye, shrugging her shoulders as if she had no idea how this situation had come about. Fanny was still holding the box of candles when the door closed behind them.

First, she threw up. Projectile vomit splattered the walls and furniture wherever Fanny turned, as she reeled around the dining room, grabbing at any surface that could hold her up. It covered the cake that still awaited its candles. Her body heaved as if it was exploding, as if it was trying to turn itself inside out, trying to rid itself of everything it had ever consumed. It continued to heave and spasm, to drive Fanny to her knees and then into a fetal position, even when there was nothing left within her, liquid or solid, that could possibly be expelled.

Next, Fanny screamed — screamed so piercingly that neighbors summoned the police, thinking that someone was being killed, not knowing how close to the truth their fears were. Fanny's wails and sobs gave the police enough of a clue to call an ambulance. She was taken to the nearest psychiatric ward, and tranquilizers did for her what nothing else would do. Fanny spent the next few days in a haze of pills, doctors' questions, and deep, drug-induced sleep.

As she gradually emerged from her stupor, reality crept into Fanny's consciousness. Her doctors gave her enough medication to get her through the necessary conversations with the attorney Carl had hired for her. She felt paralyzed — emotionally, physically, and psychologically paralyzed. Often, she couldn't put a coherent thought together, couldn't understand or respond to what was being said to her. She couldn't take anything in. It felt as though she was trapped in a never-ending nightmare, a nightmare she never saw coming. Her every thought and movement seemed to be made in slow motion, as if she was trying to run underwater, in sluggish, laborious lurches. When she managed to focus on the attorney's questions, she said that she wanted no arguments, no contact with Carl, and no prolonging of the process. The attorney told her that Carl wanted none of their joint assets or the house they had lived in, and he was willing to give all of their savings to her. She barely understood what the attorney was saying and she certainly couldn't think about anything like assets.

The divorce process began swiftly and Fanny was on her way to being free. Abe tried to comfort her but there was no sense in trying to keep her job at Goodman's. With as much focus and attentiveness as she could summon, Fanny told Abe to hire someone else. As soon as the divorce was underway, Fanny surrendered to a complete mental and emotional collapse. She was placed in a rest home in the Poconos and given the kind of caring attention she had not known since her childhood. She was examined, listened to, fed, and medicated ... and was asked for nothing in return. She was simply allowed to sleep and 'be' at her own pace. After three months, the doctors determined that she was ready to return to a life she couldn't imagine and did not want.

Fanny moved mechanically through the next weeks and months. Abe paid her bills for her and brought her food, knowing how fragile she still was. He learned to never mention Carl and never refer, even sympathetically, to the departure that had stunned him almost as much as it had stunned Fanny. He hired a housekeeper who came to Fanny's home daily to do her laundry, cook, clean the house, and assist Fanny in any way necessary. The housekeeper understood intuitively how damaged Fanny was, and she often did kindnesses, such as making a cup of tea for Fanny or wrapping a sweater around her shoulders. The housekeeper could not reconcile the beaming, pink-cheeked, dark-haired woman in the various photos around the house with the gray-haired, drawn woman to whom she tended daily. Fanny was 55 and she looked as if she was 75. She didn't care.

One year after the cataclysm, with some semblance of her strength and stability returned, Fanny walked down to Goodman's one day and told Abe that she thought it would be good for her to spend a few hours at the store, even if she only helped to stock shelves. Abe embraced her, welcomed her back, and said she could do anything she wanted. Over the course of several months, Fanny gradually assumed some of her old duties, careful not to overload herself with too many demands. She found solace and some form of relief and renewal in the comforting familiarity of her work and in the simple act of accomplishing something ... anything ... every day. Once again, she was grateful to Abe for providing her with as close to a sanctuary as she thought she would ever find in this life.

Fanny never knew when the idea first formed in her mind. Perhaps it was when she saw those candy commercials on TV. She only knew that, once it came to her, the idea would not leave her — that it burrowed itself into her brain, that it beckoned to her, gave her a purpose and an energy she thought she would never have again. She began to nurture the idea, embrace it, cultivate it, play with it, and cherish it ... the way one would, she sometimes thought, embrace and cherish a child.

Methodically, over the course of a few months, Fanny assembled almost 25 years of records of purchases that Goodman's had made from Gutekunst Candy through Carl. She had access to Carl's blank invoice and sales forms, which he had left behind in his office at the house. Fortunately for Fanny, the invoice forms were not pre-numbered. Slowly, carefully, she made exact copies of the invoices Carl had submitted to Goodman's (including the dates and invoice numbers), copying his neat, small printing precisely, and numbering them as he had. She simply doubled the prices he had charged. She also made sure that she personally attended to the Gutekunst salesman who was now assigned to Goodman's. Finally, Fanny wrote her carefully worded letter to Mr. Jonathan Butler, president of Gutekunst Candy.

Dear Mr. Butler,

It pains me to write to you about this matter, but I believe something should be brought to your attention. My ex-husband, Carl Schneider, was, for many years, the Gutekunst sales representative for the Goodman Wholesale Company.

When I worked at Goodman's, and prior to my marriage to Mr. Schneider, I received and paid the invoices submitted by him for our orders. Recently, when I returned to work at Goodman's and began to deal with a new Gutekunst salesman, I saw that the charges for our current orders were substantially different from those that Mr. Schneider had submitted over the years, even allowing for changes in pricing. I know that the integrity and reputation of the Gutekunst name matter a great deal to your company, and I do not report this matter to you lightly. Quite simply, Mr. Schneider appears to have submitted invoices to us that were more than double the amount he should have charged, double the amount he recorded on the invoice copies he submitted to you. I assume, although I am loathe to think of it, that he kept the difference for himself. That would help to explain the generous gifts he was able to make to me and the vacations that we enjoyed. Please understand that I am not reporting this to cause any difficulty for Mr. Schneider or the Gutekunst company. I simply believe that integrity, honor, and loyalty still have meaning and importance in our world and I am, frankly, deeply disturbed by the fact that I may have benefited from what appear to be ill-gotten gains.

When Fanny finished typing the letter, she calmly signed it and gathered all of Carl's blank invoice sheets and the original invoices he had submitted to Goodman's over the years. She placed these in a large manila envelope and sealed it. She took the envelope with her when she left Goodman's for the day, stopping at the post office on Fourth Street on her way home to mail the letter to Jonathan Butler.

As she walked home, Fanny considered the possibilities. Any investigation of the invoices would require the originals. These she now had and would soon destroy. She would explain that she had kept only the carbon copies for the store files in order to minimize file space. Even if she had missed some fact, some part of the puzzle, even if her scheme fell apart or was uncovered, a bevy of doctors would testify to her fragile mental state and recent nervous breakdown. The most she would have to face would be a few years in a psychiatric prison or hospital, and that prospect did not frighten her. Nothing frightened her anymore.

Carl was arrested in his new workplace two years after he started his job with Chaucer Candies in Camden, New Jersey. His attorneys told him that the evidence against him was so strong that his best course would be to plead guilty and hope for a reduced sentence in light of his cooperation. For a long while Carl insisted that he would fight the charges, insisted that he had never done anything underhanded in his life and was innocent in this matter. He begged his attorneys to believe him, and the fear and desperation in him seemed almost to consume him. Carl might not have been the bravest or boldest man in the world, but he had never felt completely helpless before. He had never been at the mercy of people who were saying and doing things that were incomprehensible to him, things he could neither understand nor control. He felt paralyzed. He couldn't, somehow, take anything in, and he felt as if he was moving in slow motion while the circumstances around him were spinning into warp speed. He felt as though he was descending into a nightmare that had no rationale, no purpose, and no ending — a nightmare he never saw coming.

Carl knew that he had never submitted a fraudulent invoice to any customer, had never stolen money from anyone, and he could only suspect that Fanny was behind this somehow. Only she would know where those files were at Goodman's, only she had access to his sales forms and records at home, and only she would have a motive to ensnare him in such a trap. But Carl's attorneys and Abe himself had told Carl that Fanny was still very fragile emotionally. "Barely managing to get through each day," Abe had said, and hardly energetic enough or organized enough to fashion such a scheme. Carl also did not believe, in the depths of his heart, that Fanny could ever really hurt him or wish him harm. He knew … he remembered … how much she loved him. In fact, in the past two years, he had recognized the difference between the deep bond he had had with Fanny and the weak and insubstantial relationship he had with Bambi. Slowly but inexorably, before this nightmare began, he had made up his mind to return to Fanny. He had resolved to beg for her forgiveness, plead with her to absolve him for his foolish mistake, and allow him to return to her. Somehow, he hoped and prayed, their love for each other would be strong enough to re-unite them.

Carl's attorneys made it clear to him that it would cost him far more than he could possibly afford to mount a full-blown legal fight in this matter, with ink dating and paper analysis and the like. The attorneys also encouraged him to think of his future, of what it would take to find another job in the wake of a well-publicized trial. "Even if you win, you'll lose," they told him.

The attorneys' recommendations were hammered onto Carl like a water torture until he relented. In light of his cooperation and his *nolo contendere* plea, the judge sentenced Carl to no more than fifteen and no fewer than ten years in prison. It would be at least seven years before he might be eligible for release.

Bambi, to whom Carl had been married since his divorce from Fanny, sobbed at his sentencing and kept asking him what was to become of her. She said that she had no security, no future, except in her marriage to him. He had no answers for her.

When their small joint savings account was exhausted, Bambi sold what she could of their possessions and moved into a single room in a blighted area of Camden. Each evening, she puts on her high heels and mini-skirt and teases her graying blonde hair into a cascading bouffant. She trolls the bars of Camden or Philly, smiling hopefully, trying to look perky, and waiting — always waiting — for a sign of interest from a man — any man — when she says, "Hi. I'm Bambi."

Carl's life in prison revolves around his memories of Fanny. He retrieves and mentally caresses every memory that he can summon of Fanny and their life together. He repeats to himself the words and endearments that they said to each other, and he can almost feel the softness of her neck and shoulders, her arms and breasts, the downy velvet of her rose-touched cheeks and warm lips. He often visualizes their wedding day, as clearly as if it was yesterday, and he relishes the image of the blue nightgown that she wore on their wedding night, smiling at the memory of their shyness. He tries to remember the smells — the scent of the roses in their garden, the aroma of pot roast emanating from their kitchen, and the fragrance of the Shalimar that Fanny wore on special occasions. Carl writes a letter to Fanny every day, even though every one of them is returned to him unopened. In each letter, he declares his love for her, admits his folly in leaving her, and begs for her forgiveness. In some letters, he assures Fanny that he forgives her, too ... knowing that she will understand what he means. Carl waits for the day when he will be released and can plead his case with Fanny in person. He waits for a day that might come much sooner, when one of his letters might not come back — might actually be read by his beloved Fanny. And almost every night, as he falls asleep on the thin, narrow mattress in his prison cell, Carl's mind replays the words and the tune of "What a Difference a Day Makes."

Carl's imprisonment brought Fanny neither peace nor victory. She spent less and less time at Goodman's and more and more time in frozen isolation in her home, until she finally stopped going to Goodman's at all. Not even her books distract her or rescue her from the disquiet that permeates every cell of her body and every corner of her mind. Abe dutifully visits Fanny, but senses that even his presence and friendship can't reach beyond the walls behind which she seems to be confined. Hoping to turn her thoughts in another direction, Abe came to Fanny's home one evening and asked her to come with him to a special memorial service at the synagogue. "A remembrance," he said, "of those who perished in the Holocaust, those that you and I and so many others lost." Fanny stared at him for a long moment and then said, "There are many kinds of holocausts. There are some that are internal and invisible. And the ovens are not the only horrible way to perish." Then she turned away from Abe and resumed staring out the window, in the gathering darkness of her unlighted living room. Abe lowered his head sorrowfully, and that evening, left without saying good-bye.

A few nights later, Fanny tried to distract herself by reading one of the countless books she had brought home from the library. Her eyes locked on the author's words: *"It is perhaps the greatest tragedy that our sins and wrongdoings do not kill us. They may destroy us, but they do not kill us. Instead, we live on, in pain that is infinite, waiting to forgive or be forgiven, to forget or be forgotten. Waiting for release. Waiting for an absolution that never comes."* She read the lines again and again. The words seared into Fanny's soul. They burned into her brain. She couldn't forget them, just as she once couldn't forget the idea of creating false invoices and writing to Jonathan Butler. The words on the page, like the idea of punishing Carl, became Fanny's constant companion, her mind's refrain, her soul's focus. And so, living out the drama which she created, Fanny sits in her home and waits.

Three lives. Suspended in waiting. As if in mid-air. As if on a web. Waiting to forgive, waiting to forget. Waiting for release. Waiting for an absolution that never comes.

Part III
South Side School Days — A Memoir

This is the land of lost content,
I see it shining plain,
The happy highways where I went
And cannot come again.
A. E. Housman
A Shropshire Lad

In every adult there dwells the child that was,
And in every child there lies the adult that will be.
John Connally

CENTRAL SCHOOL

Most of us in the first wave of Baby Boomers were blessed with golden grade school years. Before computers, before violent video games, before political correctness, before drug dealers began hanging around playgrounds ... before the world changed, it was golden for many of us.

Central Elementary School on Vine Street in South Bethlehem was a gray stone fortress of a building, the kind that would have stood for half a millennium and to hell with any hurricanes or floods that came calling. Each morning around nine, scores of scrubbed youngsters converged on the school, all of them walking there from nearby homes and apartments. Children were brought to school in cars, to their great embarrassment, only if they were relegated to crutches or if a parent suspected that playing hooky was a possibility. If a car pulled up to the curb in front of the school while we were waiting outside, we stared at it, expecting a movie star or the President of the United States to emerge. If it was only a student with a broken leg we went back to our playing.

Girls, in those 1950s grade school days, wore cotton dresses with bows tied neatly in the back, or jumpers or skirts with blouses. Socks and shoes and the occasional hair ribbon completed the picture. Boys wore slacks with cotton shirts or sweaters. At Central, there was no sense of someone's clothing being better or more expensive than someone else's. Girls might admire a friend's dress, and a boy might think his buddy was lucky to have a really neat Phillies jacket, but the word "designer" was nowhere in our vocabulary and neither envy nor shame were anywhere in our hearts. In terms of time-frame and appearance, we were halfway between the Little Rascals and the Rolling Stones. Alfalfa and Jagger. We were the Shirleys and Stevies, the Billys and Bernadettes. We came after Etta and Asa and before Tiffany and Aiden.

"What are you?" was the immediate question when a newcomer came to school. By that, we meant are you Italian, German, Greek, Hungarian, or something else? And the kids always knew what they were, unto the fourth and, yea, even unto the fifth power. "I'm Italian and German on my mother's side and my father is Hungarian and Windish, but his mother was part Polish and *her* mother came from Scotland." We knew lineage the way we knew our addresses.

The sole exception to this seemed to be Robert Chevalier. Easygoing and friendly, Robert always wore a perfectly ironed shirt and a tie to school. He could have fit in with the denizens of Holy Infancy School and looked perfectly at home there. One day, when first-grade recess boredom triggered a round of 'what are you' questions, Robert said that he didn't know. Being both bossy and helpful, I told him he was French. He looked at me as if he had never heard the word. "What?" he asked. "You know, French," I replied. "From France. Someone in your family must have been from France because your name is French." "How do you know?" Robert asked, gazing at me with astonished admiration. "Haven't you ever seen Maurice Chevalier?" I asked, introducing the cultural theme. He shook his head. I had seen Maurice Chevalier on countless Sunday nights on the Ed Sullivan television show. I proceeded to describe him to Robert, mime his elegant way with a straw hat, and offered Robert several choruses of "Every leetle breeze seems to whispah Loueez" with the appropriate Gallic accent. Having completed my performance before the bell signaled the end to recess, I told Robert again that he was French and advised him not to forget it.

POWER

Miss Curry was our second-grade teacher, and at some point during our year in her class she became Mrs. Patelis. I knew that she was going to be married, because my parents were friends of hers and socialized with her. They always referred to her as Miss Curry or Mrs. Patelis in front of me, but I knew that they called her Peggy when they thought I wasn't listening. Whether she was Curry or Patelis, she was a very nice lady and a good teacher. She really seemed to encourage everyone in the class. She was quick to praise and congratulate students when they knew answers or did something well. If she ever criticized or corrected anyone, she did it gently and with an extra helping of encouragement. I liked Mrs. Patelis.

Pleasant as Mrs. Patelis was, she was still human and she had days when she was out of sorts with the world or with us. On one such day, she told us to work on our 'circus wagon project,' stay in our seats, and be quiet. Wow! Our circus wagons! My favorite project! I couldn't have been happier if it was Christmas morning. We had each made a paper circus wagon, with carefully cut-out slits in the sides, through which animals in the wagon could be seen, and with wheels that could actually move. We had finished our wagons a few days before and had just started to draw, cut out, and color the animals we would put inside our wagons. Mrs. Patelis had promised that when we were all finished with our wagons, they would be joined and displayed — like a real train of circus wagons — above the blackboards.

I zealously started drawing a giraffe for my wagon. When I finished with the drawing, I took the snub-ended little scissors that we were allowed to use and carefully cut out the long-necked creature. Next, I was ready to color it. I put a nice base of pale yellow all over the giraffe, but

I had no brown crayon with which to make its spots. I got up from my seat to go to the back of the classroom, to the ancient, brown wooden box that held an assortment of crayons, most of them worn down to one or two inches in size. As I tip-toed back to my desk, Mrs. Patelis looked up. "Carol! What are you doing out of your seat?" she demanded. I was startled by her tone. "I just needed a brown crayon for my giraffe," I whispered. "I only went to get a crayon and I didn't make any noise." Astonishingly, she was still angry. "I told you that I didn't want anyone out of their seats!" "I'm sorry," I murmured, "but I just needed to get a brown crayon." "Don't argue with me!" she barked. "I told you I didn't want anyone out of their seats." By now the other kids in the class were listening to us and not paying any attention to their circus animals. "I'm sorry," I said again, no longer whispering. "I needed a brown crayon and I didn't know how else to get one without making any noise." "Are you still going to argue with me?" she snapped. "I ordered all of you to be quiet and stay in your seats."

Something dawned in my six-year-old mind. I walked from my desk in the middle of the classroom to the front of the room. Clutching the little nub of brown crayon in my hand, I turned and faced the class. With the confident pride of new discovery, I serenely said, "You know, we don't have to do what she tells us. There are forty of us and only one of her. We don't *have* to do what she tells us." I looked over at Mrs. Patelis. At first, her expression was pure astonishment — her eyes were wide and her mouth was open. Slowly, amazingly, that mouth formed into a smile. She actually chuckled. And in a tone more like her usual self, she said, "You have your crayon, Carol. You may go back to your seat now." More with relief than triumph I sat back down and happily started putting spots on my giraffe. I looked up a few minutes later and saw Mrs. Patelis, chin in hand, staring at me and still smiling. I smiled back and gave her a wave.

A few days later, my parents asked me what happened in class with the brown crayon. From the way they asked, I knew that they had already heard about it from Mrs. Patelis. I told them — I guess they wanted to hear my version — and they didn't scold me. "What did she say?" I asked them. They exchanged glances. Mom answered. "She said she hopes she lives long enough to see what you're going to do in the world." Then I smiled. Just like Mrs. Patelis.

NEW WORLDS

*I*n elementary school, kids usually stayed with their classmates at recess and before and after school. There wasn't much mixing between grades unless you happened to personally know someone in one of the other grades.

Sometimes, a tall girl from Central walked in the same direction I did when I walked home from school. But she was in sixth grade and I was in second grade, so I knew better than to talk to her or try to walk with her.

One day, as I walked up Morton Street, the girl came out of the candy shop near Morton and Vine as I was walking by. "Where do you live?" she asked, as we walked in the same direction. (It was fine for an older kid to talk to a younger one, but not the other way around.)

"Fillmore Street," I said. "Do you live near there?"

"Kind of," she replied. "I live on Webster Street. My name is Marilyn."

"My name is Carol," I said, still somewhat surprised that a sixth grader would talk to me.

We talked about school and about some of the teachers and soon we were at the corner of Webster and Morton.

"I live there," Marilyn told me, pointing up the street, "in the house across from the synagogue."

"The what?"

"The synagogue. My father is the rabbi for the synagogue. We're Jewish."

"What's that?" I asked. I had heard the word in Sunday School, but we hadn't been taught the actual meaning of "Jewish." We were probably still at the Jesus-in-the-manger stage.

"It's a religion," Marilyn said patiently, apparently having made the explanation before. "Just as there is the Christian religion, and other religions, there is the Jewish religion. It's really called Judaism."

"I'm a Christian," I hurriedly told her, "and I'm Lutheran. I go to St. John's Windish Lutheran Church, and sometimes we go to the Moravian Church up there," I said, pointing to the corner of Webster and Packer Avenue, where First Moravian Church was located, "because my Daddy is Moravian, so I guess I'm half Lutheran and half Moravian." Suddenly I felt almost exotic, and I was anxious for Marilyn to know that I had religious connections, too.

"We don't believe in Jesus," Marilyn continued. "We don't believe that he was the Messiah, and that's the big difference between your religion and ours. But Jesus was a Jew, so we're connected in some ways."

I thought Marilyn must be the smartest girl — besides Jackie Ruyak and Nancy Iampietro—in the whole school.

"Your church has pretty glass windows, just like our church," I said.

"Do you want to see the synagogue?" Marilyn asked.

"Sure."

Marilyn went her to house and opened the front door. In a few minutes she came out, followed by a man wearing a small black cap on his head. She introduced me to him and told me that this was her father, the rabbi of the synagogue. He smiled pleasantly and said that he was pleased to meet me. I could detect his accent as he gave a heavy 'k' sound to the 'C' in Carol and rolled the 'r' in my name, as so many older immigrants did.

"So you want to see our synagogue?" he asked, smiling as he led us in the direction of the beige-sided structure.

"Yes, sir," I replied, sensing that calling him 'sir' was proper as well as natural.

He opened the doors of the building and led us inside. Afternoon sunlight streamed through the stained-glass windows, in which bright red and cobalt blue colors predominated. He explained the design of the altar area and spoke about the Torah. He talked about the exiles of the Jewish people and he talked about Moses.

"I know about Moses!" I piped up. "He was put in a basket and left in the water so he'd be safe." I was glad I could show that I knew at least something.

"That's right," said Marilyn's father. "And he grew up to be strong and great. He led his people, our Jewish people, through the desert and away from their bondage in Egypt."

I was fascinated by the stories he told and the word-pictures he painted.

"Our two religions get along, don't they?" I asked, in innocence.

"Oh, child," he responded, stroking my hair. "In a better world ... maybe the world you will live in and my Marilyn will live in ... maybe in that world. But for many years and centuries people of different religions have not gotten along, and many have done horrible things in the name of God. Wars have even been fought in the name of God — fought between men who said they were religious."

Somehow sure that he wouldn't mind, I asked where he was from.

"Germany," he replied. "And my wife was born in Poland. We lived in Germany for many years. But our Jewish religion was not tolerated there and so we came to America. Our country was one place where people did terrible things."

I wasn't sure that I understood everything that he was saying, but I told him that I was glad he was in America and in Bethlehem, and I told him that I liked his synagogue very much. He smiled again and said that he hoped I would visit their house anytime.

I told Marilyn that it was nice to meet her and her father, and that I was glad she talked to me even though I was only in second grade.

"Thank you for talking to me," Marilyn said, suddenly growing serious and somehow sad. "You know, not everyone wants to be friends with someone who is Jewish. There are some students in my class who don't want to be friends with me."

I knew she must be telling the truth, but I couldn't imagine why something like a different religion would keep people from being friends with each other.

"I'll always talk to you," I promised Marilyn. "I think you're very smart and very nice, and you can talk to me anytime or walk home with me anytime. You can even play with me and my friends at recess if you want."

Marilyn thanked me and went into her house, while I walked back to Morton Street to complete the trek home. My mind was full of so many things as I walked from Webster Street to Taylor Street, then Taylor to Polk and Polk to Fillmore. The blocks almost seemed to divide according to the thoughts swirling in my mind — people who don't believe in Jesus, Moses leading his people, people doing bad things in the name of God, kids not liking Marilyn because she's Jewish. So many big things to think about!

When I got home and plunked my books and tablet on the kitchen table, Mom asked "How was school today?" Excitedly and in a run-on stream of words, I told her that I had a new friend named Marilyn and she's in sixth grade and she's smart and nice and we walked home together and she introduced me to her father and they live on Webster Street and he's a rabbi and they're Jewish and Jewish people don't believe that Jesus is God and her father took me into their church that they call a synagogue and it's as beautiful as our church and he told me about Moses and the Torah and he's from Germany and they did bad things to Jewish people in Germany and ....

While I was rambling on and on, with Mom listening patiently, obviously a little surprised at the extent of my after-school adventure, Dad came home from work. As always, he grinned, lifted me high, gave me a bear hug, and asked "What did you learn today?" I finally stopped prattling and sat down at the kitchen table and thought seriously for a moment. Then I said, "I learned that you don't learn everything in school." Then I told him about Marilyn and her father and how a rabbi is a Jewish minister and a synagogue is a Jewish church and how some people do bad things in the name of God ....

TAKING COVER

Occasionally we would be taken from our classrooms, single file, and marched to a large assembly room on Central School's third floor. There, we would be shown grainy black and white films warning us of the Communist peril — a peril shown as red arrows sweeping across Europe. We were dutifully warned that the Red Menace was waiting to take over the United States and the world. As a more practical step, we would participate in periodic air-raid drills. With an almost casual air, teachers told us that if the Soviet Union attacked the United States, "Bethlehem will certainly be one of the first places to be bombed because we are the home of Bethlehem Steel. They will bomb New York City, Washington, D.C., and Bethlehem." We felt something akin to pride to be included in the big three, and after a few such pronouncements, an aura of inevitability settled on the students. I don't recall anyone, not even the wimpiest of the boys or the prissiest of the girls, ever crying or fretting when this pronouncement was made. No one seemed to lose any sleep over knowing that Bethlehem had a virtual bull's eye painted on it.

There were two categories of air-raid drill. The first, something of a mini-drill, involved remaining in our classrooms and shoving as much of ourselves as we could under our desks. These were the old metal desks with attached seats — the kind with wooden tops that flipped up, revealing a deep metal storage area where books, tablets, and other necessities could be kept. The desk tops were invariably carved with several decades' worth of names, declarations of love, and the occasional announcement that "Mrs. Gorbush stinks." The round holes in the upper right hand corner of the desks were mute reminders of ink wells that had long since disappeared. Books and school supplies not currently being used were expected to be put away in your desk. When a mini air-raid drill was called, all desks were cleared and we scrunched ourselves under the metal desks as best we could. That became more difficult as we grew taller and bigger, but we did our best. These drills were always blessedly brief.

The more dramatic air-raid drill involved all classes filing, quietly and in good order, to the cavernous and stony basement of the building, where stone-sided tunnels arched off in various directions from the central lavatory area under the stairs. A few light bulbs illuminated the tunnels, and when the teachers decided that we were in the right place, they told us to crouch down on the floor. Girls had to make sure that their dresses or skirts covered their backsides so that they wouldn't be sitting directly on the cold concrete. Next, we were told to pull our knees up to our chests, put our heads down onto our knees, and fold our hands over the back of our necks. All easy maneuvers for wiry little kids. The boys usually sat along one wall of the tunnel and the girls along the opposite wall.

During one such drill in third grade, the boys who were crouched down opposite to us seemed to be collapsing. Their heads slid down from their knees and came perilously close to touching the floor. Mikey made no attempt to be subtle and basically curled up on his side on the floor, staring intently ahead at the white cotton panties that could almost be seen behind Sharon's rigidly straight legs. I nudged Sharon. She instantly sacrificed the safety of her neck in order to place a protective hand over her crotch. When the teacher walked by, her hands returned to their place behind her neck. Sharon and I both saw other boys half sliding, half lounging on the concrete floor. We directed nudges up and down the row of crouching girls. Silently, adjustments in hand placement were made. A year or so earlier, my grandmother, who wore the prospect of calamity like a favorite shawl, cautioned me furtively and without explanation to "never let a boy touch you down there." At the time, I wondered why any boy would want to, but Gram closed the subject as suddenly as she had opened it and I didn't ask her any questions. I assumed that looking "down there" was as unacceptable as touching, so I spread my hands out defensively like fans. An ant on the concrete couldn't have seen my panties.

When the air-raid drill ended, Sharon and I confronted Mikey at recess. We poked him in his bony chest and pushed him up against the chain link fence encircling the school yard. He said that a boy in the sixth grade had sent the word down that if the boys positioned themselves a certain way they "could see something." It was instantly clear that the sophisticated boulevardier of the sixth grade might have known what he was seeking, but the boys in the third grade had no idea what they were looking for. Tommy had a fleeting hope that he might find the baseball mitt he had lost, and Mikey was hoping something would appear that would make his contortions worthwhile. But all he saw were glimpses of white cotton. Disappointment reigned in the tunnels that day. By the time the next air-raid drill was called, we forgot about covering our panties and the boys forgot to look.

MRS. DELIO

Mrs. DeLio was our third-grade teacher. Rumor had it that she once taught sixth grade but had been moved to third grade and considered that to be a demotion. Whatever the reason, she was curt, moody, strict, and volatile. You never knew what would please her or what would set her off.

Mrs. DeLio played a major role with May Days; she chose the May Queen. And she made certain that the May Queen was always Italian and Catholic. There might be pretty Irish girls in the sixth grade, smart Greek girls, polished and poised German girls, even a comely assortment of Catholic girls from the Hungarian, Windish, and Polish churches. None of them mattered. The May Queen of Central School would be Italian and Catholic — the critical combination — for as long as Mrs. DeLio drew breath. In our class, Bernadette had that magic combination, in addition to being vivacious and pretty. Her future as May Queen might just as well have been written into her baptismal book. I don't know what Mrs. DeLio would have done if there had been several Italian Catholic girls in a class. Most likely she would have created multiple titles (May Queen, May Empress, May Sovereign) or used her powers to keep some of the girls back a grade so as to spread the wealth.

I was unacceptable to Mrs. DeLio for three key reasons: I was not Italian; I was not Catholic; and I was not quietly compliant. Sometimes, when she looked at me, I could almost hear her wondering how so handicapped a creature could survive in the world. But she could not deny the fact that I was smart. I could also draw well and write well, and I got along with my classmates. All of this grated on Mrs. DeLio. Whenever something went wrong in class — if something was misplaced or a noise was made — she automatically turned to me. If she couldn't find the real culprit, I would do. My third-grade report cards were uniform: an A or B in almost every subject and a bold, red U (Unsatisfactory) in Conduct. Every few weeks she found some reason to send me to the principal's office. Most kids never saw the inside of that office. I had my own chair there. Mr. Russell Bleiler, the principal, understood the situation but evidently picked his battles with Mrs. DeLio. He apparently saw no reason to challenge her when he and I had made peace with my being periodically exiled to his office. I enjoyed my time there (I was away from Mrs. DeLio) and I didn't disturb him. We even had some pleasant chats about my interests and the subjects we were studying. All in all, an agreeable arrangement. I liked Mr. Bleiler.

One day in Mrs. DeLio's class, I turned to the girl sitting behind me to ask for an eraser. It was enough. Mrs. DeLio slammed a book down on her desk and screamed "Qui-*et!*" As my punishment, she ordered me to move to the small desk placed next to hers. I did so, knowing that the class saw her for what she was and felt only sympathy for me. Next to her desk I remained, with the unanticipated result that I had welcome peace and quiet in which to do my work. She suffered the unintended consequence of no longer being able to blame me for whatever went wrong in the class. I was happy; she was frustrated. Hardly her intention. A few weeks after my migration, Parent-Teacher Night arrived. My parents came to the school and entered the third-grade classroom with me. Mrs. DeLio had placed placards with all of the students' names on their desks, and my name card was on my old desk, in its regular place in the classroom. When Mrs. DeLio came over to us, all cloying smiles and sweetness, I announced to my parents that, "I don't sit here. I sit over there, next to her desk. She put me there after I asked for an eraser." Mrs. DeLio's jaw dropped and she turned tomato red. I picked up the placard and walked over to the desk next to hers. My parents and Mrs. DeLio followed. It didn't help that she had to tell them that I was currently getting an A in each of my subjects. She suggested that I could improve my attitude a bit, and my parents nodded politely. They weren't buying it and she knew it. The next day, I was moved permanently back to my regular desk in the classroom.

From my earliest years, I loved to draw and had some natural abilities for drawing and art work. At Central School, I was sometimes asked to go to the blackboard and draw whatever visuals we were studying. I drew African and Caribbean villages (palm trees a specialty), Spanish galleons, birds, blast furnaces, Pilgrims, and horses. I loved doing the drawings and the class seemed to enjoy watching them emerge on the blackboard. Other kids in the class had their wonderful gifts: they could sing, play piano, tap dance, or hit a baseball over the fence. I had my skill: I could draw.

One day, Mrs. DeLio seemed especially irritated and touchy. She snapped at everyone. Finally, she decided to keep us quiet by giving us an art project. She handed out sheets of drawing paper and told us to draw an American Indian. At the blackboard, she carefully drew an oval for the Indian's head, a horizontal oval for his neck, elongated ovals for the upper arms, smaller ovals for the forearms, an oval for the chest and so on. By then I was happily drawing away. My Indian looked terrific. He had high cheekbones, a headdress, a leather vest and a spear. He was tanned and strong looking. When Mrs. DeLio passed my desk, she demanded to know why I had not drawn my Indian in the way she had shown: with ovals for body sections. "I've drawn a nice Indian," I replied. "But you didn't draw him the way I wanted you to draw him," she shouted. "Your Indian does not look the way I want him to!" Now she was in my area of aptitude. "Your Indian has a circle for a head and a circle for a neck and circles for arms and hands," I told her, "and no one has circles like that for body parts. My Indian looks like a real person." By now the class was looking at us instead of at their drawings. I didn't care. I got up from my desk, taking my drawing with me. "Where are you going?" Mrs. DeLio demanded. "To the principal's office," I said. "That's probably where you were going to send me anyway."

Through the classroom door I went. I climbed the wide wooden stairs to the second floor and knocked at Mr. Bleiler's office. His secretary said, "Come in." As soon as I entered his office, I headed for Mr. Bleiler's desk. "Look at my Indian," I said. "Mrs. DeLio yelled at me because I didn't draw him the way she drew her Indian. But my Indian looks like a real Indian. Hers is a bunch of circles and no person looks like a bunch of circles. All

I did was draw a nice Indian and she yelled at me. Which do you think looks more like an Indian? Mine or something that's all circles?" For the first time in my many trips to his office I was genuinely upset, and Mr. Bleiler could see my exasperation and resentment as well as my trembling chin and the tears forming in my eyes. He took my drawing, looked at it carefully, and said, "This is very good, Carol. You draw very well and you've drawn a fine Indian." I thanked him, still trembling with hurt and indignation. He stood up and came around the desk. He reached down, gave me his handkerchief and a hug, and said, "Why don't you just stay here for a while and draw some more. Draw anything you want." His secretary, smiling, gave me some sheets of paper and a pencil and told me to sit on the red leather sofa under the wide windows in the office. I wiped my tears with the handkerchief and settled myself on the large sofa — with my legs sticking straight out because they were too short to touch the floor. I put the papers on my lap and began drawing with the pencil. Mr. Bleiler patted my head, seemed to chuckle a bit, and then turned to his secretary. "Tell Mrs. DeLio to come to my office after school today." I never had trouble with Mrs. DeLio again.

NO GOOD DEED

Springtime at Central School brought two special events: May Day and the Ice Cream Festival. Of the two, May Day was the most important, but the Ice Cream Festival was the most fun.

For the six years of my elementary school stint, my Dad and another father, Mr. Kienzle from Webster Street, manned the soda stand at the Ice Cream Festival. Mom helped with the cake walk. I made repeated trips to the "fishing booth," which was a crudely constructed three-sided cardboard box set on top of a table. Behind the box sat Mr. Zsilavecz, my friend Sheila's father, who attached small toys to the fishing lines kids cast over the top of the box. It must be a measure of my joyful nature – or my stupidity — that I squealed with delight every time I caught a toy on my line. I'd run off to show Mom or Dad my catch and get another penny or two to fish again. I could have done that for days on end. I think I was in fourth grade before I figured out that I wasn't catching anything and Mr. Zsilavecz was tying toys to all of our fishing lines.

May Day was much more complicated. It involved having every grade learn and perform a dance, with every grade taking its turn doing a dance around the maypole, weaving intricate designs around the pole with long streams of brightly colored crepe paper. By the time we were in fifth or sixth grade, the dances were more complicated and our weaving around the maypole was more elaborate. Classes practiced their dances for weeks on end, usually with little evidence of progress. It seemed to me, early on, that the Sunday School admonition to have "faith the size of a mustard seed" was nothing compared to the faith of teachers who thought they could coax a credible performance from forty or fifty youngsters who were distracted, uncoordinated, uninterested, and incapable of remembering their dance steps.

May Day in the fifth grade taught me one of life's unavoidable lessons: No good deed goes unpunished. For five years, I had dutifully sent penny valentines to all of my classmates. Each year, in early February, a foil-covered Valentine's Day box, decorated with red construction paper hearts, would appear in every classroom. Kids would drop their penny valentines into the box. Penny valentines were sold by the box or bag, and they probably cost less than a penny each. They were small, brightly colored, one-sided cards that featured such zowie illustrations as a duck holding a heart and saying, "Valentine, you quack me up!" Most kids filled out valentines for all of their classmates, scrawling the recipient's name in pencil on the little white envelope, and most would sign their names to the cards, with some turning shy and simply signing, 'Your Valentine.' The unspoken hope was that on February 14th, you'd get a valentine from everyone in the class, with exceptions made for kids who might be too poor to afford the valentines. I filled out cards for everyone, even Lenny Houser. Lenny was stocky, quiet, wore horn-rimmed glasses, had thick, dark hair, and kept to himself. No one bothered much with Lenny because he picked his nose. At recess, kids kicked at the balls Lenny threw to them rather than catch the balls. I didn't want to get near Lenny, but I felt sorry for him and always sent him a valentine. Five years. Five valentines.

For our fifth-grade May Day dance, I was assigned Lenny as my dance partner. Lenny! I would have to hold hands with Booger himself. It was unthinkable. So this is what I get for being nice to him. Fate could not have smacked me with a bigger custard pie. I asked the teacher for another partner. In the absence of an actual allergy to Lenny, I had no case. "Yeeeeeewwww!" exclaimed Sheila and Bernadette and Nancy, grateful that they had been paired up with non-boogery boys. At our first rehearsal in the schoolyard, I held a pencil in my hand and made Lenny hold onto the other end of the pencil. The teacher never noticed. By the second rehearsal, she told me to lose the pencil and I held Lenny's hand through the pocket of my dress. In all of this, Lenny was mutely compliant. Then the light dawned — an idea!

I arrived at rehearsal number three with a pair of white gloves. I told the teacher that I wanted to wear gloves on May Day and I was getting used to them. She looked puzzled but was soon re-focused on thirty-nine other rambunctious kids. I told Sheila and Bernadette that I wanted to look like Audrey Hepburn. They bought it. For the entire month of May Day practices, I wore my white Audrey Hepburn gloves. On May Day itself, Sheila, Bernadette, Anna, Nancy, and Donna also showed up with white gloves. We looked like pint-sized debutantes. I never forgot the lesson of Lenny Houser: No good deed goes unpunished.

"BLUCK, BLUCK, BLUCK, BLUCK, BLUCK"

Bullying is not a humorous matter, and I'm sure that most children who are bullied experience real trauma from it. I also suspect that bullying — in delivery if not in intent — has become more vicious in recent decades. Social media devices have apparently raised humiliation to an art form. Things were simpler in the 1950s. Then, it was often a matter of simple teasing ... and simple solutions.

With the last name of Henn, I suppose it was inevitable that I would be the object of occasional chicken jokes and nicknames. There was the occasional Henny Penny, but for the most part, I had little teasing and I usually just laughed with whoever was trying to be funny. Except for Tommy Dolan. Except for his "bluck, bluck, bluck, bluck." Tommy had what must have been a God-given gift for making sounds like a chicken. His "bluck, bluck, bluck, bluck" sounded as if it came straight from the barnyard. Loud and high pitched, his voice was one that anyone within a half-mile could hear, and they would know who he was tormenting. Usually, I just told him to knock it off and then waited until his attention wandered to some other target or object of interest.

One day, I was walking to Central School with my friend Christina. We were walking on Packer Avenue, a broad tree-lined street bordered by Lehigh University on one side and by neat brick houses, the Windish Hall, and First Moravian Church on the other side. Soon, from somewhere behind me, I heard the familiar screech of "bluck, bluck, bluck." Tommy was walking behind us with some of his buddies and he was giving a bravura performance.

"Please stop it," I told him. "I just don't think it's funny and I wish you wouldn't do that anymore." He took it up an octave. "Bluck, bluck, bluck, bluck, bluck!" he screeched, even louder. "Stop it!" I shouted. "I mean it. Stop it!" He laughed and added chicken-wing motions to his performance. That was it. That was enough. For some reason, that day in the sixth grade was my breaking point.

I stopped in my tracks and put my tablet and books down carefully at the base of a tall maple tree. Next, I took off my shoulder bag, worn, as required by my mother, cross-body so I wouldn't lose it. The purse was placed on top of the books. I turned around and walked toward Tommy and his friends. Not the brightest kid in the class, Tommy lacked the perception to see whatever glint was in my eye. His friends were sharper, and they scattered backwards and sideways away from him. With the innocence of ignorance, Tommy continued with his blucking and wing flapping. He never saw the punch coming. I grabbed him by the front of his shirt with my left hand and yanked him toward me. With vague images from the *Gillette Friday Night Fights* racing through my mind, I pulled my right arm back, my hand tightly balled into a fist, and did the best imitation of Rocky Marciano that I could manage. My fist landed solidly on his nose and sent blood flying everywhere. The punch also sent Tommy airborne and into a spread-eagle landing on his fanny. With my hands still curled into fists, I stood over him and said, "Don't you ever say 'bluck' again." Then I walked back to the tree, calmly picked up my purse, put it over my shoulder and adjusted it properly, then picked up my books and tablet and walked toward Christina. She was still staring, wide-eyed and open-mouthed, at Tommy.

Things were simpler then.

BROUGHAL JUNIOR HIGH

Before the powers-that-be re-named them as "middle schools," schools like Broughal were called junior high schools — in some ways, a more accurate name. Junior high schools were a pre-high school but clearly post-grade school experience, and they encompassed seventh, eighth, and ninth grades. We attended junior high from roughly the age of twelve (or eleven, if you started first grade at age five) to age thirteen or fourteen. This transition into the teenage years was made bearable by the fact that everyone else around you was going through the same angst and confusion, and there was an unspoken understanding that we would tolerate almost any behavior from each other as we navigated our way through adolescence.

James Collins was our seventh-grade homeroom, geography, and world affairs teacher. He was the first male teacher we'd ever had and he seemed to bring — and require — a new level of respect and seriousness in the classroom. The first thing that amazed and impressed me about Mr. Collins was his easy and flawless pronunciation of Russian and Eastern European names that seemed to be comprised of all consonants and no vowels. He had obviously worked at knowing and being at ease with names such as Krasnoyarsk, Vladivostok, Khabarovsk, Novosibirsk, Kosygin, and Khrushchev. This mastery seemed to reflect a respect for his students as well as his subjects.

Mr. Collins expected serious effort and good work from his students, but he had a sense of humor and the ability to laugh with us and connect with us. Sometime in the middle of seventh grade, he decided that we would put on a play that linked world affairs, the environment, and geography. He cast me as Mother Earth. I remember little about the play, but I remember the unmistakable thrill of being on Broughal's huge, wonderful stage. Before my turn as Mother Earth, I had only had two brushes with performing: once as Mary in the Sunday School Christmas pageant (when the only emoting I did was to make faces at my friend Sheila who was portraying the angel Gabriel), and my brief radio career at age three. The latter was an example of pure serendipity.

A few blocks away from our house on Fillmore Street was a steak sandwich shop called Freddy's, near the corner of Polk and East Fourth Streets. Freddy and his wife, Miriam, ran the shop but also had a country and western band, Freddy and the Range Riders. The band appeared on local radio every Saturday. One day, when I was about three, Dad took me down to Freddy's to get steak sandwiches to take home. I wore my cowgirl outfit — a white blouse, a burgundy vest with white fringes, a burgundy skirt trimmed with white fringe, and white cowgirl boots and a white cowboy hat. At about two and half feet in height, I must have been quite a sight. This was in the brief period when I wanted to be a cowgirl. I loved my cowgirl outfit and would have worn it every day if I could.

On this particular day, Freddy shared my enthusiasm for my outfit. And he had an idea. Freddy and the Range Riders had a female vocalist — Miriam — and plenty of musicians with neckerchiefs and cowboy hats, but they didn't have a child as part of the entourage. I don't know how easily or reluctantly my parents agreed to the idea, but a few Saturdays later Dad was taking me to the radio station, all dressed up in my little cowgirl clothes, to appear with Freddy and the Range Riders. My part in the show was fun if unremarkable. I'm not sure I was old enough to even understand what it meant to be on the radio. Freddy would hoist me up to the microphone and introduce me as The Littlest Cowgirl and I'd lean into the mike and say, "Howdy, pardners!" Then the Range Riders would play on their guitars and fiddles and such, and Freddy and Miriam would lead in the singing of "Home on the Range." Almost every week we also sang "Red River Valley," "I'm An Old Cowhand," "Ghost Riders in the Sky," "Tumblin' Tumbleweeds," "Happy Trails to You," "Yellow Rose of Texas," and other western standards. I'm not sure how long my stint on the radio lasted, but I enjoyed going to the station on Saturdays and being part of the excitement of doing the show. I shouldn't have been surprised that playing Mother Earth brought long-dormant yearnings to the surface. There was a performer somewhere in me. Stage or soundtrack, pulpit or podium, I loved performing.

Mother Earth was followed by plays and comedy sketches in various follies-type shows at Broughal. Frank Ofchus, an English teacher who also served as the drama director, allowed me to be in several plays. He also taught me to PROJECT my voice. To this day I can whisper on a stage and have it be heard in the balcony. Thank you, Mr. Ofchus. I could add nothing to the wonderful musicals presented by the students with real talents for singing and playing instruments. Even now, my friend Sheila's beautiful voice can give me goose bumps. Carlton Weaver, the school district's music director, enlisted me to be the announcer at several musical productions and that was fine with me. I was happy to be part of the presentation, even though I had nothing resembling the talents of the student singers and instrumentalists. But I was really in my element when we had variety shows with comedy sketches. I discovered the addictive rush that all comedians know: the sound of laughter in response to what you are saying or doing. Laughter! There could be no better feeling than making people laugh. Once again, my focus on being a fashion designer was de-railed, this time by the determination to become an actress and a comedienne. My parents were patient with this ambition until I announced that I saw no reason to go to high school and preferred to move to Greenwich Village immediately. That got their attention. It also put my Thespian ambitions on ice.

One day as we sat at our tables in Mr. Collins's homeroom, Marvin Reffert, who sat across from me, motioned for me to duck under the table so he could tell me something. What he told me was, "I really want to grab your boobs." I was so shocked that I banged my head hard on the underside of the table in my rush to get away from him. "Are you crazy?" I finally screeched at him when we were topside again. "How dare you say something like that?!" He gave me a leering grin and said, "Someday you're gonna want me to." "Never in a million, billion years!" I assured him. Marvin was one of the kids who were bused in to Broughal from Freemansburg, and for a while I attributed his sins to the fact that he wasn't from the South Side like the rest of us. I was sure that no South

Side boy — not Michael nor Robert, not Alan nor Francis nor Wayne, not even Tommy — *no* South Side guy would ever be so crude. Little did I know that Marvin's leering was an introduction to subject matter awaiting us in the eighth grade.

THE BIRDS AND THE BEES AND BELLYBUTTONS

*I*n junior high, all of our classes were co-ed, with one exception: eighth-grade Health and Hygiene. That class, invariably taught by the gym teachers, required the boys to be in one classroom and the girls in another. Those classrooms were actually widely separated in the building, as if to protect one gender from overhearing whatever was being said in the other gender's classroom.

After reviewing the rudimentary requirements of hygiene — regular brushing of teeth and laundering of undies in hot water — we moved into the materials concerning reproduction. I don't think our teacher, Miss Courtwright, looked anyone in the eye for the entire span of our education in reproduction. She tended to lower her voice and mumble a bit when she got around to specifics, but she drew very nice sperm on the blackboard — they looked like balloons with wiggly tails. They looked like parts of Mrs. DiLeo's Indian. Miss Courtwright's reticence and embarrassment seemed natural at the time. Many years later, when I worked at Moravian College, an older colleague of mine who attended Moravian in the late 1930s told me that female students routinely passed out in class when Dr. Katherine Miller, the biology teacher, described in detail what happened to cause conception. "They dropped like flies," she told me. "Dr. Miller would call for assistance, and several students from other classes would come over and carry the collapsed girls out, like so many corpses." All things considered, feminine sensibilities must have progressed nicely from the late 1930s to the late 1950s; no one passed out in Miss Courtwright's class.

If anyone in the seventh or eighth grade actually knew how reproduction worked, he or she was keeping quiet about it. Even the kids who had younger brothers and sisters, and who had seen their mothers' bellies swell before the baby's arrival and shrink afterward, seemed only to know that the baby came from somewhere inside there. How it got there was another and unknown matter. I thought that I had at least part of it figured out. I guessed that some kind of coupling between a man and a woman was involved, and Sherlock-like, had deduced that some type of insertion had to happen. Because babies grew inside the mom's belly, I had figured out that whatever was being inserted had to go into the bellybutton. To my eleven-year-old mind, it was the only logical port of entry. I was quite proud of myself to have figured that much out on my own. It also made sense because bikinis — made famous at the time by French actress Bridget Bardot — seemed to come in two versions: the kind with panty-like bottoms that covered the whole tummy and the kind with skimpy bottoms, tied on the side, which showed the bellybutton. Good girls like Doris Day and Annette Funicello wore the full-brief bottoms; vixens like Bardot wore the kind that showed the bellybutton. It all seemed so clear to me. The bellybutton was clearly an erotic and off-limits part of the body, befitting its role in reproduction. When I finally learned The Truth, I actually didn't believe it for several weeks. The bellybutton made so much more sense.

We were each given small, illustrated booklets to guide our studies in Health and Hygiene. The booklets enabled Miss Courtwright to refer to "page 17" instead of having to actually explain too much. The booklets were a nice mix of biological drawings of ovaries and Fallopian tubes and illustrations of girls in fancy dresses with crinolines. The booklet I remember best had photos of actress Sandra Dee telling us about her grooming routines and offering suggestions about clothes and hairstyles. I actually still adhere to two of her suggestions from that booklet: I use a separate washcloth for my face and I never put anything that needs to be mended into the closet before that mending is done. Fifty years later, I'm still following advice from Gidget.

In some ways, I was a little ahead of Miss Courtwright, although I certainly didn't know the details of copulation or the names of body parts. I'm not certain of exactly when I began to notice boys as other than classmates or pals in the neighborhood, but I distinctly remember how I knew things had changed.

In the early 1950s, we got our first television. We were one of the first households in the area to have cable TV. It seemed that everyone with a television had an antenna, and that was something my grandmother would not permit on her roof. So my father signed on for this new-fangled way of getting TV reception: cable TV. Although the television screen was small, the ability to see films in your own living room was mesmerizing. Frankie from next door and Glenny and Butchy from across the street came over to our house and we sprawled on the floor in front of the TV to watch *Davy Crockett* with Fess Parker and Buddy Ebsen.

Friday nights were the best TV nights. At 7:30, I'd watch *Wyatt Earp* with Hugh O'Brian, and at 9:00 Dad and I would watch the *Gillette Friday Night Fights*. For a long while, I thought about becoming a U.S. Marshal, just like Wyatt Earp. Until then I had wanted to be a fashion designer, but something about getting rid of the bad guys spoke to my child's depths. When *Sea Hunt*, with Lloyd Bridges as scuba diver Mike Nelson, debuted at 7:00 on Friday nights ... I was genuinely torn. I really, really, really wanted to be a scuba diver, too. I wanted to breathe underwater from a tank and see fish and kelp and coral. Blessedly, that was one dream I would fulfill and enjoy many years later.

Then, unexpectedly and almost imperceptibly, I noticed that my feelings were changing. I no longer wanted to be Wyatt Earp. I wanted to be Wyatt Earp's girlfriend. When I looked at Hugh O'Brian, I no longer saw him as a U.S. Marshal, I saw him as a very desirable male. I didn't know if it was the black hat or the brocade vest or the handsome face. I only knew that the sight of Wyatt Earp triggered reactions in me that I had never felt before — reactions I could actually feel in my body. I was eleven or twelve and I had the hots for Hugh O'Brian. For a while I wasn't sure I liked these new feelings and urges. Even at that tender age, I understood the odds against my ever meeting Hugh O'Brian, and I wasn't sure I wanted to be in love with someone I'd never meet. Not to worry. A few months later, as I watched the *Gillette Friday Night Fights* with Dad, I noticed that Swedish boxer Ingemar Johansson was really very good-looking. Wisely, I said nothing to Dad. For a while it was a tight race between Johansson and O'Brian for my affections. Eventually, I stayed true to Hugh. But I had come to understand that this was more about my changing feelings than it was about whatever male happened to catch my fancy at the time. I was growing up. For the first time in my life, as the next year came around, I realized that I was getting older, and not just in the sense of moving from one grade to the next or needing a larger shoe size. I was growing up. I was changing. Life was changing. We were all changing. It was the exact right time for Miss Courtwright to draw the sperm on the blackboard and guide us through the booklets. I don't know how the school district knew that this was the right time, but it was.

JANICE

*I*n the wonderful mix of personalities and perspectives that was our little community at Broughal, one person seemed distinct, and not just in our class. Janice was, hands-down, the prettiest girl in the school, probably in the whole city. She also had a mature sophistication that the rest of us could only dream of. At age thirteen she looked as though she was eighteen or twenty. She had a natural prettiness and a personality to match. She could have walked the halls of Liberty High School and passed for a student there; heck, she could have strolled onto a college campus and no one would have questioned her being there.

Janice wore make-up and she wore it flawlessly. A touch of lipstick and mascara simply heightened the prettiness nature had already given her. She had a Barbie-doll figure and a model's carriage, and I was not surprised that, when she started to date, she dated high school boys — including one from a posh private school.

Janice and I had gone to different grade schools, but we became friends at Broughal. We talked and laughed and shared the silly secrets that adolescent girls have. One day, I happened to go to the Girls Room (lavatory) when Janice was there. She was re-applying her lipstick and took the tube from a small, cloth cosmetics bag. I watched her with fascinated concentration. Janice was as intuitive as she was pretty. She looked at me in the mirror and asked, "Want to use my lipstick?" I nodded mutely. I touched the colored tube to my lips and applied it carefully. Suddenly I didn't feel quite as ugly-duckling as I usually did. Somehow, Janice knew. Somehow, she had guessed at how I felt. "You can borrow anything from me anytime," she said. "My Mom doesn't let me wear make-up," I confessed to her, as though she hadn't already guessed that fact. "I know," she said, "and that's okay. But you can use any of my make-up anytime you want." Thus began my external transformation.

If Janice was the prettiest girl in the school, I was surely the homeliest. I had problem skin, unruly brown hair that curled and waved too much when straight hair was the style, and — to top it all off — eyeglasses with aluminum frames that were only seen on old ladies with bad taste. ("They're sturdy," my parents had said, "and they'll last a long time.") Add a crook to my nose and a hump on my back and I could have played Richard III at Stratford, no questions asked. The acne that was supposed to start at age thirteen and disappear at sixteen came at age ten and has never left. When my first gray hairs appeared in my fifties, I joked that I must be the only female to be buying hair dye and acne remedies at the same time. Somehow, it mattered more in junior high. In junior high, it hurt.

Janice's offer turned into a settled routine. I'd get to school a little earlier every morning and she would hand me her make-up bag. I'd go to the Girls Room and cover my face with powder, add some blush, put on eyeliner and mascara, and finish with a touch of lipstick. In a few minutes, before the start of the school day, I'd be back in homeroom and returning Janice's cosmetics bag to her.

I was actually aware, after a few weeks of my magic morning makeovers, of looking up at people when I spoke to them instead of staring at their feet, hoping they wouldn't see my latest zit. I found myself smiling more. Enjoying people more. Liking myself more. I didn't turn myself into a beauty on those mornings. I simply, because of Janice's kindness, hid my flaws a bit. I made myself look more like a young girl, more like the other girls in school. And I made myself feel different. I'd wash the make-up off my face before going home after school, but that didn't matter. I had moved through my day with a face that wasn't as bad as it could have been. It was enough.

With no way to buy make-up to give to Janice, I simply accepted the sample lipsticks from the Fuller Brush man, when he came to deliver whatever products Mom had bought, and I gave them to Janice. It was a small gesture, but it was the only one I could make at the time. I think she understood.

Sometime in ninth grade, one of the myriad dermatologists my parents patiently took me to prescribed a face lotion that was flesh-colored and actually served as a kind of make-up. It was the equivalent of holy water to me. It really covered my problem skin. Before the ninth-grade dance, I asked my mother for two things — lipstick and permission to shave my legs. The latter, for a lot of girls in the 1950s-60s, was something you got permission to do at a certain age regardless of how much you might have needed to shave before that time. Miraculously, Mom said yes to both requests. She said that she hadn't wanted me to start shaving because, she explained, it was thought that hair grows in more after you start shaving. "More than the chimpanzee legs I have now?" I cried. She saw the point and apologized for not letting me de-fuzz my legs earlier. Perhaps as penance, in addition to lipstick I was allowed to buy eyeliner and mascara. I was in Heaven!

I headed to the ninth-grade dance with silky legs, glossy lips, and kohl-rimmed, long-lashed eyes. I wore a beige silk dress and kitten heels. I looked and felt like a real girl. Janice's brunette hair was done up in a French twist, and she wore a sleeveless black sheath, a beaded necklace, and high heels. She looked like Natalie Wood. No, she looked better. Broughal's dimly lighted gym was decorated with crepe paper and a mirrored ball for our dance. Our dance theme was "The Twelfth of Never." We probably did as much talking as we did dancing. We knew that, with a few exceptions, we were headed to Liberty High School, which had thousands of students. We were likely to lose each other in the ocean of people and experiences that awaited us. Intuitively, we knew that this night was one of our last times together.

During one break in the music, Janice and I huddled together with our punch cups in our hands. "Your friendship means so much to me," she said. "You really understand me. You always have." I choked up a bit. "No," I said, "I'm the one who is grateful to you. You did more than let me borrow your make-up. You let me feel like a person instead of a pariah. You'll never know how much your kindness has meant to me, and I'll never forget how much it can mean to be kind to someone who needs it." A half-century later, Janice lives thousands of miles away, in another country. We still exchange occasional cards and notes, and on her rare trips back to Bethlehem, we make a promise to see each other. How long will I remember her kindness to me and the importance of such thoughtfulness toward others? Until the twelfth of never.

THE VIEW FROM THE WINDOW

*I*t was one of those dark, drenching afternoons, when the rain poured down incessantly and the sky — what could be seen of it — looked in early afternoon as it should have looked at dusk. In contrast, the fluorescent ceiling lights in the classroom of our ninth-grade English class were glaringly bright, and seemed to give the comfort of warmth as well as light on that dreariest of days.

The gloom outside seemed to have affected people inside as well. The class clowns were, for once, subdued and quiet. There was no chatter, no passing of notes, no giggles or surreptitious whispers. Our teacher, Mr. Zuk, who could have been a body double for Oliver Hardy, sans mustache and derby hat, was usually animated and ebullient. But on this day, he too seemed listless and disinterested in us or our class.

After some perfunctory review of the previous day's assignments, Mr. Zuk sighed heavily and stared out the wall of windows facing Packer Avenue. "Let's make this a quiet day," he said. "Write an essay for me on what you see when you look out these windows."

We took our tablets out of our desks and began to write, looking intently at the granite gray scene outside the windows. Everything appeared to be dark and muted. Even the trees, not yet wearing their autumn colors, seemed to have lost their green, their vibrancy. They appeared to be indistinguishable from the dark sky that pressed down on them.

Across the street, facing our school, was the spreading campus of Lehigh University. Usually a beautiful sight in any season, the campus on this day looked almost Gothic. Its stone buildings blended with the leaden gray sky. Yellowish lighting in scattered classrooms in those buildings provided the only touch of color or warmth in the scene.

As several of my classmates began to write their essays, I continued to stare through the windows, looking past the zig-zags of rain racing each other down the long, glass panels.

"The heartbreak of a good-bye, a parting so painful that it cannot be made in person, only at a distance, in hurried words spoken with cowardice or sensitivity or both. Other words, exchanged by other people, are redolent of love and almost giddy with plans for the future. For others, the ordinariness of life unfolds with comforting predictability — favorite recipes, news of a grandchild's birth, baseball scores, plans to go to the movies, complaints about rheumatism or the influx of immigrants. Sprinkled throughout, like flecks of well-chosen spices, the tidbits of gossip — some helpful, some hurtful — that flavor conversations and relationships."

The next day, Mr. Zuk called me to his desk. Holding my essay in his hand he looked up at me, puzzled. "What is this?" he asked. "How could you see this from the windows?"

I pointed toward the now sunny scene outside. "There," I said, "running straight across the whole view. Telephone wires. Telephone wires carrying conversations."

Mr. Zuk looked out the window for a long moment and then back at me. With a red pencil he marked my paper. When he handed it to me, he looked at me strangely without saying anything.

I always knew I could write. That was the day I knew I could see.

AFTERTHOUGHTS:
SOUTH BETHLEHEM REMEMBERED

"*Um-brel-las! I can fix your um-brel-las!*" I can still hear the sing-song voice of the peddler and fix-it man who drove through our South Bethlehem neighborhood every week from the 1910s through the 1950s. His horse-drawn wagon — and later, his ancient truck — rattled along slowly, loaded to overflowing with brooms, pots, pans, washboards, bolts of cloth, and tools to repair almost anything.

When he stopped at the corner of Morton and Fillmore Streets, women came to look at his wares and make their purchases. Money came from leather coin purses tucked into their apron pockets. He spoke with an accent, doing transactions among the Windish, Hungarians, Slovaks, Polish, and Portuguese in a broken English that sufficed for everyone. He seemed to have no name and was simply called 'the boney man.' Word preceded him from backyard to backyard as women called to each other over fences and hedges: "The boney man is coming!"

There have been many changes in South Bethlehem since the decades in which the Oilcloth Stories take place: decades when Baby Boomer kids filled Central, Broughal, and other schools to overflowing.

New stores and restaurants, the brownfields redevelopment of the Bethlehem Steel site, and the expansion of Lehigh University have enhanced the South Side. At the same time, macadam lots, deteriorating buildings, and the flip-side of expansion have replaced what were once hundreds of homes, gardens, and flourishing stores and shops. Absentee landlords intent on profiting from student housing have turned well-tended private homes into often neglected rooming houses. They've dumped hundreds of tons of gravel on top of lawns, landscapes, and gardens to accommodate students' cars — replacing trees and greenery with the ugly visual scar of haphazard parking spread over whole blocks and neighborhoods, helping to drive more families away from their homes. As Joni Mitchell sang in the 1960s, *"They paved paradise and put up a parking lot."*

South Bethlehem certainly wasn't paradise, but it was one of those iconic American neighborhoods where people came, stayed, and made a life — a place to which many returned after they'd left. It was a place that became part of your identity for a lifetime. South Bethlehem was part Brooklyn, part Bleecker Street, and part Bowery. In the heyday of its industrialization, it had more pollution than Foggy Bottom. In South Bethlehem's wicked and wayward years, when it was known for its bars and brothels, when special trains from New York City brought people to Bethlehem to 'have a good time' — before the crime-busting reforms of Mayor Robert Pfeifle, who closed 241 speakeasies and brothels in 1930 alone — it was rumored that South Bethlehem had more brothels per square mile than the South Side of Chicago and more bars than Bourbon Street. The area was urbane and complex in other ways, with the Windish alone maintaining connections with Windish communities in Europe, in other states, and in South America.

In the 1920s, my mother attended Quinn Elementary School on East Fourth Street, located where a parking lot now serves St. John's Windish Lutheran Church. She wore a tag showing her name and address, labeled like a piece of baggage in danger of being lost in a new country. This was typical for children of immigrants who were not yet accustomed to their new language, English. For all of her life, my mother could recall the humiliation of having to walk into an assembly at Quinn School wearing a pink dress with a large red gingham patch sewn on the back of the skirt. It was the closest color her mother could find to match the dress. Hand-me-down and patched clothing was something else that immigrant families often had in common. They wore clothing until it was almost worn out. Then they sewed or patched it and wore it a little longer. Mom also remembered the requirement for high school girls to wear silk stockings. At that time, nylon was not yet used for the mass manufacturing of stockings. Because silk stockings were too expensive to throw away when they had a run, they were sewed when they were torn. It was easier to sew them if the tear was near the seam going down the back of the stockings.

Next door to the enormous (195 vendors) Bethlehem City Market at Third and Adams Streets was the tiny A&P store with its gigantic — to a five-year-old — red coffee grinder. Snyder's and Thomas's Delicatessens always had a free pickle from the barrel for a kid. Across Third Street, at Alexy Shoes, you could look at the bones in your feet through the magic of the wooden x-ray machine, intended to show whether your toes had enough room in the shoes you were trying on. Walk another block eastward and you'd be across from the rickety, wooden building that was the chicken house — a dilapidated structure housing crates filled with chickens that would be killed when customers made their choices among the screaming fowl. Feathers filled the air around the chicken house like so many snowflakes. After one childhood visit to the chicken house with my grandmother, I never went near the smells or the sounds of that place again. It may have been the only structure in South Bethlehem whose demise was not mourned.

Movie theatres abounded in South Bethlehem, and none more colorfully nicknamed than the Bughouse — officially named the Lehigh Theatre. There, you could see movies for 25 cents and get free dishes. South Bethlehem families dined for decades on Bughouse dishes, just as they served food from platters advertising Miller's House Furnishings and poured beer and soda from pitchers advising them to "Bank on Banko." Other movie houses were the Palace, the College, the Victory, and the Globe Theatres.

"Miller's House Furnishings" was a broad definition. With everything from wooden ice boxes and wringer washing machines to clocks, stepstools, and small appliances, tiny Miller's, in the seven-hundred block of East Fourth Street, was more like a general store right out of the Old West. Fourth Street also offered, among other sites, the Royal Restaurant, Archond's Ice Cream Parlor, Zavacky's Shoe Repair, Devers Drug Store, Dorolee's Ladies Shop, Renee's Gift Shop, Giers Jewelers, the Fabric Center, Korpics Clothes, the New Merchants Hotel, the Bouquet Shop, Lehigh Stationery, Figlear's Bridal, Gasdaska's Menswear, Kauffman's

Electric, Ritter's and Oravec's Pharmacies, Fella Photographers, and Cantelmi's Hardware, which still does a brisk business.

Long-gone stores along Third Street included Tom Bass, Egan's Men's Shop, Le-Roy Women's Shop, Alice Kay's Dress Shop, Cottoncrest, the Victory Shoppe; Refowich's, Subko's, and Bimby's men's stores; Muhr's Meat Market, Phillips Music Store, the HUB Store, Finkelstein Jewelers, Glazier's Furniture, Kroope's, Lonstein and Triplex shoe stores, The New York Department Store, Sears Roebuck, Josephine Harris Beauty Salon, Coleman's Furniture, and 5- and 10-cent stores, including the 'up-and-down fivie.' Martin's Furniture remains a multi-generational icon of the area. Evans Street had cigar factories and Fourth Street had silk mills. Every block had its grocery store. In our neighborhood these included the Purity, the Pure Food, Kay-Gee's, Greger's, Albert's, Jerry's, Zrinski's, Patsy's, and Gergar's. On Fifth Street, the Roosevelt restaurant specialized in home-made crab patties and Theresa's Fillmore Street Restaurant had the best food on the planet. Period.

At various times in the 1920s and '30s, my paternal grandfather, Earl Henn, owned a taxi cab company, several car dealerships, and the Globe Theatre at Fourth and Wyandotte Streets. The economy took its toll on the cab company and the car dealerships, but even in the Depression people paid to go to the movies. My grandfather once placed an ad in the *Bethlehem Globe-Times* newspaper announcing that, "America's only female projectionist" would be showing movies at the Globe. It was only his wife, my grandmother, helping in the projection booth, but people lined up to see movies shown by a woman. Granddad understood marketing instinctively before it became a science.

South Bethlehem was a place where many doors were left unlocked. My aunt, Mary Kuzma Hassay Susa, who lived on Morton Street and later on Webster Street, left her front and back doors unlocked all day, well into the twenty-first century. It was a place where people who lived six blocks away from us knew my name and what time I had to be home for supper, where I could sit in the sun with white-haired Mr. Connell in front of Connell's Funeral Home and tell him about my school day — a school day created by students' curiosity and teachers' skills, not by state tests. South Bethlehem schools produced workers for Bethlehem

Steel, the railroad, Laros, and Sure Fit, but they also produced scores of doctors, lawyers, educators, artists, and engineers. From that immigrant community came, among others, Pulitzer Prize winners, the head chef of the famed 21 Club in New York City, and the Senior Research Scientist in Pediatrics/Endocrinology at the Yale School of Medicine.

In the midst of the gray soot of the foundries and factories of South Bethlehem — soot that my grandmother unfailingly wiped off every windowsill of her house every day — there was no shortage of spectacular color ... color provided by hundreds of pocket gardens at the front, sides, and rear of the homes that covered the area. Cascades of fragrant roses spilled over the fences of the houses I passed on my daily walk to Central School. Huge shrubs of delicate spirea provided a pristine, white counterpoint to the reds, pinks, and corals of the roses, the blues and purples of irises, and the yellow and orange of the daylilies that abounded in these gardens. In many South Side backyards, grape arbors provided shade as well as a bounty of grapes used to make home-made wines.

In the same way that colorful flowers and gardens counter-balanced the dinginess of industrialization, the music that seemed to always be in the air in South Bethlehem was a welcome distraction from the harsh and incessant roar of the foundries and furnaces of the steel company. On many evenings and on weekends, polka music and other dance music could be heard in clubs and halls all over the area, their names reflecting their origins. Among them, there was the Croatian Hall, the Hungarian Hall, the Polish Club, the Russian Club, the Ukrainian Hall, the Italian Club, the Windish Hall, St. John's Windish Club, the Sokol Hall, and the Mexican Club. When it wasn't live music filling the air, it was music emanating from radios in almost every home. Grape festivals, a harvest-time tradition brought from the old countries, offered day-long playing of music, often by several orchestras. When Czipoth's Music Store on East Fourth Street had its windows open, sounds of children practicing on the violin or accordion could be heard for a full block. And scattered here and there, people who loved music could be heard playing musical instruments for their own pleasure in living rooms and backyards throughout South Bethlehem. A half-block away from our home, on dusky summer evenings, Mr. Jaroschy sat in his backyard playing his violin and filling the firmament with sounds of love and loss and longing. People in the neighborhood came outside to sit tranquilly in their backyards, listening to the concert he provided, and watching the evening close in as the skies darkened and the stars came out in the velvet canopy overhead.

Three times each day — at 6:00 a.m., at noon, and at 6:00 p.m. — the churches of South Bethlehem created a miles-long span of chiming and pealing as their bells rang out to mark the hour. In addition to heralding the beginning and ending of worship every Sunday, churches used their bells to convey news to their immediate neighborhoods, where most of their parishioners lived. Most old-timers could decipher each church's bells. They would know if a church was tolling out the news of a death, announcing that someone in the congregation had passed away, or ringing out to call people to a meeting or special worship. Specific bell sequences accompanied the somber occasions of funeral services; other sequences conveyed the joyful occurrences of weddings or confirmations. The daily ringing of the bells filled the air with a sound that was both sacred and musical — a sound that caused many people to pause and recognize that another day was beginning or ending, and that life was being marked and moved by a God who watched over the sad and difficult parts of life, as well as the times of joy and celebration. There was comfort and continuity in the sound of those bells. In some ways, they symbolized the reality of a community — a community comprised of numerous and diverse neighborhoods and ethnic groups, a community that evolved and thrived in a remarkable place called South Bethlehem in the first half of the twentieth century.

Portions of this essay appeared as an Op Ed in the Morning Call newspaper in 2010.

Wedding photo of Dean Richard Henn and Irene Caroline Kuzma Henn who were married on December 31, 1941.

ACKNOWLEDGMENTS

My first and deepest thanks go to my parents, Dean and Irene Henn. Although they are no longer present in this life, they are with me every day in their love, faith, and in the strength of their spirits. My mother, known to friends and family as "Iggie," read many of the Oilcloth Stories as I wrote them. She smiled then and I can see her smiling now. My parents not only loved me, they believed in me. They thought that I could do anything I wanted to do. Because they believed that, I did, too.

Many thanks to the dozens of friends who read these stories at various stages and who gave me encouragement as well as their candid and constructive opinions. Special thanks to best friend Llyena Boylan, who has always been a cheerleader for my writing aspirations and who patiently listened to stories and story ideas through scores of weekly coffees and lunches.

I am grateful to my good friends, retired English professors Dr. Carole Koepke Brown and Dr. Robert T. Burcaw for their review of much of the text and their insightful, helpful suggestions.

Thanks to Bette Kovach, Patricia McAndrew, Charlene Donchez Mowers, and Ralph Grayson Schwarz for their guidance and expertise in my references to the history of Bethlehem, South Bethlehem, and Bethlehem Steel. I am grateful to attorneys Ellen M. Kraft, Judith Harris, Dolores Laputka, and Jeanne Hamburg for their guidance on legal references in these stories.

My gratitude to Maria Skrilec for her assistance with my writing phonetic Windish, to Julie Fortley for reviewing "Theresa," to Judith Morecz Simpson for blessing "Morecz-nina," and to Ron Hari for sharing his "Ghost" experience with me. Thanks to friends and fellow South Siders

Amparo Martin Harpel and Kenneth B. Irvine, Jr. for their recollections of the South Bethlehem neighborhoods we knew and loved.

Thanks to Jack Hodgins, Ray Huston, Wally Ely, and Bruce Boyer for their memories of Allentown and the wonderful music and orchestras of yesterday.

Ken Raniere, designer extraordinaire, has been an advocate for the publication of *Oilcloth Stories* as well as a valued and important artistic influence. The maps Ken created for this volume not only help to bring some of the people and locations of *Oilcloth Stories* to life, they help to preserve a time and a place that could too easily be lost.

To the editors and staff at FriesenPress, I give my sincere thanks, for their professionalism and the respect which they accorded to me and to my book at every stage of the publication process.

Finally and somewhat whimsically, my thanks to the late John Updike. Many years ago, he told me, "There are many people who want to write. There are some people who actually do write. And then there are a few who have to write. You're one of those. You're one of us. Go write your books."

Carol Dean Henn
Bethlehem, Pennsylvania
2015

CPSIA information can be obtained at www.ICGtesting.com
Printed in the USA
BVOW05s0400010516

446210BV00001B/17/P